Fort Cracks Up in North Sea, But Crew Comes Sailing Home

By Andrew A. Rooney
Stars and Stripes Staff Writer

U.S. BOMBER STATION, Ill., dropped his 60,000 and it floated for Air/Sea Rescue n Casey at

Fortress into the North Sea last Forty-five minutes after the Fort boat on parachutes to the crew, cross a southwest wind for d.

here 45 miles off the English Casey had to ditch the plane. e just about shot off and the w.

time we looked at the gas it was now, the tanks are empty. Our tanks were hit worse than we thought."

Before the plane hit the water, eight of the crew, all except pilot and co-pilot, had time to get to the radio room. When the plane struck the sea, there were two sep rate jolts—first as the tail and again when the nose settled do The plane skimmed along the water about 100 yards before it was pulled to a gentle coast.

The eight men in the radio roo lowed ditching instructi all climbed out. and got into t

In the pilot, 2

STRIPES 1D.

opean Theater of Operations

Friday, April 21, 1944

---

fight
waffe operating against the
they have a will to win that c
be beaten—and a flying 29-year-old colon
more colorful sitting at a desk than a
trapeze art t is between swings.

y of the top-scori

By Andrew A. Rooney
ars and Stripes Staff Writer
Drawings by Clark Fay

F three-quarters of the colonels in the
ETO could see the knit wool cap Col.
Hubert Zemke kicks around this station
in, Gen. Marshall would probably find
himself with a handful of memorandums
—SUBJECT: Colonels Hats.

And if three-quarters of the officers in
the Army commanded as Zemke does we'd all
be living on per diem in Paris by now.

Zemke is the leader of the United States
Army Air Forces' crack fighter group
operating against the Luftwaffe. Pilots of
the Zemke outfit have knocked 86 German
fighter planes out of German skies in the
few months they have been operating to
establish themselves as the top-ranking
high-altitude fighter group in the world.
Twenty of their boys have gone down over
enemy country, but the record stands better
than four to one.

The story of the group goes, hurriedly
like this: It was activated Jan. 1
Zemke was a first lieutenan
of the officers with the c
around. Virgil Durranc
Schilling. Zemke's left-ha
last of the originals.
Almost a year later it wa

Then He Woke Up

Each jeep was equipped with a blow torch instead of the regular GI stove, and the canteen cups they heated their coffee in were of a new design which did not burn the lip when full of hot coffee.

In winter the men were issued German sheep-lined coats and every man got one of the armored-type combat jackets instead of the regular or irregular field jacket. Issue shoes were always para- troop boots instead of the cold, leaky, buckle-top boots.

48-Hour Laundry Service

Underwear, towels and handkerchiefs were white, not OD, when issued, and to keep these dainties clean the Quarter- master provided the division with a mobile, foolproof, 48-hour laundry se vice. The laundry almost never made mis- takes except when some careless worker slipped an extra shirt or pair of shorts in a bundle.

Because of the division's experience, it often was given towns to take which were being defended by Italian prisoners whom the Germans had ordered to fight. By a great stroke of luck the cellars in the towns were always as full of good things ink as was the cellar of the Excelsior Cologne.

vision's actions were closely and owed in The Stars and the average day most of sion had their names The paper always ay it was pub- points day he ed

ise that they would e for the war first thing

officers in the division eekly liquor ration and ad no tropical chocolate ach man got a carton of week and if he didn't himself he could turn them officer whose job it was to the best local market and The soldier was given all but nt of the return on sales. The per cent went into the division n gave every man $100 when his e to go home on a 30-day every six months. The arrangements were made with master in New York to have the s mail sorted there, and it was ut on special planes which flew y into a field near the division CP. g the boys four-day mail service even the West Coast.

ach infantryman who received four or air mail letters each month got ly- re air mail and the Air Force fellows were pay and the very dickens about it, because ad as the very many letters they got they o matter how the infantryman's $10 com- couldn't get the dreamer was heard t bat pay. The sleep by a chamberm chickle in his passing the door with four sho who was whistling "Off We Go over her arm, Yonder," in Fren the Bright Blue got in a ti When the division Class B the cooks were issued a chicken in ev usually, however, Some rations with who x every Sunday. fellows who issued the friendly animals th feed K rations were and prisoners who would

THE STARS AND STRIPES

Dog Is Eager Passenger on Ra

Bombsight Cover Is Flying Suit For 'Mister'

By Andrew A. Roo
Stars and Stripes S

A U.S. BOM
When

Gen. Rose KIA Due to 'Error'

By Andy Rooney
Stars and Stripes Staff Writer

WITH 1st ARMY, Germany, Apr: 3
—Maj. Gen. Maurice Rose, 3rd Armored
Division CG, whose death was announced yesterday by the War Department, was killed Saturday by a Nazi
tankman who apparently misunderstood
the general's action of unbuckling his
pistol holster to hand to his German
captors.

Details released by 1st Army said Rose
had been visiting a task force in Welborn
when tanks ran into an enemy armored
concentration.

The general was in a jeep with his
aide. Maj. Robert
Bellinger, and the
driver. They started
off, followed by
several staff officers
in a half-track,
through a patch of
woods east of
Kirchenborchen,
d came point-

Wednesday, July 7

MY
WAR

MY WAR

ANDY ROONEY

TIMES 𝕿 BOOKS

RANDOM HOUSE

Library of Congress Cataloging-in-Publication Data

Rooney, Andrew A.
My war / Andy Rooney.
p.   cm.
Includes index.
ISBN 0-8129-2532-7
1. Rooney, Andrew A.   2. World War, 1939–1945—Journalists—
Biography.   3. World War, 1939–1945—Personal narratives, American.
I. Title.
D743.R63   1995
940.54'8173—dc20   94-41322

Manufactured in the United States of America
9   8   7   6   5   4   3   2
First Edition

To my friends who will never read this because they died
in The War: Obie Slingerland, Charley Wood, Bob Taft,
Bob O'Connor, Bede Irvin, Bill Stringer, Bob Post,
Jack Frankish, Tom Treanor, Pete Paris

My thanks to Peter Smith, without whose help
Peter Osnos could not have edited this book.

CONTENTS

PREFACE

I F YOU'RE PLEASED with the way you've been remembering some of the major events in your life, don't set out to write a book about them. The chances are, they weren't that way at all.

This is a memoir, not a history book, but in an effort to make it accurate, I've tried to check my memory against the facts. It is distressing for me to note how infrequently the facts concur with my memory of what happened. I assume, in cases like this, that the facts are wrong.

I attended a symposium of distinguished historians in Chicago in 1994. Some of them were in their sixties, marginally too young to have served in World War II. I was in awe of their intellectuality until they started lecturing specifically about the war I knew. If you break your leg and go to a doctor who knows all about broken legs but has never broken his own, you know just a little bit about broken legs that the doctor does not. I thought about that listening to the historians. They had read and studied all about the war for years and had a great grasp of the overall picture. There was only one advantage I had over all of them. I was there when it happened.

On several occasions I've actually ended up convinced that my memory serves history better than the historians. They can write their books, I'll write mine. I have complete file copies of most editions of the World War II *Stars and Stripes* and because I wrote more than 200 stories for the paper, they have served me as a diary of where

I was and what I was doing. The best thing they did was remind me of things I never wrote.

World War II and my memory of the four years I was involved with it has not dominated my life, although I haven't spent any other four years into which so many memorable events were crammed. I've told stories about the war to my family and to a few friends, but months go by when it never comes to mind. I don't belong to any veterans organizations, and when I get together with the few remaining friends I have that shared some part of my war experience, we almost never talk about it. There have been times since 1945 when I've gone for months without thinking of the war. Until I started writing this, I hadn't read many books about it. I've never enjoyed seeing war movies. Several years ago one of the big Oscar winners was a movie called *Platoon*. It was a good movie by the standards of professional movie critics but I didn't consider it entertainment. I associate entertainment with pleasure and war movies are no fun. I'm not haunted by the horrors of war of which I saw so many, but I don't need to be reminded of them. I saw everything there was to be seen in a war during my four years in the Army and any reaction I have to seeing a war movie is not pleasure but revulsion. I could not imagine any Vietnam War veteran enjoying *Platoon*. It would be like renting a nightmare on videotape. Noël Coward made a great remark when a reviewer criticized his play *Blithe Spirit* for being nothing more than light entertainment.

"I am not interested," Coward said, "in proving how sad life can be to people who already know it."

I am not interested in being shown how horrible war can be. I already know it.

The language in war movies is always unremittingly profane and accurate. It would be just as accurate half as profane, and I haven't used much of it. I know all the words, but they make me uneasy out of their milieu. Soldiers used words we couldn't use in *The Stars and Stripes,* and they use words in movies that I'm reluctant to use here. It has always struck me as strange that newspapers read by a lot of people don't print words used in motion pictures that are seen by the same people. Americans accept vulgarity in the dark that they won't take with the lights on.

Having said all that though, I can't deny that The War—we call World War II "The War," as though there had never been another— was the ultimate experience for anyone in it. If you weren't killed or seriously wounded, it was an exhilarating time of life. Most of us live our lives at half speed and on schedule. We sleep when we aren't tired, eat when we aren't hungry and go to the movies or watch television to laugh or cry in order to transport ourselves out of our real lives into someone else's as if our lives were not interesting, funny, or sad enough to satisfy us.

Life is real at war, concentrated and intense. It is lived at full speed. Most people don't understand how terrible parts of it are because the stories about war are almost all concerned with the drama of survival and victory over great odds. If you read about war, you get more of an impression of winning and of the heroes who lived to be honored than of the losers and the dead who were buried.

War brings up questions to which there are no good answers. One question in my mind, which I hardly dare mention in public, is whether patriotism has, overall, been a force for good or evil in the world. Patriotism is rampant in war and there are some good things about it. Just as self-respect and pride bring out the best in an individual, pride in family, pride in teammates, pride in hometown bring out the best in groups of people. War brings out the kind of pride in country that encourages its citizens in the direction of excellence and it encourages them to be ready to die for it. At no time do people work so well together to achieve the same goal as they do in wartime. Maybe that's enough to make patriotism eligible to be considered a virtue. If only I could get out of my mind the most patriotic people who ever lived, the Nazi Germans.

For three of my four years in the Army, I saw the fighting from close up. I can't forget much of what I saw and I want to write it down. For one thing, writing is a cathartic experience. Once you've put something down on paper, you can dismiss it from your mind. Having told it, I'll be able to forget it.

I

DRAFTED

PEOPLE WHO HAVE lived well and successfully are more apt to dismiss luck as a factor in their lives than those who have not. It's clearly true that over a lifetime the same things keep happening to the same people, good and bad, so it can't be luck. The process by which each of us acquires a reputation isn't independent of our character. It almost always depends more on the decisions we make than on chance occurrences.

The trouble with this smug thesis is that anyone crossing a street can be hit by a truck and the accident alters the person's life no matter how wise he or she was in making choices, so we can't claim luck never enters in. Maybe my life wouldn't have been much different if "Doc" Armstrong hadn't owned the pharmacy and been head of the draft board in the pleasant college town of Hamilton, New York.

It was sometime in May and there were still a few weeks of classes left of my junior year at Colgate University. My life was never the same again.

Most of my classmates had registered for the draft in their hometowns. Thinking the draft board in a college town would be sympathetic to the idea of letting students finish college before serving, I had chosen to register in Hamilton instead of in my hometown, Albany.

I had come to Colgate fresh out of The Albany Academy, a private school. My friends at public school thought The Academy was elitist, which I thought was wrong at the time. Now I think they were right but that there's a case to be made for the kind of elitism that existed there. In some part, at least, it was excellence. The Academy was an exceptionally fine secondary school that graduated a high percentage of people who succeeded in making good lives for themselves. Everyone in the senior class, known at The Academy as the Sixth Form, went on to college. The other boys and girls in Albany thought of us as rich kids because the tuition was $400 a year. Some few classmates were from rich families and no one let them forget it. We kidded Walter Stephens about being brought to school every day in a chauffeur-driven Pierce Arrow and our remarks to him were not very good-natured. In a world where everyone strives to make money, it's strange that a family with a breadwinner who achieves that goal is stigmatized and charged with the epithet "Rich!"

My father's $8,000 a year was considered good money during the Great Depression. When I was eight or nine, we moved out of a respectable middle-class house in the residential heart of Albany to a much nicer one with chestnut woodwork, a fireplace, and downstairs playroom, still in the city but further out. In addition to that home in Albany, we owned a cottage on Lake George, seventy miles north. There we had a Fay-Bowen, a classic old wooden boat, and I had my own outboard attached to a sturdy rowboat. My sister, Nancy, had a canoe. She wanted a fur cape for Christmas when she was seventeen but she didn't get that.

Dad traveled through the South for the Albany Felt Company as a salesman and he was worldly wise but my mother ran things. Part of her expertise was making Dad think he was boss. She was a great mother to have and I've often wondered how she was able to get so much satisfaction from doing for us what so many mothers today do without satisfaction. She liked to play bridge but I don't think she ever read a book. Being a mother was her full-time occupation.

Life at The Academy was very good. We used the school almost like a country club, often meeting there on Saturday morning to use the facilities or plan our day if we didn't have a team game scheduled. The Academy was not a military school, but it was founded in 1812 and during the Civil War it had formed a student battalion. The tradition was continued and once a week for about an hour and a half we put on funny old Civil War–style formal uniforms and marched in practice for Albany parades and our own competitive Guidon Drill. It was my first brush with military life. Although it was years before the thought ever occurred to me that I'd ever serve in the U.S. Army, I learned to detest everything about anything military at an early age. One day when we were to parade on the football field, I even refused to march because I claimed it would damage the carefully kept field.

In the student battalion, everyone's aim was to become an officer in his Sixth-Form year. The choices were made by two military aides who came to the school just once a week and a committee from the regular faculty. Shortly before the choices were to be made as to who the officers would be, Colonel Donner, the school's military adviser who was with the New York State National Guard, lined up the Fifth Formers in the battalion and said that anyone who did not want to be considered for a position as one of the officers in his senior year should step forward.

It put me in a terrible spot. Everyone wanted to be an officer. I wanted to be one but my negative attitude toward the battalion was so well known to everyone that the colonel was, in a way, challenging me to put up or shut up. I had no choice but to step forward as the only person in the school announcing that he did not want to be considered for the honor of being an officer in the battalion.

The colonel thanked me for being honest and dismissed us.

It was lucky for me that several teachers on the faculty disliked the battalion as much as I did. When the announcement of their choice for officers was made three days later, my name was on the list. Because I was captain of the football team, president of the Beck Literary Society, and "one of the guys," it would have been difficult for them to leave me off the list because it would have called for an explanation to the younger kids in the school. And then some of the faculty members like Herbert Hahn were my friends. They knew, even though I had stepped forward in that bravado gesture, that I desperately wanted to be chosen. (Mr. Hahn otherwise distinguished himself in my eyes by stating in class one day in about 1936, "Hitler will get nowhere in Germany.")

The only problem for me at The Academy was that my marks were poor. That was a constant problem. My mother always signed my report cards and hid them from my father when he returned from a trip because she knew Dad would be angry about them. He had successfully made his way from the tiny Ballston Spa High School to Williams College and he couldn't understand my bad grades. Although I was puzzled over them, I never gave in to the idea that I was stupid even though there was some evidence of that. There were things I did well and it was easy for me to think about those and ignore failing marks in Latin, geometry, and French. It was further depressing evidence of how much we're like ourselves all day long, all our years. I still see traces of the way I performed in The Academy at age sixteen in things I do today at age seventy-five. We're trapped with what we have and with what we have not. No amount of resolve changes our character. I do a lot of woodworking as a hobby and, considering how different the craft is from writing, it's interesting— and sometimes discouraging—for me to note, in introspective moments, how close my strengths and weaknesses in making a chest of drawers are to the strengths and weaknesses in my writing. I feel the same helplessness with my shortcomings on paper and in my shop as I do when it occurs to me that I'm overweight, not primarily because I eat too much but that I eat too much primarily because of some genetic shortcoming I got from my father and share with my sister.

Football was one of the things I liked best at The Academy. We had a good bunch of fellows on the team and a coach known as "Country" Morris who was just right. He knew the game and he was a decent man who expected decency from all of us. He had been a football star at the University of Maryland and he looked just the way a coach should look on the football field with his leather-elbowed jacket and his baseball cap pulled down over his eyebrows and cocked at a jaunty angle.

I was five feet nine inches, weighed 175 pounds, and played guard on offense and tackle on defense. Because of the attitude other kids in town had toward us at The Academy, it was particularly satisfying to beat one of the public high schools or a parochial school, and we did that quite often during the four years I played. My friend Bob Baker was a good football player but his family fell on hard times and he had to leave The Academy in the Fourth Form and go to Albany High and then play against us.

I was in or near tears for three days after the high-school game my senior year. We were undefeated during the season and heavy favorites to beat the high school. The high school game ended in a scoreless tie and it was as if we had lost fifty to nothing. It seemed so important. Bob Baker was exultant and I suppose it took away some of the pain of his having had to leave The Academy.

In college, I soon realized I had conflicting interests. I was interested in writing, football, and philosophy. I thought I wanted to be a writer but didn't know where to start. What is called "English" in college is generally disappointing to anyone interested in learning how to write because, while I enjoyed having to read Byron, the English courses I was taking didn't have anything to do with learning how to put words down on paper in an interesting way. The courses I was getting were in English reading, not English writing. I didn't know at the time that you can't teach someone how to write. And I was discouraged to find grammar and English usage so much more complex than I'd previously thought it was.

Looking back at some of the things I wrote for Porter Perrin's "creative writing" classes, it's difficult to know why he thought I was worth encouraging. A good teacher hands out more encouragement than pupils deserve as a matter of teaching technique. You hear it from the teacher on the tennis court next to you. "Nice shot!" he says to the pupil who finally gets one over the net. Mr. Perrin did that with me and at least it gave me enough confidence, false though it may have been, to keep going.

Philosophy was all new to me. I had not known there were ideas like the ones we argued over in class. The great philosophers seemed to be maddeningly fair and indecisive, always too willing to consider another explanation. I had not known there was such a thing as pure thought for thought's sake only, independent of any practical result of having had it. I was fascinated by the application of philosophy to religion and became more convinced than ever that the mysteries of life, death, and the universe were insoluble and that God was as much a question as an answer.

Football was the thing I knew most about although some of the courses were easy. I took a biology course that was almost identical to, but simpler than, one I'd passed in The Academy. This was a freshman's dream come true.

At The Academy the linemen had already begun to trap block, which was considered a fairly sophisticated maneuver at the time, but my career as a football player at Colgate was checkered. I'd been heavy enough to be good in high school, but now at 185 pounds going up against linemen weighing 220 and 230 was a different experience. The first time I tried to move Hans Guenther out of the hole I was supposed to make for the fullback, Hans grabbed me by the shoulder pads, threw me aside, and tackled the fullback behind the line of scrimmage. Colgate had had an all-American guard a few years before my class who weighed even less than I did. The press had picked up the Colgate press agent's phrase "watch-charm guard" to describe him and it caught on. He was small but very fast and quick—not the same thing on the football field. The freshman coach, Razor Watkins, thought he had another watch-charm guard in me because I was small. He was not prepared for a player who was small and neither fast nor quick.

No matter how I did on the field, I was determined not to be a jock and let football dominate my life. A lot of the young men on the team were scholarship players who had been recruited to play football. They seemed crude to me and I became more aware than I had been at The Academy that I'd led a sheltered high-school life. None of my friends there had smoked, we didn't say "shit" or "fuck," and we didn't sleep with our girlfriends. Sex was only a rumor to us. I felt a sense of superiority that I recall now with a mixture of pride and embarrassment. I was right but it was self-righteous of me to think so.

It was nonetheless true though that college often brings out the worst in perfectly good young men and women. First-rate colleges like Colgate that get three times as many applicants as they can accept choose what they think are the best prospects. Go to one of those colleges on a party weekend and you wonder what the college applicants who weren't selected must be like if these young people attending the college are the cream of the crop.

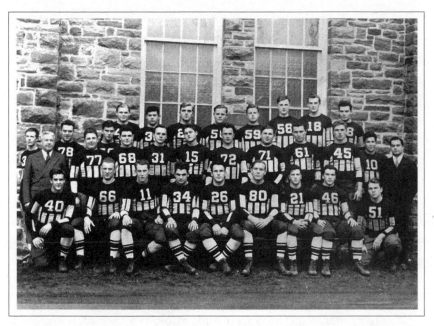

The Colgate football team. I'm number 51. Carl Kinscherf, Number 15, played for the New York Giants and Bill Geyer, Number 21, played with the Chicago Bears. Jack Scott, Number 80, was killed flying as a tail gunner in a B-17. Dick East, Number 10, was a fighter pilot, shot down and killed flying with the Eighth Air Force.

I don't know what happens, but too often kids who have been bright and decent in high school turn into something else in college. I remember hearing of "Pig Night" at Yale where club residents were expected to bring a woman to the party who'd lay anybody. Colgate had fraternities, and there's some collective evil spirit that prevails in many fraternities and clubs. They offer sanctuary for boors and boorishness.

Colgate didn't bring out the best in me. I liked several of the teachers and their courses but I felt superior to a lot of what I saw there because I was looking at superficial things about the college and the students. It had a lot to do with my getting involved with a pacifist movement there.

Toward the end of my freshman year, I joined the Sigma Chi fraternity even though I felt the fraternity idea was foolish. Our house had been one of the fine old homes in town, and the fraternity had divided it up into a clutch of rabbit warrens that housed fifty of us in near-slum conditions. It was a good group of young men though, and it was an economically and socially practical way to live. The whole hocus-pocus of the fraternity mystique was foolish but dividing a campus up into groups of forty or fifty students and letting them work out their own food and housing is not a bad system.

For many years now I've returned all the Sigma Chi material that comes my way from the national headquarters with a note DECEASED on the envelope but nothing discourages the national organization from trying to honor anyone like me who they think might give them money.

When I got to college my marks improved dramatically, not through any genetic transformation but because I chose courses suited to a deformed intellect. This was one of the changes college life brought me. Another way I hoped to prove I wasn't a jock was by deciding to take piano lessons between classes and football practice. The wife of one of the professors undertook, at $2 for each one-hour lesson, to teach me. During my first lesson, I recall thinking that I clearly had more potential as a football player than I had as a musician. Piano playing didn't come easily to me. The teacher was quite a pretty woman and I was disappointed at myself, considering my motive for taking the lessons, for being thrilled when she put her hand over mine to move it over the keys. I found myself thinking more of the professor's wife than of the piano.

My third day of piano lessons turned out to be my last. I went directly from that lesson to football practice. It was a game-style scrimmage between the second team and the first team. During the second half of the scrimmage that day, I was playing opposite Bill Chernokowski, one of those gorillalike athletes whose weight was mostly at or above the waist. He had short, relatively small legs and a huge torso with stomach to match. There are potbellied men who are surprisingly strong and athletic and "Cherno" was one of those. At 260 pounds he was the heaviest man on the squad.

As things turned out, it didn't matter where he carried most of his weight. When he stepped on the back of my right hand in the middle of the third quarter, that ended, for all time, any thought I might have had of being another Vladimir Horowitz.

At our fiftieth class reunion I had to revise my long-held opinion of Bill Chernokowski when I learned that his daughter was an outstanding cellist and Bill had season tickets to the New York Philharmonic. I couldn't have been more surprised, as my friend Charlie Slocum used to say, if I'd seen Albert Payson Terhune kick a collie.

Football became less important to me as I realized I was never going to be an all-American player. My career as a pianist now over, I began to think more about writing. There were two professors who interested me.

One was Porter Perrin, who was writing a book called *A Writer's Guide and Index to English*. He became the closest thing I had to a friend on the faculty. The other was a Quaker iconoclast, Kenneth Boulding, who taught economics for the university and pacifism for his own satisfaction at night in meetings with students at his home. I don't know firsthand that he was brilliant, but it is an adjective that almost everyone used in referring to him.

When the college opened after preseason football, I had classes with both men. Boulding stammered badly and even though you knew it shouldn't have, it influenced the way you thought about him. During a class lecture, you were driven to pay careful attention because of the difficulty of following his broken speech. He was always surprising us, too. He'd be expounding some theory of economics that we barely understood when suddenly and unexpectedly he'd drop in some mildly witty or unexpected remark. The class would erupt in raucous laughter, more from the sense of relief the class felt when Boulding got it out than by the humorous content of it.

When Boulding posted a notice on the bulletin board about a meeting of all those opposed to our entry into the war, I took that second opportunity to separate myself from the other football players and started going to his meetings. For some reason opposing the war seemed like an intellectual stand to take. It still seemed that way to Vietnam protesters. It was almost like not watching television now. There's a whole subculture in America of people who are proud of themselves for not watching television. They take every opportunity to tell anyone they can get to listen. I suffered something like that syndrome in opposing the war.

Boulding was a good teacher. The best teachers are not the ones who know most about the subject. The best teachers are the ones who are most interested in *something*—anything, and not necessarily the subject they teach. Boulding was consumed with the idea of pacifism and I've often thought of him as a good example of how little it matters that a college teacher is professing theories that are counter to popular and acceptable ideas of economics, religion, race, or government. His students were constantly propagandized by him but they ended up sorting things out for themselves. Being exposed to a communist professor in the 1930s didn't make communists of many students. Being exposed to the pacifist ideas of Kenneth Boulding didn't do his students any harm although if the parents of many of my classmates had sat in on some of those evening sessions in Boulding's home, they might have been reluctant to pay the next tuition bill to Colgate.

Quakers, like Christian Scientists, are frequently such decent, gentle, and seemingly reasonable people that they are not often considered to be religious fanatics. But they are generally more zealous than other Christians—most of whom, God knows, are zealous enough. The further a religion is from mainstream, the more devoted its followers are likely to be to it, and Quakers are down a long little rivulet.

Boulding may have been an economics genius, but he was definitely a religious nut. I was caught up with some of his ideas before I knew that and became convinced of the truth of one of his statements I've since seen attributed to both Plato and Benjamin Franklin: "Any peace is better than any war." I liked that a lot.

It was Boulding's contention that the conflict in Europe was none of the United States' business and even if it had been, war was an immoral way to pursue interests. The argument made sense to me, which gives you some idea how sensible I was when I was twenty.

On September 1, 1939, the day Hitler invaded Poland to begin World War II, I was in Hamilton where I'd arrived three weeks before classes began for football practice under the legendary head coach, Andy Kerr. I was so consumed with the game that one of the most momentous events in all history, Hitler's blitzkreig, barely got my attention. I'd buy *The New York Times* several days a week but I didn't read much of it.

NAZIS TAKE BREST-LITOVSK

TURKS MASS ON SYRIAN BORDER

I couldn't have told you what country Brest-Litovsk was in nor did I have any idea what disagreement the Turks had with the Syrians.

It still was ten years before Senator Joseph McCarthy aroused the moderate and liberal population to protest his demagogic effort to expose and make jobless any American who ever had a conciliatory thought about socialism or communism. Before the war the isolationist Congressman Martin Dies of Texas had already formed an Un-American Activities Committee that was McCarthy's forerunner. Isolationism was a popular movement, and outside the House it was organized as a group called "America First."

I participated in a debating society contest and the issue of the argument was "Resolved, that the American Press should be under the control of a Federal Press Commission." I'm pleased to be able to report that I was on the right side of that argument although I think the sides were chosen by a flip of a coin. We won the debate, but the fact that it could have been proposed as a subject for debate says something about the times—and we didn't have any easy time winning. The proposition would not be seriously considered today.

I didn't want to go to Europe to fight and die for what seemed to me to be someone else's cause. I hear the faint, far-away-and-long-ago echo of my own voice every time a congressman proclaims that "we shouldn't sacrifice the life of a single American boy" when the question comes up about our moving in to save a few hundred thousand poor souls being slaughtered in some foreign land. I decided I must be a Conscientious Objector. It was always capitalized because it was a formally recognized category of draft resisters.

This was when "Doc" Armstrong ended up forcing my hand, although he couldn't have known it since I'd never spoken with him. I had no idea that "Doc," the friendly, homespun tradesman with the gold-rimmed spectacles, was the head of the draft board. If "Doc" was around today, he could step into a role as the druggist in any pharmaceutical company's television commercial. His was the first drugstore I'd ever seen that didn't have a soda fountain, and that should have made me realize that "Doc" was a no-nonsense guy. There was something else I didn't know about "Doc" that I learned later. He was commander of the Madison County chapter of the American Legion and thought that every red-blooded American boy should serve his country—as he had in World War I—and right now.

He was not impressed by my attempt to delay enlisting by registering in Hamilton instead of Albany. It seemed to me as though I'd been hit by a truck the day I got the draft notice, sometime in May, a few weeks before the end of my junior year, stating I was to report for duty in the United States Army.

I had long, sophomoric, philosophical discussions with my friends about resisting the draft. A young man I'd been in school with at The Albany Academy, Allen Winslow, had already refused to serve and was the first person to go to prison for that offense during World War II. I admired him.

Unwilling as I was, over the few months I had between the time I was drafted and the day I had to report, I wisely concluded that I probably wasn't smart enough to be a conscientious objector even though I agreed with those who were. All the conscientious objectors I knew, like Boulding, seemed bright, deep, introspective, and a little strange. I liked those traits in a person even though I didn't have them myself.

One of my dominating characteristics has always been that I'm not strange. I'm average in so many ways that it eliminates any chance I ever had of being considered a brooding, introspective intellectual.

When Boulding died in 1993, several people wrote me saying I'd been unfair in some of the things I'd said about him. Our opinions of people tend to alter slowly over the years and, if we don't update our relationship by talking to them, become untrue. I have opinions of a great many people that must be unfair and untrue, but I've repeated them so often they're set in my mind and serve my purpose when I'm casting characters for stories that illustrate a point. My opinion of Kenneth Boulding settled and changed moderately over the years without my having come on any new facts to justify the change. It may not be accurate. On the other hand, of course, it may *be* accurate.

After months of anguishing over it I realized that, while I was an objector, I could not honestly claim to be a conscientious one. On July 7th, 1941, I reported for duty.

II

PRIVATE
ROONEY

T HE SMALL GROUP of about eight young men who had been chosen for service that day met in front of the Colgate Inn in Hamilton. I was the only college student among them, and "Doc" Armstrong immediately thrust leadership on me by announcing to the others that I was in charge during the bus trip to Buffalo. This was my first and last Army command position. I got it because I'd bought my Forhan's Toothpaste and what the sign out front of his apothecary shop called "sundries" from him. It was more or less typical of the way command was assigned in the military. The United States was scrambling to get together the biggest fighting force it had ever had and there wasn't time to find out who the leaders were. The military needed leaders and they were assigned, often arbitrarily.

That first night in the Army, we slept on canvas cots in the armory in Buffalo. The following day, we were put on a train for Fort Bragg, North Carolina. My friend Charles Kuralt is a native and an incurable booster but he has never convinced me that North Carolina is first among states. We all make instant love/hate decisions about places we have visited, based on small things that happen to us while we're there. We liked the hotel room. The newsstand at the airport had *The New York Times*. The restaurant we ate in had good rolls. We keep our geographical prejudices all our lives even in the face of persuasive evidence that we're wrong. My feelings about North Carolina were set

in stone during the six months I spent at Fort Bragg, and I have hardened them over the years by reading about Jesse Helms and the
tobacco industry.

For three months I was assigned to a basic-training unit of the field
artillery. The corporals and sergeants in charge were North Carolini-
ans who had joined the Army in peacetime, during the Depression,
because jobs were so scarce. The defense of our country should never
be left to soldiers who join up because they need the money. The
North Carolina noncoms and I didn't take to each other.

The officers were mostly recent college graduates who had been
in the Reserve Officers Training Corps and had received their commission there. The three lieutenants were basically civilians, as different from the Regular Army officers they mingled with at the officers'
club as the enlisted draftees were from the enlisted men who had
joined the Army by choice. It occurs to me for the first time, all these
years later and after having used the phrase "enlisted men" thousands
of times, that it has a voluntary connotation that is unwarranted and
that makes writing "enlisted draftees" contradictory.

The fourth officer, a man named George Creel, was a Regular Army
lieutenant and liked to act the part. He had some old-line Confederate
Army heritage with which he was more familiar than we were.

There were about 130 men in our two-story barracks and when
reveille sounded it was the alarm that indicated we were all supposed
to scramble into our uniforms and fall out in the company street
where a first sergeant named Fischuk called the roll. I was never on a
first-name basis with a first sergeant and don't recall Fischuk's. He
may not have had one, and even if he did, Sergeant Fischuk's first
name wasn't part of my life.

Sergeant Fischuk had been in the Army, by his own choice, for
fourteen years and he didn't have much sympathy for the young men
lined up in front of him who had been forced into service by the
draft. There was a sharp division in every unit between the draftees
and the volunteers, and each felt superior to the other. Sergeant Fischuk felt superior to both and must not have liked the young Reserve
Officer Training Corps lieutenants over him, either, and I noticed a
special bond between the sergeant and Lieutenant Creel. Despite his

Regular Army attitude though, I sensed a certain compassion in Sergeant Fischuk that was not always evident in the other noncommissioned officers.

The rifles assigned to us wouldn't have helped much in combat because they hadn't been fired since World War I, but we were lectured about their importance and how crucial it was for us to keep track of ours at all times. Lieutenant Creel called the rifle a "piece" as in "keep your piece at your side at all times."

On the third morning, at the sound of the badly played but live bugle, I pulled on my clothes in a hurry, which wasn't too fast, and went directly to the barracks door and out onto the red clay "street" that separated row on row of the two-story wood barracks. In my haste to get out there and line up for roll call, I failed to bring my rifle. It was the recruit's cardinal sin.

Sergeant Fischuk looked at me with a mixture of contempt and pity.

"ROONEY!" he bellowed at the top of his lungs. "Where's ya goddamn rifle? Get your goddamn rifle on the goddamn double!"

I fell out and ran back into the barracks. Behind me, I could hear a disgusted Sergeant Fischuk saying, half to himself and half to the assembled troops, "How do you like that. A college education and he don't even remember his rifle."

My second run-in with Sergeant Fischuk was more serious and it was unfortunate that it happened shortly after I had been elevated from the status of recruit at $28 a month to the honorable status of just plain Private Rooney at $35 a month. A soldier's bunk in those barracks was four feet from the bunk next to his. All a soldier's possessions, including his uniform changes, had to fit in the foot locker, two feet high and the width of the bed.

There was some time for reading after training and before or after meals and I had a collection of seven books. There wasn't room for the books in my foot locker so I put them under the bed, immediately behind the foot locker, where they were least visible.

In a routine inspection one day, Sergeant Fischuk spotted my books and blew up.

"What are books doing under your bunk, Rooney?"

"I read them," I said.

"Get them out of there," Fischuk said and started down the line.

I knew as soon as I said it that it wasn't a wise remark but it popped out before I thought.

"You're just sore," I said, good-naturedly I thought, "because you can't read."

Good-naturedness was lost on Sergeant Fischuk. He spun on his heel and confronted me in an apoplectic rage. With his nose six inches from mine, he shouted about disrespect, discipline, and college punks who thought they were smarter than anyone else. At the conclusion of his tirade, he told me I was busted back to a $28-a-month recruit. It might sound as if I was impervious to the hurtfulness of a $7 cut in pay but I was not.

The officers assigned to our battery had little in common with Sergeant Fischuk, but all four had access to the orderly room and must have shared with him some opinions about specific soldiers under their command.

One of the lieutenants had graduated from Cornell and was no more than two years older than I was. I had played football against him, but when I reminded him of the game, probably in an attempt to bring myself up to his level or bring him down to mine, he looked at me and said simply, "Yes." He never said anything more about it than that one "Yes." I think his answer emanated from the memory he had of an ROTC course he'd taken in military discipline recommending that officers not become friendly with the enlisted men they were to lead.

There was another lieutenant named Millar who apparently thought he'd made the mistake of being too approachable. I remember his name because his family ran a company that installed and repaired elevators in New York and I saw him a few times in Grand Central Terminal after the war. Early in our training Lieutenant Millar got everyone together in front of our barracks to have a heart-to-heart talk with his recruits. He explained that this was the Army, which we knew, and that in the Army a soldier does what he's told to do. He had noted in the past few weeks, he said, a disrespect for officers on the part of some of the new recruits.

Laundry was picked up twice a week and normally returned four days later, but something had gone wrong with the system and our laundry had been out for a week. As an example of the kind of insubordination he meant, Lieutenant Millar cited the case of one private who had approached him in the company street to ask where our laundry was and when it would be coming back.

In his address to us, the lieutenant made it clear to the assembled soldiers that their laundry was not *his* problem.

Lieutenant Millar spoke seriously to us about discipline in general, weekend leaves, the condition of our barracks, and what he felt was our failure to grasp the importance of the order of command in the Army.

He finished his long, rambling lecture and appeared to relax with the contented feeling he'd done a good job. He was a pretty good guy.

"Now," he said, "are there any questions?" He surveyed the men sitting in front of him. There were no hands. "Any questions at all," he said. "This is the time to get them off your chest."

I raised my hand tentatively.

"Rooney!" he said, pointing toward me. "You have a question?"

"Yes, sir."

"Go ahead."

"Sir," I said quietly, "when *will* our laundry be back?"

Lieutenant Millar took it better than Sergeant Fischuk had taken the books under my bed. Everyone laughed and he laughed.

ONE OF THE noncoms I liked least was a North Carolinian bully named Wray Funderburk, a corporal. I got off to a bad start with Wray when he yelled at me one day for not having my shoes shined. The details are vague but the argument between us got nasty when I childishly suggested that he ended up being called Wray because his family didn't know how to spell Ray on his birth certificate.

That night I wasn't sleeping. I'd heard there was usually an all-night poker game in the small furnace room underneath the barracks so I decided to check it out. The men playing were mostly North Carolina noncoms and, while I knew I wasn't welcome as the college guy, they were happy to take anyone's money and, anticipating that they had a pigeon in this green recruit, they asked if I wanted to play.

On rainy summer days as a kid at Lake George, my friends Buster Scovill and the twins Caroline and Eunice Robinson and I had often played Michigan or a game called Pounce! and less frequently poker to pass the time until the sun came out. This was my only poker experience so I knew what a winning poker hand was but I knew almost nothing about the intricacies of the game.

Soon after I joined the five men sitting around a circle on the sandy floor of the furnace room, I was dealt three kings and two tens. I knew a full house when I saw one.

When the bidding started, I decided the best thing to do was sit tight with my full house to see if I could fool the others into thinking I didn't have much. It seemed like a logical tactic and it worked. On my right Funderburk plunked down a dollar and said "Raise you" to the player on his right.

To stay in the game without giving away my strength, I put down a dollar and said, "I'll see you."

The betting went around again. "Cover and raise you a dollar," Funderburk said when it came to him.

This second time around I decided I had their ante up as high as it would go so I said, "See you and raise you two dollars."

I didn't really even understand the lexicon of the game.

Funderburk glanced at me sideways suspiciously and put down three nines. The others laid down their hands. The best was a plain flush—all cards the same suit. I laid down my full house and it was the winner.

"Ya sonofabitch!" Funderburk screamed. "Ya sandbagged me. Ya said ya never played the goddamn game and ya sandbagged me."

I'd never heard the expression "sandbag" but quickly grasped its meaning and realized that's what I'd done by first passing and then raising. I had no idea it wasn't done in a friendly poker game.

Funderburk jumped up, grabbed my shirt, and was ready to fight.

The other players on the floor didn't care whether we fought or not but they wanted to play poker. They separated us and it was agreed that Funderburk and I would fight in the company street the following morning after breakfast.

Funderburk had a reputation as a fighter. He was a beefy man with a heavy, round face and he probably weighed 190 pounds. I was 180. He had fought in the brigade boxing championships and I was nervous. I knew less about boxing than I knew about poker but I'd wrestled at Colgate in the 175-pound class. I was scared.

Funderburk made the mistake of thinking it was going to be a fist-fight. As we squared off, he hit me once on the left cheekbone. I rushed in to tackle him and, with my shoulder in the pit of his stomach, brought him to the ground in a cloud of red clay. There was a crowd of perhaps seventy-five soldiers now in the company street in front of the barracks. They surrounded us, yelling and laughing.

Funderburk got to his hands and knees with me riding his back. I wrapped my legs around his midsection, hooked my right foot behind my left knee, put my arms under his armpits, and then clasped my hands behind his neck. In wrestling there is a hold known as a half nelson and figure-four scissors. It's a tough hold to escape from and very uncomfortable for the man caught in it. It's called a "half" nelson because you have only one arm under your opponent's arm and up behind his neck.

What I had on Funderburk was a full nelson with both my arms under his armpits and up around the back of his neck. The full nelson is illegal in amateur wrestling because you can force a man's chin down onto his chest and by applying pressure with your legs around his middle, make it almost impossible for him to breath. It might even be possible to break his neck. We weren't fighting by the rules and no one in the audience would have known what the rules were anyway. They could have been watching a cockfight.

I could hear Wray gurgling and gasping for air as he struggled to get free of me with a dwindling supply of oxygen in his lungs. I squeezed harder with my legs and forced his head down until his chin was digging into his chest.

The crowd around us was cheering now, sensing a kill. I had been the clear underdog in the fight and they liked the surprise.

"Okay," Funderburk grunted.

"Okay what?" I said, squeezing harder.

"Okay . . . you win," he said, just barely audible.

"Say uncle." I thought I might as well humiliate him.

There was a pause. "Uncle," he gasped.

I unwrapped myself from around him. We both got up and without saying another word, Funderburk walked off. The crowd, mostly recruits like myself, applauded and life in the barracks was a lot better for me from that moment on. I don't know where Funderburk kept himself but I seldom saw him again. But I never went back down to the furnace room to play poker, either.

The nights were sweltering hot and two hours after taps one evening I knew I wasn't going to sleep and I started thinking about ice water. I couldn't get ice water off my mind. The canteen was down at the end of the company street and one row of barracks over from ours. It closed at 9 P.M. and when it closed the soldiers running it cleaned up and dumped tubs of ice out the back door before locking up.

I was determined to get ice. I put on my shoes and, still in my pajamas, went down the aisle of the barracks, between the rows of young soldiers lying there in the heat. Very few were sleeping but they didn't pay any attention to me. I could have been going to the latrine at the end of the barracks by the door leading to the company street. I slipped quietly out the screen door, bent over, and crawled on my hands and knees under the barracks, which rested on stilts the size of telephone poles, pounded down into the sand. They were left so that about two and a half feet protruded for the crossbeams. The company street was on a slight incline and, by the time I got to the bottom end of the barracks near the street, those supports on which it was built were high enough so I could stand erect.

I looked both ways up and down and saw the sentry walking the red clay street 100 feet away. I dashed across the opening and crawled under the building immediately next to the canteen. Quietly I made my way until I was opposite the back end of the canteen and there, like gold in a fairy tale, huge, beautiful chunks of ice glistened in the dim streetlight. Each weighed several pounds.

I was too pleased to be nervous now. I took off my pajama top, tied the arms together, and made a makeshift bag of it. I heaped as much ice as I could carry into it and started the dangerous trip back across the company street and under the barracks up to the side door. On this reverse trip, the floors overhead got lower and lower and I was crawling by the time I reached the door with my frozen treasure.

I don't know what would have happened if I'd been caught with the ice or caught out of the barracks at all. I suppose I'd have lost my weekend privilege of going into nearby Fayetteville and might even have drawn a few nights in the stockade. Not being able to go into Fayetteville was hardly capital punishment.

In all the years I've watched movies in which an actor darts across an opening trying to avoid being seen by a sentry, I've never seen anyone who was caught. They always manage to avoid being seen in the movies. I was pleased that the cliché held up that night and the sentry didn't see me, either.

I got back into the barracks and walked down between the row of beds to my bunk. My friend Bob Stouffer, lying in the bunk next to mine, was worried about where I'd gone. Bob was always looking for something to worry about. He had served in the peacetime Army in Panama during the Depression. At twenty-nine, he was the oldest man in our barracks and didn't really belong with the recruits.

"You better watch it," he said, looking suspiciously at my dripping shirt. "What have you got?" he asked.

"Ice," I said. "Lots of it."

By this time I'd attracted a crowd. We broke up the chunks of ice with our rifle butts and twenty-five or thirty of the men in the barracks took big pieces of ice in their canteens, went to the latrine to fill them with water, and came back to their bunks to savor that beautiful, cold, clear ice water. I don't ever recall having a drink as good.

It was one of the high points of my Army career, not so much because the ice water was good but because I'd added to the prestige I'd gained a few days before during the fight in the company street. Even among the men who'd enlisted, I'd about licked the epithet "college guy."

The most dreaded event on our training schedule was the full-field inspection in the hot sun on the red clay drill field a quarter mile from the barracks. You put down your olive-drab blanket on the hard clay and laid out on that every single item the Army had issued you, each in its specified position in relation to the others. It was a tedious experience. Your canteen had to be in exactly the right place on the blanket in relation to your rifle, and your clean underwear had to be parallel to your mess kit. This is how a peacetime Army thinks wars are won.

As with most Army inspections, it was a staged event. The colonel who reviewed our persons and our possessions chose an occasional soldier to ask some questions. His choice was supposed to be random but in actual fact the company commander steered him to a model soldier he'd chosen for that purpose.

One of the standard procedures during the inspection involved a blindfolded soldier assembling a rifle that had been broken down into its component parts, its pieces carefully laid out on the soldier's blanket.

Bob Stouffer was the only soldier in our unit who could take his rifle apart and put it back together again under any circumstances, and Bob had been chosen in advance to be inspected by the colonel for obvious reasons. There was no attempt to deceive the colonel because Bob's rifle was already taken apart and lying in something like sixty-four separate pieces when the colonel approached him.

There are half a dozen things I've done in my life that embarrass me to think about and what I did to Bob is one of them. If I wasn't writing a book I wouldn't tell the story.

I liked Bob. He was a good friend. He worried about me and the Army and tried to protect me from myself. I have no idea why I thought it was funny, but in an instant when Bob was fixing a belt loop, I slipped the metal pocket clip off a fountain pen I had in my pocket and put it in among the parts to Bob's rifle along with a small, plain key ring from which I'd removed the keys.

As the colonel approached, a sergeant, by prearrangement, tied a blindfold over Bob's eyes. The colonel stopped in front of him.

"All right, soldier, let me see how long it takes you to reassemble your piece," the colonel said.

Bob reached for a few familiar pieces and put them in place. Then his groping right hand fell on the clip from the fountain pen. You could almost see the hand wondering what it had come on. It felt, fingered, and then put it down and reached for another part.

Within thirty seconds Bob was lost. He fumbled among the pieces and kept coming on the ring or the clip, unable to figure what part of the rifle it was or where it fitted in with all the other parts. Finally, the colonel shot a disapproving glance at the lieutenant and strode off down the line of blankets and men.

"Is he the best you have?" he asked.

No one had seen me slip the clip from the pen in with the rifle parts, but with his blindfold off Bob recognized what had happened and he knew who had done it. I wasn't sure what anyone else's reaction would be and I wished I hadn't done it. Bob wasn't Wray Funderburk. He was puzzled, not angry, and to this day I wish I could take back that clip from the pen and the key ring.

After three months of basic training, I was assigned to Battery C of the Seventeenth Field Artillery Regiment, part of the Thirteenth Field Artillery Brigade. Unlike a squad, a company, or a division, a brigade seems to vary in composition. The Thirteenth was the administrative headquarters for just two artillery regiments, the Seventeenth and the Thirty-sixth. At the time I was assigned, I would not have been able to tell you whether a regiment was part of a brigade or vice versa. A battery is the artillery equivalent of an infantry company.

We took some tests driving the big Diamond-T trucks that pulled the 155mm howitzers, the regiment's weapon, and I was assigned to drive one. It was the first good job I'd had in the Army. I was much impressed by the truck's power. In its lowest gear it would idle up a steep incline carrying eight men and pulling the two-ton howitzer behind it without my having to depress the accelerator. I enjoyed learning how to jack the howitzer into position by turning the wheels of the truck one way if I wanted the weapon to go the other. I still stand on a New York City street, with memories of that, and watch as a truck driver tries to put his ten-foot-wide rig into a loading dock eleven feet wide. He faces the same problems I had with the howitzer and when I see a driver having trouble I have the urge to say, "Here, let me at that thing."

The gun crew of eight men sat in the body of the truck behind me and the sergeant sat up front with me. Mine wasn't considered a position of much authority but even so, there was something to the phrase "in the driver's seat."

These were the months between fall and Christmas 1941. The United States was not yet at war and most of us were hoping this whole unpleasant episode would blow over and we'd be sent home. I had no grasp of what was going on in the world although I read Walter Lippmann and Dorothy Thompson regularly in the *New York Herald Tribune*.

It gives me a sense of inadequacy, even now, to think back and recall that I was having no thoughts of any consequence. I was trying to live with as little unhappiness as possible under the circumstances and I had no grander plan in my head than that. I got up in the morning, ate three times a day, and did what I had to do in an ordered military society I detested. It was a bad time in my life.

I was in the battery recreation room reading shortly after eating dinner in the mess hall on December 7 when I heard a commotion over in the corner where a few people sat listening to the Atwater-Kent radio.

The Japanese had attacked Pearl Harbor and then declared war on the United States. I had that awful feeling of fear in my stomach. I don't know why fear strikes there.

The following day President Franklin D. Roosevelt told an assembled Congress that December 7th was a day that would live in infamy. I heard it, not as a speech of historic significance, but as the end of my hope that this desperately unhappy Army experience I was having would shortly be done with and we'd all be discharged and sent home.

MY FIRST MODERATELY good break in the Army was when I was given a part-time job helping a friendly and bright lieutenant named Jim Bickers do some kind of morale-building job for the regiment. I can't remember any single thing I ever did in that office, but I was out of the mainstream of military life and Lieutenant Bickers was the kind of guy I could call "Jim." He treated me as more or less his equal instead of like a drafted private, but it is not my impression that Jim and I accomplished a great deal toward winning the war in the brief time we worked together, and when the regiment went out on some kind of maneuvers, I was still driving the Diamond-T.

It doesn't take much to get the reputation of being experienced in some area in the Army and, because I'd helped Jim Bickers get out press releases about the regiment, in January I was assigned to help a sergeant, Ken Giniger, get out the Thirteenth Field Artillery Brigade weekly newspaper. Calling it a newspaper may be giving it more than it deserved. It was four pages of mimeographed material about the two regiments in the brigade and most of it was something Col. Reese M. Howell, who commanded the brigade, wanted printed.

My new status was something called detached service, a status much to be desired in the Army because it might also be called "out from under." When you're on detached service, it is considerably less apparent to your immediate superiors, both enlisted and commissioned, what you are doing. I was on detached service from the Seventeenth Field Artillery Regiment and assigned to the Thirteenth Field Artillery Brigade headquarters. My only obligation to the Seventeenth was to line up for roll call at reveille and then disappear to brigade headquarters for the rest of the day.

The colonel who commanded the Seventeenth Field Artillery Regiment was a silver-haired, Regular Army martinet who looked like Mickey Rooney's father in an Andy Hardy movie but without his charm. I don't know how smart a colonel should be but Reese Howell wasn't smart enough to be in command of several thousand men. He was the prototype of the know-nothing, midlevel career officer who stayed in the Army during peacetime, waiting to retire with a brigadier general's pay because there was nothing out in the real world that he knew how or could learn how to do.

The war had moved him quickly from major to full colonel. My friend Bud Hutton, who I was to meet several months later, liked to say "The trouble with a peacetime Army is, the enlisted men are no smarter than the officers." Howell was the kind of peacetime Regular Army officer whom a good many of the drafted privates were smarter than.

I cannot recall now any conversation I ever had with Colonel Howell that led him to think so but at one point Ken Giniger told me that the colonel thought I was a communist. He probably realized I hated the Army and in his mind this alone was subversive. After the war I'm sure he joined the John Birch Society and applauded Senator Joseph McCarthy's witch-hunts.

There have been a lot of times in my life when I've been slow to catch on. I have looked at other people who are more or less in my situation in life—age, education, and general background—and wondered why they learned how and I didn't. I remember thinking that in 1941. I did not rise above my surroundings and view them intelligently or dispassionately and I was even aware that I was not doing it. I've always been more aware of problems than smart at doing anything about them. I suppose it's a common shortcoming. That thought came to me frequently then because in another area at Fort

Bragg, Cpl. Marion Hargrove, a young man with more or less my civilian and Army experience was working on a publication similar to the Thirteenth Field Artillery Brigade newspaper and he had already written a book called *See Here, Private Hargrove.* It was a runaway bestseller and, by making him a celebrity, had lifted Hargrove out of the miserable life I was trapped in. Why was I, I wondered, helping put out a mimeographed sheet of trivia that was nothing more than a unit house organ? Why had Hargrove caught on to the possibilities of writing about the humor in Army life when I had not? The possibility that he was more talented than I was occurred to me but I pretty much dismissed it and consoled myself with the thought that I'd always been slow to grow up.

I'D BEEN WRITING to Marge Howard, a girl I'd first met in Mrs. Munson's dancing class when we were thirteen. We had gone together, off and on, all through high school and college. I'd frequently made the drive from Colgate to Bryn Mawr, outside Philadelphia, where she was in college. She still points out that she was a year ahead of me in college although a year behind in age. It was a seven-hour drive each way and that took a lot of time out of the weekend.

One Friday afternoon I'd left after my one o'clock class and was driving a little too fast somewhere between New York and Philadelphia. In order to get to Bryn Mawr by 6 P.M. I was saving time by changing my clothes as I drove. This was before highways were "super" and at a time when all state policemen rode Indian motorcycles. A lot of the young men who showed up at Bryn Mawr weekends were from nearby Princeton and, in order to fit in and conceal my Colgate affiliation, I had brought gray flannel slacks and a sports jacket and I wore Spaulding dirty white bucks (from buckskin) with red rubber soles. They were part of the Ivy League uniform of the era. It was said of a well-dressed Princeton student "He's really 'shoe.' "

With my knees raised, I was holding the steering wheel on a straight course while I pulled my old corduroy pants down around my ankles with my two hands in anticipation of changing them for the gray flannels. I knew when I saw the flashing red light on the trooper's motorcycle behind me that I was in big trouble. The corduroys were in a never-never land, half on and half off, and when the cop came up to the side of my car and looked in the window he must have decided I was not only a speeder but a sex pervert. He ordered me to follow him to the house of a justice of the peace, with whom I assumed he had a business arrangement, and I paid a cash fine of $12, which was all but a few dollars of the money I had.

MARGIE GRADUATED IN the spring of 1941, a short time before I got my draft notice, and she was using her Bryn Mawr degree in art history to teach French, a language about which she knew very little, in a girls' school in Albany. In February or March we decided, long distance and me on a pay phone, to get married. I forget why we thought it was a good idea. Most of our friends were delaying marriage until after the war.

There was a major family argument over who would perform the ceremony. I was already set in disbelief and Margie, although brought up Catholic, had stopped going to church when she was sixteen. Margie's mother had always served fish on Fridays and was a serious mass-going Catholic. She was adamant that her daughter be married "in the church."

My mother's strongest religious belief was that she was not Catholic. She had always gone to great pains to point out that, even with the name Rooney, we were Presbyterians. My father and mother both grew up in the small town of Ballston Spa, New York, and there had been a moderate influx of Irish immigrants to the area in the late 1800s. My mother's parents were English and my father's had come from Scotland although their Irishness was not far behind them. When my father and mother were growing up, most of the Irish in Ballston were doing what first-generation immigrants have traditionally done in America—working at menial jobs and doing the housework for the establishment. It was a desire to distance herself from them that produced this Irish-denial in my mother. It made me understand how benign prejudice can be at its inception.

After a lot of letter writing and telephoning during which we tried to come to some amicable agreement, Margie's father, an eminently sensible orthopedist who was in no way religious, wrote me a letter that was not unfriendly but was brief and to the point. He was obviously tired of the dinner-table conversation he was getting on the subject from Margie's mother.

"I don't give a damn who performs the ceremony," he wrote, "but if you're going to do it, I wish you'd do it and get it over with." I wish I had the letter. I don't know what happens to life-altering pieces of paper like that. I suppose I threw it away.

After reading Dr. Howard's letter, I realized that I didn't really care who married us either. It was a ceremonial formality, the religious overtones of which meant nothing to me.

Travel was difficult and the prenuptial negotiations had been so contentious that neither my parents nor Dr. Howard came to the event conducted in a bare-bones Army chapel used for Catholic, Protestant, and Jewish services. The priest, a lieutenant named Joseph Farrell, who was chaplain for the regiment, assumed that Margie was Catholic through the circumstance of birth, and inasmuch as I had told him I was not Catholic or anything else, decided it was what he called a "mixed marriage."

He was very friendly and casual about it, but he thought he ought to get permission from some higher authority in the church so he called the living quarters of his bishop. The bishop was on the golf course at the time but someone on the other end of the phone said he was commissioned to act in his name.

"Mixio religione," our priest said. "Okay?"

Evidently it was okay with this anonymous and somewhat suspect stand-in and we were married on the authority of a cleric well down the hierarchical ladder from the pope. I suppose I was predetermined to dislike this likable priest, and it seemed to me that Chaplain Farrell had a condescending air about himself during the ceremony which suggested that he felt marriage was for lesser mortals than himself.

We had dinner that night with a group of friends of Margie's father and mother who were staying at The Pinehurst Inn, near Southern Pines, North Carolina, which was for a time one of the great resort hotels in the country. Most of them were doctors and their wives, and I was uncomfortable with what I considered the off-color stories they were telling. "Off-color" is what we used to call a dirty joke. After dinner I returned directly to the barracks at Fort Bragg and, on the very next day, before we'd had a chance to live any married life, the Seventeenth Field Artillery was ordered south from North Carolina to Camp Blanding, Florida, and we were all restricted to the base until the move, which took place ten days later.

ON THE FIRST morning roll call at Camp Blanding, I realized that as far as the Seventeenth Field Artillery Regiment's books were concerned, I was still on detached service to the Thirteenth Field Artillery Brigade. It mattered not to any superior of mine that the brigade had been left back at Fort Bragg or that the Seventeenth was no longer an element of it. Immediately after breakfast I wandered off, as I had been doing all the previous months at Bragg, and didn't come back until late afternoon.

After thinking about it for several hours, I called Margie, who had gone back to Albany, and suggested she come to Saint Augustine, about twenty-five miles from Camp Blanding, and get an apartment. I said I thought if she did I could get down there so we could have some time together before I was shipped out. We found a small, pleasant apartment on a little alley running parallel and immediately adjacent to the inland waterway in Saint Augustine. Every morning I reported in for roll call and then caught the first bus to Saint Augustine and joined Margie there. Except for weekends, I returned to Blanding in time for a nine o'clock bed check.

Saint Augustine was an interesting and pleasant not-very-Florida town with a lot of good history and we enjoyed ourselves there.

Saint Augustine must be the most authentically old Spanish town in the United States. Our apartment was at the dead end of a short, cobblestone street lined with brick-walled gardens. The history of the place interested me as an idea but I began a long career of not going to see well-known tourist attractions by failing to walk through the famous fortress, the Castillo de San Marcos.

Saint Augustine was the nearest big town of any interest to Blanding so a lot of married officers lived there and enlisted men liked to come there on two-day passes. Traffic between Blanding and the city was heavy and I wasn't commuting alone.

I was nervous about what would happen if I were caught going AWOL every day but it was such a curious technical situation I decided I couldn't be in any really serious trouble. No one had told me I was relieved of my detached-service status.

My father had traveled extensively through the South when I was in school and on several occasions he had taken me along so I knew a little about how things were in the South but it was still a shock for me to see water fountains and rest rooms in Florida marked WHITE and COLORED.

Race had never been an issue in my life. It was easy since I never knew any black kids. (Years ago I went to Harry Reasoner's hometown of Humboldt, Iowa, and people told me there was absolutely no anti–Semitism in Humboldt. They quickly added that there were no Jews, either.) There were no black kids in The Academy. I know now that was not normal but it seemed normal then and I had never given the question much thought. There was one black family about two blocks from Partridge Street in Albany and we used to say how nice they were. I didn't even know what condescending meant yet.

The first time I recall consciously thinking there was something wrong was when I heard one of my father's friends in Asheville, North Carolina, refer to a black man as a "shine." It was a generic term he used for any black man, not just the ones who hung out around the hotel hoping to get a job shining a white man's shoes. There was no doubt that's where the word came from though. My father used the term "shine" himself. I don't think he would have used so opprobrious a term as "nigger." His use of "shine" was more thoughtless than vicious. I never said anything to him about it even though it seemed wrong to me even at age fourteen. I don't know what his reaction would have been if I had said something. I liked Dad but we never had an easy kind of relationship. It was a help with our relationship that my friends liked him. He took me to school one day with two other boys in the car. When a car stopped in front of us, the driver stopped to reach into his pocket while his son waited. "Hittin' the old man for a touch," my father said, and my friends thought it was funny and that he was one of the boys.

I became increasingly aware of black and white in Saint Augustine and, while I didn't anguish over it, I was disturbed. I've been more pleased in recent years with having felt that way than I was at the time. I often felt an anger welling up in me at the way Negroes, which was the accepted term at the time, were treated.

One morning in Saint Augustine, I was waiting for an early bus back to Camp Blanding. There was a crowd at the bus station. I was one of the first people in line, and when the driver opened the door I got on and went immediately to one of the side seats near the back of the bus. "Back of the bus" was not yet a phrase anyone used as pejorative slang.

A dozen more soldiers got on before the driver looked back and saw where I was sitting.

"Hey!" he yelled at me. "You can't sit there, soldier!"

I knew what he meant.

"Well, I'm going to sit here," I said.

I could feel the nervous bubbles effervescing in the pit of my stomach. I knew there was going to be trouble.

The driver came back and stood over me.

"Sit up there," he said, pointing to one of the forward seats. Bus drivers in uniform think of themselves as having some authority.

I didn't move and I didn't say anything. He walked forward, got off the bus, and strode into the small bus station and returned a few minutes later with a Saint Augustine police officer. The other soldiers on the bus were not interested in the issue, but they were unhappy about the delay.

"Stand up and turn around!" the cop said to me.

Saint Augustine was not Jackson, Mississippi, but when a cop in a southern town says "Stand up and turn around," it's best to stand up and turn around. He snapped handcuffs on my wrists behind my back and led me off the bus. Handcuffs are a bad experience. We walked a few blocks to a police station—this was back in the days before every cop had a car—and when we came in I was relieved that the sergeant on the desk didn't seem to approve of the arrest. He wasn't friendly toward me, just unfriendly toward the arresting officer.

"This isn't for us," he said to him. "Take off the cuffs and bring him to the MPs."

The military police were people I didn't want to face, either. I saw my whole world crumbling. I'd lose my detached-service status to a nonexistent brigade and maybe even get thrown in the stockade for a few weeks. The good life in Saint Augustine would be a thing of the past.

"Look," I said, copping out, "I'll sit where you want me to sit. I had a bad night." I thought it was best if I copped out. I've always known you have to once in a while but it didn't make me proud of myself.

The sergeant hesitated a minute and then said to the cop, "Let him go." He looked at me and said, "Next time, do the right thing."

His thought was that observing segregation customs in Florida was doing the right thing.

Rationalizing my caving in was easy. We're all confronted with so many opportunities to take a stand in our lives that we have to choose them wisely. This didn't seem like a propitious time for me to go any farther with this one. It wasn't as though I'd have single-handedly ended segregation on buses in the South if I'd stuck to my principles and been thrown in the guardhouse for insisting on sitting in the COL-ORED ONLY section of the bus back to Camp Blanding that morning.

The first signs of trouble with my ideal living arrangement came in the first month when I learned that a brigadier general from Camp Blanding lived just across the courtyard of the small apartment complex and that the medical officer of the Seventeenth Field Artillery, a captain, lived in the apartment above us. Margie and the captain's wife had become friendly and she asked Margie how I was able to spend so much time away from Camp Blanding.

From that day on I was very careful to keep a low profile in Saint Augustine but my part of the war fought there didn't last long anyway.

On about July 10 we got word that the Seventeenth Field Artillery Regiment was moving out. It was all supposed to be secret but we learned we were being moved to Indiantown Gap near Harrisburg, Pennsylvania. Only an Army with money to burn would have moved a major unit like ours south from Fort Bragg to Camp Blanding so it could be sent north to Harrisburg a few months later for shipment overseas from Newark. No one making decisions has to pay the train fare in the Army. No one even knew which sea we were going to be shipped over, either. It could have been the Pacific.

One of a great number of miserable times I remember in those early days in the Army was the train ride from Florida to Pennsylvania. The temperature when we left Florida was in the high nineties and it didn't get much cooler going north. The train was made up of ten old passenger cars with worn, red-velvet seats that must have been plush when they were new. The backs of the seats were the kind that could be flopped over when the train reached its destination and started back the other way so that passengers were again looking forward. The red velvet had been turned a greasy gray-black from where ten thousand heads had rested against it in the past. Because of this condition of their construction, the seats were straight-backed with no suggestion of a contour and about as comfortable as a church pew.

We were crowded onto the train, two in each seat with no empties, and our duffel bags were thrown up in the racks overhead. I was in the third car from the front and I remember estimating that it must have been the worst car to be in. The train windows were all open, as they had to be in the heat, and the soot from the coal-burning steam engine went up in a black plume from the smokestack but then, just as quickly, settled back down with the weight of the black coal particles in it. Most of it, it seemed, came in the windows of the third car. I sat there, sweating profusely, enveloped in a shroud of soot and grime.

WE WERE AT Indiantown Gap for only ten days before being shipped to England. We spent most of the time getting shots as if we were more apt to be struck by some dread disease in a foreign country than by enemy fire. At one point during the third day, I'd been working all day loading equipment into trucks when the squad I was with was called in to have mug shots taken. You can see the result, which accurately reflected my attitude at the moment. We were loaded onboard a British ship, the *Orcades,* in Newark for the trip to Liverpool, England. I had never been on an oceangoing ship and the thought of it was exciting but the fact of it was that with 4,000 soldiers jammed into what was formerly cargo storage space it was unpleasant below. When I read stories of boat people making long

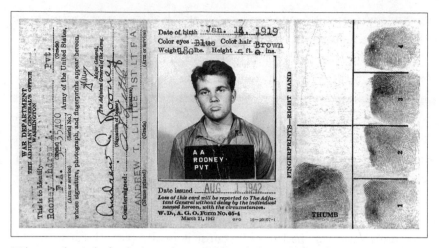

Taken at the end of a day's work as a battery clerk just before shipping out of Indiantown Gap on a hot day in July 1942. The picture accurately captures my attitude toward being in the Army.

voyages to the United States stuffed in the holds of old freighters, I wince. Canvas hammocks were slung between pipes that had been welded to the structure of the ship. A hammock is a comfortable place to read a book in the shade at a country home, but our bodies were not designed to lie, like bananas, in a curved position all night. You can't lie on your side in a hammock because the body doesn't bend sideways.

The first night out of New York was stifling hot and the hold already smelled of bodies. Many of the soldiers who had never been within 500 miles of an ocean were seasick. I couldn't begin to sleep so I climbed up the metal ladder out of the hold and onto the deck. The ship's progress through the water created its own breeze and the salt spray felt cool and good. After standing near the bow for more than an hour, I began to roam.

The British crew in the main galley was baking bread, and watching bread rise was more fun than trying to sleep below so I stayed with the British bakers, talking for most of the night.

With the exception of that bread, the food onboard was poor. It was the first of many experiences I've had with English food. The smell of lamb that had been around too long and too far from refrigeration before it was stewed permeated the ship. I don't think anyone was freezing food yet in 1942. The malodorous fumes invaded every compartment that didn't already reek of some other foul smell.

By morning of the second day out, I was ready to sleep. All but a few of the other soldiers were above deck now. I climbed into one of the hundreds of hammocks that had been slung in the hold and slept for five hours. I had almost instantly reversed day and night and that's the way I continued to live for the ten days it took us to reach Liverpool. I roamed the deck and various working areas of the ship by night and slept during the day.

In England we were shipped by train to Perham Downs near Tidworth and put up in old British army barracks. My first sergeant now was Hardy M. Harrell, Regular Army, and he was a lot like Sergeant Fischuk except that whereas Sergeant Fischuk had a sort of charming way of becoming exasperated with me, Harrell became enraged at any unsoldierly act of mine. Of which there were a great many. He was the cartoonists' prototype of a first sergeant.

I had written Margie and told her how hard the cots were in the barracks and how difficult I found it to make a bed that satisfied Sergeant Harrell, who was constantly inspecting it. I explained to her that, in the Army, the blankets were supposed to be stretched tight enough across the valley in the middle of the bed so that, when an inspecting sergeant flipped a quarter on it, the quarter would bounce. I could not make a bed that made a quarter bounce.

Within ten days I received what seemed to me at the time to be a great gift from her. It was a package from Abercrombie & Fitch, the sporting-goods store in New York, containing an air mattress. It was the answer to my problems with the hard bed and the difficult sergeant.

I dragged the thin, hard, GI mattress to an area under the barracks where a lot of trash had been dumped and put the air mattress on the cot. The air mattress was a pleasure to sleep on and it made quarters bounce like no other bed in the barracks.

On the third day, Sergeant Harrell became suspicious of my new-found talent for making a bed in such a manner that quarters flipped. He pressed down on it, suspiciously, with his fingers extended.

"What's this, Rooney?" he snorted.

"My bed, sergeant" I said.

"What have you got in here?"

He ripped the brown Army blanket off and exposed my puffy prize. The cachet of Abercrombie & Fitch was lost on Hardy M. Harrell. That was the end of my good nights' sleeping and the bouncing quarters. The air mattress was confiscated and I had to go back down under the barracks and retrieve my thin, hard mattress. For the second time in my brief career in the Army my pay was reduced to that of a recruit. It made the difference between being able to buy a Coke and a hamburger at the canteen or just a hamburger.

Aunt Anna used to send me cookies and brownies. I liked the sentiment and enjoyed getting a box of anything from home but Aunt Anna was at the same time the worst cook in the family and the only one who sent me food. Her cookies tasted more like the writing-paper box she sent them in than like chocolate or molasses. This was before the days of plastic wrap, and aluminum foil was scarce. Aluminum foil was called "tin foil" and everyone at home saved it to give themselves the illusion they were helping the war effort. There was often a picture in the newspaper of someone who had rolled together a ball of tin foil six feet tall. Patriotism was rampant, but it was tough on cookies from home.

It was fun being in a strange country. England has everything that makes a foreign country interesting without the inconvenience of having a foreign language, and the prospects of being killed at war seemed remote. We were vaguely aware that there would be an invasion of France if the war lasted, but it seemed far off and we knew that the artillery would be a safer place to be than the infantry because the artillery never wades ashore with the first wave.

Shortly after we arrived in England, our equipment followed us to camp. When we got our howitzers and our heavy trucks, I was put back behind the wheel of a Diamond-T again. We'd left the Thirteenth Brigade and the cushy job I had on detached service to it back in Blanding. I don't remember worrying about our mission or being afraid of anything.

In the barracks at Perham Downs, I occupied some of my spare time filling out an application for officer candidate school. In retrospect I can't imagine why I thought I should be an officer except that I did have part of an education and none of the officers I was exposed to seemed to have any exceptional leadership quality that I didn't have or couldn't generate.

The application went first to the clerk sergeant in the orderly room. Some compulsion to be fair must have come over him because he passed it along to a lieutenant instead of discarding it out of hand. The lieutenant was George Creel, my least favorite of all the officers I'd had. He took being a lieutenant very seriously. He was aware of my attitude toward officers, the Army, and him personally and did not take kindly to me or my application.

The next day he called me into his office in the orderly room just behind the sergeant's desk. He had the application in his hand.

"Private!" he said with loathing, shaking my application papers at me. "What the hell makes you think you could be an officer in this man's Army?" He was the type who used that phrase every time he referred to the Army.

I don't recall what I answered but there was nothing I could have said that would have mattered. I turned on my heel and left without saluting. I was angry and disappointed although, in retrospect, I realize he may have been right.

Because of the limitations in places we could travel to in England, we didn't participate in a lot of training exercises using our equipment and I was taken off the Diamond-T several days every week to do the work of a battery clerk. The job of battery clerk was much to be desired and mine was particularly desirable because I was made clerk for the regimental band.

It's hard to believe a regiment kept thirty-one musicians on the rolls at a time when we were getting ready for a big-time war, but the Seventeenth had a band and I was its clerk. The musicians were mostly Filipinos. They had been in the Army for more than twenty years and were substantially older than the rest of the regiment. I made out the payroll, typed up passes, and did the general bookwork for them. My typing was weak but the practice I got paid off in an unexpected way within a month.

The adjutant, 1/Lt. Claude B. Morris, was an exceptionally decent person. He had assigned me the job and, in recognition of my work

on the brigade newspaper, also made me regimental historian. I was
to make notes on all the activities of the regiment and send them to a
storage facility in the United States. A field artillery regiment's activities in training camp are not the stuff of history and I don't recall
making many entries.

A steady stream of directives, memos, and advisories came into the
headquarters building where the battery clerks worked and I was
elated and as hopeful as I have ever been the day I spotted a memo
from Special Services headquarters in London asking that all newspapermen make their whereabouts known for possible reassignment to
The Stars and Stripes, the Army newspaper.

The Stars and Stripes had begun publication as a weekly in Belfast,
Ireland, with a staff of five people and shortly moved to the area of
London known as Soho. With more than 2 million American soldiers
about to be dumped into the British Isles, the Army recognized its
need for a daily newspaper and set out to assemble a staff.

Before the war was over, *The Stars and Stripes* had an editorial
department of more than 150 and double that number of circulation
and business people. It was not a small-time operation.

I wrote my résumé in the traditional manner of résumés, blowing
it as full of hot air as I dared, and Lieutenant Morris wrote me a good
recommendation. I had worked as a copy boy one summer for the
Knickerbocker Press in Albany. I'd edited the college magazine and, of
course, I had my vast Army publication experience, several months
with the Thirteenth Field Artillery Brigade mimeographed sheet. I
tried to keep hope out of my mind but could not.

Two weeks after being turned down for OCS, and the same week
I applied for the reporter's job with *The Stars and Stripes,* the regiment
started out in a long caravan of vehicles for the uninhabited moors
near Okehampton where we were to have target practice with the
155 howitzers.

The trip down the narrow roads to the south-central moors in
Dover, with me at the wheel of the Diamond-T pulling the howitzer,
was a test of my driving. A 155 howitzer is no toy gun. We, of course,
had to observe England's rules by staying on the left side of the road
and I was relieved to get the gun crew and the equipment to our des-

tination without hitting anything more serious than a few curbs on sharp right turns.

Once out on the desolate moors, we set up for target practice. I recall thinking how strange it was that, in a small country with so many people, there would be a spot so isolated that you could shoot off an artillery piece and not hit anything. Because there was a captaincy open in the regiment, it became widely known that this maneuver and target practice with the big guns was a test for the four lieutenants. One of them, probably the one with the best score on the range, would get the promotion.

I did my job of jacking the howitzer into place and then parking the truck in a clump of trees where it wouldn't be immediately visible to the hypothetical enemy.

The eight crew members and the sergeant who rode up front with me hopped out when I had the howitzer close to its proper position. (The commands given to soldiers to get in and out of a truck in the artillery were "Mount . . . UP!" and "Mount . . . DOWN!")

The projectile for the howitzer was thirty inches long. It must have weighed 250 pounds. It was lifted into the breech on a cradle designed for it by four men. The powder for the shell came in eight cloth bags, each bag a different color and of varying thickness. They looked like small round pillows or beanbags. The bags of powder were stored in an olive-drab, tubular, fiberboard canister four feet tall and ten inches in diameter. Taking care of the bags of gunpowder was my only other responsibility once I'd hidden the Diamond-T.

Sitting at four folding field tables behind the four gun positions were the lieutenants who wanted to be captains. My lieutenant, by chance, was George Creel, the man who had turned down my application for OCS. It was worse luck for him than for me. We prepared for the exercise and in about half an hour everyone was ready for the contest.

He noted a few numbers on a pad in front of him and shouted the command. A typical command to a howitzer crew would be:

"Range three . . . nine . . . two . . . five.
"Elevation, one . . . six . . . eight!
"Charge . . . five!"

He put emphasis on the "charge five!" because that was the end of his direction to the gun crew and "charge five!" was my cue to place five powder charges, pillows of powder, in the breech behind the projectile. He had judged that's how much powder it would take to blast the shell out that distance.

I was still burning mad over his decision to turn down my application for officer candidate school and angry with the manner in which he had done it. I put in just four powder charges.

"Fire!" he commanded.

With a deafening roar and a puff of smoke the 250-pound shell was hurled into the air toward the target. Only toward the target though, not to it. Not with only four bags of powder to propel it.

Of all the shells, Creel's was the only one to fall substantially short of the mark. He cursed audibly, bent over the paper on his work desk, wrote down a few numbers, then looked up, called out substantially the same directions with the exception of the charge.

"Charge six!" he yelled at the top of his lungs.

I put in seven bags of powder. No one was in a position to see how many I used.

On command, the shell was sent soaring a quarter mile past the target.

It was one of the most viciously vengeful acts of my life and wonderfully satisfying. I didn't get to officer candidate school but Creel didn't make captain that day either. I justified my actions in my own mind by thinking he wouldn't have made a good captain anyway. It was a patriotic act of mine. I have no idea where he is or even if he's alive and reading books like this.

Several years ago I was invited to speak to the graduating class at West Point and I told that story. I thought it might be a valuable lesson for them to learn that there are things the military experts at West Point would never teach them. I pointed out that they should keep in mind that there would always be one sonofabitch like me in their command.

When we got back to our base at Perham Downs the order for my transfer to *The Stars and Stripes* had arrived. Glory, glory hallelujah! There was a God in heaven.

I packed my duffel bag, caught the train for London, and left "this man's Army" forever.

III

THE AIR
WAR

THE LONDON EDITION of the World War II *Stars and Stripes* probably had the best printing facility in the world because *The Times* had abandoned its newly installed presses on the ground floor to move back to their old press two stories underground in order to be safe from bombing attacks.

The Stars and Stripes inherited the new, though vulnerable, ground-floor plant. Having been exposed to the tradition of that fine old British newspaper, *The Times,* by working in proximity to the staid, green-eyeshaded inhabitants of its library-quiet newsroom, I cannot, to this day, call any other newspaper simply *The Times.* I don't qualify it with "London." There's *The Times* and then there are other papers that have assumed its name—like *The New York Times* and the *Los Angeles Times.*

The Stars and Stripes had attracted a dozen reporters and editors who could have written for any of the best newspapers in the world. Bob Moora had come from the *New York Herald Tribune.* Charles Kiley from the *Jersey Journal.* Ben Price had worked for the *Des Moines Register,* Bob Wood for the *Detroit Free Press* and the *New York Daily News,* Len Giblin for the Associated Press. Ham Whitman was an old-school rewrite man from the *New York World Telegram.* Bud Hutton had been editor of the *Buffalo Evening News.* Mark Senigo had been with *The New York Times.* It was one of those typical Army stories of a bungled assignment that put me in their midst. My experience as subeditor of the *13th Field Artillery Brigade Bulletin* hardly qualified me to be one of them. Some Army clerk who didn't know or didn't care was probably leafing through the applications. He looked at my résumé and, because the paper was desperate for help in a hurry, made a paperwork decision that changed my life.

There were a few other staff members who got to *The Stars and Stripes* by accident or ignorance on the part of some Army clerk. Bill Estoff had been a bookmaker in Syracuse. He wasn't ashamed of it and listed himself on his personnel form as "Bookmaker." That's what he said he was anytime he was asked for his civilian occupation. It caught the eye of someone riffling through the files. The clerk must have decided there wasn't much difference between making a book and making a newspaper, so this Syracuse bookie was assigned to the circulation staff of the paper.

Bob Moora and Bud Hutton sat at big desks facing each other in the newsroom, each with a wide green lampshade overhead. Bob was the general news editor and Bud handled all "local" stories. Local for *The Stars and Stripes* meant the troops in Great Britain and the war. One of my early impressions of their newspaper expertise was seeing both Moora and Hutton standing across from the font in the composing room where the printers were building headlines by hand with pieces of type. I had not known that a good newspaper editor had to know how to read type that was upside down and backwards, and Bob and Bud were proud of their ability to do it. They also liked doing it in front of the able British pressmen.

Each of us has a few significant rooms in his or her life, and the newsroom of *The Stars and Stripes* in *The Times* building in London was as important to my life as any room I've ever known. There was only one door, a great advantage to any room because it was not a hallway to anywhere else. The room was thirty feet deep and fifty feet wide with not a single window. In addition to the main news desks, there were eight smaller desks, two or three of which were for transient reporters like myself. There were six Underwood #5 typewriters and two L.C. Smith typewriters. The Underwoods were roughly my age, twenty-three, but had lived a harder life. Hutton and Moora each had their own. Ham Whitman, the rewrite man, had one. Mark Senigo, the sports editor, had one and the others were up for grabs.

Those old Underwoods were the best typewriters ever built—one of the best of anything ever built. Even when you weren't writing anything interesting they were satisfying to pound on and I never outgrew my sentimental attachment to them.

I was immediately impressed and somewhat abashed, that first day, to note how fast everyone typed, considering that there wasn't a touch typist on the staff. Bob Moora sat sidesaddle in his chair because he liked to cross his legs and they wouldn't fit under the desk crossed. The typewriter was on his right. His eyes squinted to keep the smoke from curling up into them from the cigarette he always held between his lips. Bob typed faster than I could imagine thinking of anything to say. I thought at the time that he was fast because he'd done so much of it but by now I must have done more of it than he had at the time and I still don't type half as fast as he did. You reach your full typing speed early in the game.

I was out of the office, on assignment, more than I was in it and I used any available desk or typewriter when I came in with a story. Among the things I learned was the personality of each typewriter. We all knew which machines had the best action, which the worst. The typewriter you chose had a marked effect on the speed with which you could turn out a story. One would have a sticky *e*. Another had been in London too long and had a key for a pound sign but no dollar-sign key. The left-handed newsmen didn't like to use the L.C. Smith because the device you used to return the carriage was inconveniently located for them.

To this day, I have in my possession seventeen Underwood #5 typewriters and I'm reluctant to admit that I'm writing on a Toshiba T3200SX computer. Evidence of the swift passage of time is pressed on me often now because people come into my office and ask where I got the old computer.

I love my Underwoods but you can carry the good old days too far. I still write letters on my typewriter so I won't forget how. I wish Underwood had made the keyboard on my Toshiba. My old computer. I'll never have seventeen of these.

There were four upright, pipe-like steel ceiling supports in the newsroom that helped define working areas. Someone had broken the bottom out of a wicker wastebasket and fastened it with wire and

From left: Ben Price, at typewriter, New York Herald Tribune; *Hamilton Whit-man,* New York Telegraph; *I'm looking over Bud Hutton's shoulder; Bob Moora,* New York Herald Tribune, *and far right, Russell Jones, who won the Pulitzer Prize with UPI reporting in Hungary.*

tape near the top of one of those pipes where it served as a basketball hoop. We didn't have a basketball, but reporters working on stories routinely tore bad takes out of their Underwoods, crumpled up the yellow copy paper, and threw it in the direction of the basket. By the end of the day there was more paper on the floor under that hoop than in the wastebaskets provided for the purpose.

I came to London by train and finally found *The Stars and Stripes* office in the maze of narrow, wood-floored corridors that seemed to run in random directions through *The Times.* You'd be walking down a hallway the width of outspread arms and often, for no apparent reason, come on three or four steps that took you up or down to another slightly higher or lower level.

I introduced myself to Hutton and Moora and sat down with the distinct feeling that neither of these editors to whom I'd be answering had chosen me to join the staff. There had been no interview and I'd obviously been thrust on them when I was hastily chosen from a piece of paper that arrived on the desk of Col. Ensley M. Llewellyan, the officer in charge—although he wasn't in charge of much. David Lilienthal said during the war and about the war that decisions made from paper have been responsible for many of the world's ills but Grand Truths like that are always being undermined by small events in real life. I approved of the paper-made decision that put me on *The Stars and Stripes*.

That first day turned out to be an inauspicious beginning for my career in journalism. I sat at an empty desk and rolled a piece of yellow copy paper into the Underwood and started pecking awkwardly at keys with the index finger on my left hand and the index and middle finger of my right hand, a three-finger pecking order I maintain to this minute.

I caught Bob Moora's eyes rolling to the ceiling as he looked first at me and then across his desk to Bud. He said nothing but the thought was clear.

"My God. He can't even type."

I was further terrified about my incompetence when, within my first few days at the paper, Hutton exploded at Phil Bucknell after he'd turned in a piece of copy. Phil was an American by birth but he'd lived and worked in London most of his life. He had a good flair with a feature story, but he was a London newspaperman and no one who knows newspapers thinks this is a compliment.

Bucknell had made the mistake of writing the report he gave Hutton in the chatty, first-person style, including personal opinion, used by the London tabloids.

"Bucknell!" Hutton screamed. "A British sheet says 'I understand Hitler has declared war on Poland and I think it is terrible.' The London *Times* says 'Hitler has declared war on Poland and it is terrible.' An American newspaper says 'Hitler has declared war period' and you, goddamnit, are writing for an American newspaper."

I often thought of the incident afterward because the more I read London newspapers, the more amazed I am that the British people are as well informed as they are. They knew then and still know what's going on in their world and are generally better informed than Americans. They certainly don't get their information from anything I ever saw in the British press. It is, beyond question, the world's worst. If there are worse newspapers, they're not printed in any language I can read. The best London papers make *USA Today* read like the *Encyclopaedia Britannica* by comparison. The most popular London newspapers make our supermarket tabloids seem like models of journalistic integrity.

IT ISN'T EASY or even possible to sort out and categorize the people you have met in your life and assign them labels like Most Unforgettable, but if my life was a play, Bud Hutton would be one of the lead players in it. His name was Oram Clark Hutton, but he was known far and wide and all his life, which ended at age seventy-three in 1984, as Bud. We all have good friends we don't really like and that's the way it was with Bud and me. I couldn't stand being with him for long and yet we were close friends. I greatly admired and liked him in many ways and detested him in others.

It seems likely that as an editor and reporter for *The Stars and Stripes* he, more than any other person, gave 2 million American soldiers in the European Theater of Operations their idea of what World War II was like. A lot of older Americans who still talk about the war are remembering not what they saw but what Hutton told them about it in their newspaper.

When I first met Bud, he was twenty-nine and he often spoke of what he'd done with his life as though it was about over. It was true that he'd had a lifetime of experience at an early age and, while his statement struck me as funny at the time, it turned out he never did do much after the war. He worked a few years for *Time* magazine and was married twice more, for a total of four, but his life as a working newspaperman *was* closer to over than it should have been by the time he was thirty-two.

When he was seventeen, Bud went to work for his father, Tom Hutton, who was editor of the *Binghamton Press,* in Binghamton, New

York. He was living at home but on one occasion he'd been out with a girl he liked and spent the night at her house. He was, in all ways, precocious. Even at that age he was responsible enough as a newsman to have left the girl's phone number with the city desk in case of an emergency and he was awakened early the next morning when the girl's phone rang. Bud's father was furious, not so much because Bud had spent the night with a woman but because there'd been a bank holdup and he didn't have anyone down at the scene.

Bud decided to placate his father by faking it until he could get downtown and find out what happened. He waited a few minutes and then called in to a rewrite man named Kronk and started dictating a story.

"An angry mob of creditors swarmed around the First National Bank of Binghamton today, following an early morning robbery."

At this point, Hutton's father, listening to his call, broke in.

"Goddamnit, Hutton," he yelled at his son, "how many's in an angry mob?"

Bud began again. "A large, angry mob of creditors . . ."

"You're off the story, Hutton," his father yelled. "Get back in here."

Bud says he returned to the newspaper office, threw his Underwood typewriter across the desk at his father, and left home for good at age seventeen. He came to New York to look for newspaper work in 1937 and not only failed to get a job with the *New York Herald Tribune* but was treated so rudely by the person who interviewed him that he never forgave the paper. In desperation, he took a job with the Cleve-O-Rock Construction Company, operating a jackhammer. The *Herald Tribune* offices were on 40th Street between Seventh and Eighth Avenue in Manhattan and, by luck, the company assigned Bud to work on a pedestrian tunnel connecting the subway stations on the two avenues.

"I dug every one of those holes for the dynamite six inches deeper than they were supposed to be," he said. "Broke every goddamn window in the *Herald Trib* building up to the third floor."

He was working with the jackhammer several weeks later when there was a cave-in further along in the tunnel and several men were trapped and it was uncertain how or when they could be rescued. Bud left the tunnel, ran to a nearby phone in the street, and gave a detailed story of the disaster to City News, an important agency in town at the time. It paid off for him because he got a job with them two days later and left the tunnel and the jackhammer with some reluctance because he wanted to start on those fourth-floor windows in the *Herald Tribune* building.

Two years later, Bud became the youngest city editor of any major newspaper in the country when he was at the *Buffalo News,* an afternoon paper. He was proud of how he got the job and often told about it. As assistant city editor, he started early every day. By the time the city editor came in at nine o'clock, Bud had assigned most of the stories to reporters and had things in order for the morning meeting.

The editor became more and more dependent on Bud and, confident things were in good hands, started coming in later and later. One morning before anyone else was in, a fire broke out in downtown Buffalo. It was a major blaze involving several of the big stores on the main street. All of Buffalo's fire equipment was called to the scene, and help came from neighboring towns.

"I came in that morning, saw what was going on," Bud said, "and decided to go out and have a second cup of coffee."

When the city editor arrived, Bud was still at breakfast. No reporters or photographers had been called in or assigned to the fire, and when the paper came out early that afternoon, it's coverage was a poor second to the opposition Buffalo paper.

The next day Mr. Nice Guy was city editor.

It amused Bud to tell the story.

By the time I met him in London, Bud Hutton had long since left the Buffalo paper and had spent several years in New York writing pulp fiction. Zane Grey, the Western novelist, had died and he was so popular in the 1930s that an agent named Steve Schlessinger had bought rights to the name Zane Grey from his estate so he could continue to sell books using the name. For several years Bud was "Zane Grey."

Hutton had also written a lot of what were called Little Big Books. They were the shape of four inches cut off the end of a two-by-four and designed to be read by young teenagers and were very popular for a while.

The Little Big Books were about 10,000 words long and I remember being impressed when Bud told me he could write one in a day.

He was easily the fastest four-finger typist I ever knew and by sticking at it he could write 1,000 words in fifty minutes.

He'd start writing at 8 A.M. At the end of fifty minutes, he'd sit back and take precisely ten minutes drinking a cup of coffee and smoking a cigarette. By noon, he'd have 4,000 words written and he'd stop work for lunch and a brief nap. At one o'clock he'd resume writing, smoking and drinking coffee until 5 P.M., at which time, with 8,000 words completed, he'd stop working until 8 P.M. At exactly 8 P.M. after several drinks and dinner, he'd go back to work and by 10 P.M. he'd have the book written and go to bed.

In 1941, Bud volunteered for the Canadian army, a fact he never let anyone like myself, who'd been drafted, forget. He was contemptuous of draftees. After less than a year in the Canadian army Bud transferred to the U.S. Army and was assigned to *The Stars and Stripes* where, as a master sergeant, he quickly became its chief editor. M/Sgt. Oram Clarke Hutton. It was Hutton who established the style "M/Sgt." in designating rank in our newspaper. Our style book, which Bud had drawn up, called for "Pvt.," "Cpl.," "Sgt.," "S/Sgt.," "T/Sgt." (for technical sergeant), and "M/Sgt." Officers were "2/Lt.," "1/Lt.," "Capt.," "Maj.," "Lt. Col.," "Col.," "Lt./Gen.," and "Gen."

While he was writing and editing, Bud liked to say that he was the best farmer in the newspaper business. Years later I visited him on his farm on the Eastern Shore of Maryland and he told me then that he was the best newspaperman in the farming business.

Over the years I worked with and for him, Bud and I had a lot of rocky times and were often close to actually fighting.

"Don't ever fight with me," he'd say in calm moments. "I'd kill you. I'd do things to you in a fight that you wouldn't do to me."

For some perverse reason, Bud enjoyed the image of himself as a rotten bastard. He liked to promote that idea and then surprise people by giving candy to babies. In some ways he was a bastard, often petty, selfish, and totally egocentric, but he was also the consummate newsman. His counterpart across the desk, Bob Moora, was in many ways as good and steadier but Hutton dominated the editorial pages of the paper through the assignments he handed out and the choices of stories he made. Hutton and Moora seldom disagreed on any basic news decision and I think that's because they were both good and there are absolutes in newspaper editing. It is not a question of "That's what you think."

When Republic Aviation's P-47 fighter planes first got to England and were assigned to Brig. Gen. Frank Hunter's Eighth Fighter Command in January 1943, it was an important story for us. The presence of this powerful, four-ton fighting machine, armed with eight 20mm cannon in its wings, meant that the B-17s and B-24s would have better air cover deep into Germany than they'd ever had before. More than half again as heavy as the P-51 and with a dive speed up as close to compressibility at the speed of sound as a pilot dared push it, the P-47 was a monster fighter plane that made it a new and different war in the air over Germany. The P-51 was a good aircraft and more maneuverable but it was liquid-cooled instead of air-cooled as the P-47 was, and more easily brought down when the metal tubes carrying its liquid coolant were pierced by enemy fire. The P-47s made it more difficult for the Luftwaffe to shoot down a big, slow-moving bomber because our own fighter planes were now sitting up there, a few thousand feet above our bomber formations, waiting to dive with all eight guns blazing, at any ME-109 or FW-190 that ventured up to intercept the bombers.

On my Air Force beat, I heard early that the P-47s had arrived and told Bud about it. He was an airplane buff and already knew more about it than I did but he pressed me for any details I could give him about its performance and about what the pilots flying it thought. I told him a lot of pilots had been killed when they crashed trying to learn how to fly this juggernaut but the ones who had mastered it, like Col. Hubert Zemke, loved it.

Because it could no longer be kept secret from anyone—it's hard to keep so obvious and dramatic a weapon secret for long—Fighter Command announced a press junket at which the P-47s would be shown to reporters with the understanding that it was a hold-for-release story. We couldn't print it until they gave us the okay. There were about twelve reporters looking over the P-47s that day and we were all properly impressed and a little grumpy about not being able to release our stories immediately.

Back in the office, I spent the next day writing what I'd learned about the P-47, and I made it clear to Bud that there was an absolute hold on the information until Eighth Fighter Command cleared it.

More than three weeks later, the Air Force had still not given us permission to go with the story. Interest in the plane's existence in the British Isles was at a peak because the success or failure of the heavy bombers' raids might depend on the protection the P-47s could give them. We knew that two P-47s had been forced down in Germany and there was no question that the Germans knew we had them and knew their performance capabilities. The two planes had landed intact. As soon as any aircraft of ours was forced down and landed in one piece in Germany, the Luftwaffe fixed it up and flew it to find out all about what it could do and could not do.

Hutton was one of those airplane nuts who knew everything about anything that flew. During the time after I had seen the P-47 and before news of its presence was officially released, he kept a folder in his desk. He asked the New York office to collect everything they could find that had ever been written about the P-47's development and production, and he clipped everything he could find in aviation magazines. Over the period of the plane's development, there had been a lot published about it in various technical journals devoted to aircraft. Bud had them all.

His anger over the stop on the story grew as the days went by, and he finally sat down and wrote a long article on the P-47 with a great many specific details. It was an authoritative, masterful job of journalism, and I was envious of it though I'd actually seen the aircraft and Bud hadn't.

At about six o'clock, on a Wednesday, four hours before the paper went to press, Bud gave his story to the censors and told them he was going to use it in the next day's edition. Their first reaction was "ABSOLUTELY NOT!" Hutton argued forcefully and the young officers were no match for his anger or expertise. The censors in *The Stars and Stripes* office took the story by hand to their headquarters in the British Office of Information building. Their chief of censorship hit the ceiling when he read it and demanded that Hutton come over.

Gathering together his voluminous notes, Hutton packed them in a briefcase and headed out. He told me to come with him to testify to the fact that I hadn't given him any information that he had not or could not have obtained from previously printed articles and technical journals. At the censors' office, Hutton made sure he exhibited a higher state of anger than they did. Page by page and line by line, Hutton gave them a printed reference for every fact he'd used in his story.

The hard rule was that censors would pass anything that we could prove had already been printed somewhere else. Hutton proved that what he had written had been printed—even though it had never been collected and printed in one place. It was the kind of job someone in German Army Intelligence would already have done.

The rule of our Intelligence people was that we did not confirm anything when we simply knew the Germans had a secret of ours. We waited until we knew that they knew we knew. Intelligence people go through some convoluted thinking processes. At this point, the P-47 had been flying for more than six weeks and the Air Force had evidence that the Germans had their hands on those two P-47s that had been forced down in good condition.

The one single thing Bud had not said in his piece was that the P-47 was there in England and flying missions. He asked the colonel in charge of the censors' office to point out where there was even so much as a hint that the plane was in Great Britain. Of course the censor couldn't put a finger on anything like that. It was so clearly apparent in the articles that the P-47 was in the United Kingdom that it was unnecessary to say so. The absence of such a declaration might easily have escaped the notice of any reader.

Bud was adamant. Where had he written anything that wasn't already in print? Where had he said the P-47 was operating out of the UK? The censors finally wilted before Bud's convincing argument and the story appeared in the paper the next morning.

Before 7 A.M. that day, I got an urgent call from a public-relations captain at Eighth Fighter Command. He was livid and I was nervous. I hadn't betrayed the trust but I had known Hutton was writing the story. All day long there were calls between Fighter Command, SHAEF, and the officer-in-charge of *The Stars and Stripes,* Ensley M. Llewellyan. Llewellyan had never known how to handle Hutton and he had no idea what to do in this situation. While the colonel was nominally the sergeant's boss, the sergeant knew so much more about almost everything than the colonel did that rank was not effective. Llewellyan also appreciated the fact that Bud was good and essential to the operation of the newspaper so he hedged and did nothing.

On the second day a half-inch-thick manila envelope marked THE EDITOR was hand-delivered by Fighter Command headquarters to the offices of *The Stars and Stripes*. It was routinely handled and Joe McBride put it in Hutton's IN basket on the news desk.

In the course of getting started on the day's work, Hutton routinely tore open his mail and that's what he did this day, including the manila envelope. Inside was a sheaf of papers constituting a formally drawn up request for a court-martial of M/Sgt. Oram Clark Hutton.

Hutton looked through the legal document, put it down on his desk, and thought a minute. At that point he picked up a pen, and scribbled on top of the document DISAPPROVED! Under the word he wrote his initials, "BH."

Bud put the official-looking batch of papers into his out basket with RETURN TO SENDER noted on the outside of the fat, brown envelope. No further word was ever heard about General Hunter's demand that Sergeant Hutton be tried for treason.

I don't know what it was about Bud but his idea of a good time was to present himself as an overbearing, egotistical faker and then have the person to whom he'd appeared so objectionable realize that he was as good as he boasted of being.

Bud fell in love frequently during the time we spent in London and usually had a woman he was living with. He was always on the prowl. I watched one night as he put the moves on an attractive Red Cross girl and as usual he posed as someone who knew everything about everything. He had a way of directing any conversation to topics he was familiar with so he could display his knowledge. He wasn't much interested in any subject about which he knew less than the person he was talking to and he'd change the subject if one came up.

Toward the end of the evening the young woman was fed up with Bud.

"I've met thousands of soldiers since I've been here," she finally snapped, "and you're the most conceited fool I've ever met."

Bud took genuine pleasure from the fact that the girl thought he was the most of something. That's what he took from her remark. He wouldn't have been happy if she'd called him "one of the most" of anything.

If he sounds like a terrible guy, he was in a way, but his intelligence and his sense of humor about himself or anything else, saved him. He had a kind of universal awareness, including an awareness of the kind of person he was, that made him more than acceptable as a friend. I cherished the bastard.

M Y FIRST ASSIGNMENT was to cover the ETO bowling championship among the teams competing from several Air Force bases. Obviously, it was a test for me because neither Moora nor Hutton knew or cared anything about bowling and not much more about sports of any kind.

I spent several hours watching the event and took what notes I thought I should. The job wasn't made any easier for me by the fact that I didn't know a strike from a spare or how many pins were considered a good number to knock down in a game. When the winners were announced I was close to panic. I clutched my notes in my hand and tried to decide what to do. The paper closed about 9 P.M. and it was then sometime after seven. Was I expected to return to the office and write my story under deadline pressure? I couldn't ask Hutton. He'd covered the Lindbergh trial.

In desperation I called the office and had good luck. The phone was answered by one of the friendliest voices I've known in my lifetime and one I still hear regularly fifty years later. It was Ralph Martin, who has distinguished himself in the intervening years by turning out highly readable biographies, including his memorable two volumes on Winston Churchill's mother, *Jenny.* I've distinguished myself by remaining one of his best friends but his friendship, barely established at the time, never meant more to me than it did that day.

I'd seen movies about newspapermen and in almost all of them the reporter in the phone booth, with his fedora on the back of his head, shouted to the man on the other end of the phone in the newsroom "Stop the presses! Flash!" The reporter then dictated his story nonstop with nothing on paper in front of him. He wrote the story in his head as he spoke it into the telephone. I was afraid I was expected to do that and I couldn't.

"Ralph," I asked, tremulously I imagine, "do I have to dictate the story to you or should I come in and write it there?"

"Who won, Andy?" Ralph asked.

I told him.

"Spell that," Ralph said when I mentioned a name.

He asked several more questions and said, "Thanks, Andy. Good job. I'll put down a few 'graphs and give it to the desk."

It was the beginning of my education as a reporter.

My lifestyle has never changed so abruptly as it did the day I moved into a small flat in London. The Army gave *Stars and Stripes* editorial people food and a quarters allowance and we all lived independently. We could eat at one of the Army mess halls around London if we chose but we seldom chose. This was some exotic arrangement for a private just out from under reveille, nine o'clock bed check, and the unrelenting eye of Sergeant Harrell in the Seventeenth Field Artillery barracks.

Money never seemed to be an issue. I don't recall how much we got for a living allowance (per diem) or that I ever had to do without anything because I couldn't afford it. We had access to a good PX (post exchange) in London that had all sorts of good things that the British couldn't get and there was a great barter market. Each GI could buy seven packs of cigarettes a week and, although I never smoked, I always bought my share and gave them away or traded them with some British acquaintance. Dead now, I suppose. Two of the few foods the British have mastered are marmalade and black currant jam. I swapped cigarettes for marmalade.

I loved London from the first day, a love affair that obtains to this day. When I arrived I had not known that so much of the city had been destroyed by Luftwaffe bombs, and when I go to London now I'm acutely aware of the buildings whose reconstruction after the war is made apparent by patches or whole walls of brick that don't match the rest of the building. I'm not sure anyone who hadn't seen the walls down would notice their reconstruction. The grayness of London has, over the years, turned the new brick closer to the same color as the rest of the city, but if you're looking for evidence of World War II, you can see it everywhere.

In 1994, after the celebration of the fiftieth anniversary of D-Day, I went to London and walked some familiar streets. *The Times* is gone and Printing House Square is gone, but the area along the wide street running perpendicular to the Thames in front of St. Paul's Cathedral still has patches of rubble where buildings that I once knew stood. I had taken what I thought was an arty picture of St. Paul's in 1942, through the bomb-broken facade of a stone building on New Bridge Street and Apothecary Street. I could have come close to duplicating it in 1994 because the vacant lot and some of the broken stones were where they fell fifty-two years before.

The whole scene in London was a constant source of interest to any young American living there. Tens of thousands of Londoners routinely brought their mattresses, blankets, and burners with which

This view of St. Paul's Cathedral was close to our office at The Times *in Printing House Square, just off Fleet Street. It was one of very few pictures I took in London.*

to make hot tea down into the cavernous subway stations, known there as the Underground. Many of those stations are hundreds of moving steps down into the bowels of the city. The tunnel walls of almost every Underground station were lined with steel-framed beds facing the advertising on the walls across the tracks that advised riders to BUY BOVRIL! or to DRINK GUINNESS! The word "Underground" itself was an initiation to the wonderfully direct and literal way the English have of naming things. A restaurant that sells food packaged to bring home is a take-away.

I often used the Bethnal Green Underground station and sometimes at night I was the only person going down the long stairway. One night the terrifying wail of the air-raid sirens sounded when rush-hour traffic on the Underground was at its peak. I was walking toward the station but stopped short when I saw the terrified crowd pushing its way, like water hurrying down a drain, into the Bethnal Green station. I decided my chances of surviving the air raid were better if I walked partway home and then took a bus the rest of the way than they would be if I went down the drain into that trap, so I kept going past the pushing and shoving mob.

Bethnal Green was one of the most underground of all the Underground stations in London, and there were two flights of about thirty steps each on the L-shaped stairway before you got to the escalator. I have a nervous habit of counting steps wherever I go.

Almost simultaneously with my arrival at the entrance, a woman carrying a baby fell on the L-shaped landing at the bottom of the first flight of stairs. I didn't know this detail until the following day when I read it in the papers. After she fell, the people kept crowding in from above. Those stopped on the landing where the stairs turned and where the woman had fallen were crushed up against the wall by the mass of people pushing down the stairs because they couldn't move. The escalator below couldn't begin to move people down as fast as others were piling into the entrance above. Within a short time the escalator itself jammed and stopped. That night 178 people were crushed to death in the Bethnal Green station.

No bombs fell and the air-raid siren turned out to be a false alarm.

There are times when a number takes the place of a name. There have been half a dozen numbers in my life that were as important as any name I ever knew and 20 Grosvenor Square was one of those. There were lots of buildings on Grosvenor Square. The "20" had a meaning all its own. This was Supreme Headquarters Allied Expeditionary Force (SHAEF), where Dwight Eisenhower had his office, and it was the most important address in the world for two years. There were four unmanned blimps floating over the little park in the center of the square. They were designed to obstruct any low-level bomb run by the Luftwaffe, but in fact they made an obvious target of the headquarters building. HERE! HERE! HERE! the balloons shouted to the bombardiers.

I shared a basement flat on Clarges Street with Dick Koenig, a photographer who came to the paper at the same time I did. He was the perfect roommate. We didn't hang out together but we got along for more than a year without an argument. Clarges runs off Piccadilly opposite Green Park. Piccadilly was the playground for prostitutes looking for GIs and they prowled the streets there. Shortly after we

My roommate, Dick Koenig, took this in our basement apartment on Clarges Street, just off Piccadilly, in London. The glass of wine and the cigar were a joke because I neither smoked nor drank. Dick put up the picture showing Ronald Reagan and his wife, Jane Wyman, taking daughter Maureen for a walk. I did not yet have an opinion of Ronald Reagan but I would not have put his picture on the wall.

rented our flat, we began to hear strange noises emanating from the flat just above ours. Not strange, really.

It became apparent we had a business operating overhead and the rhythmic thumping four or five times between nine at night and 6 A.M. began to get to both Dick and me. One night about 2 A.M. the businesswoman upstairs had an especially active customer. Not knowing whether or not Dick was awake, I said nothing.

"Jesus, Andy," Dick finally whispered softly, knowing I couldn't be sleeping through it, "she's doing it again. We gotta get out of here."

We moved to a nice, big, one-room flat on Bayswater Road with a good bathroom (bathrooms were scarce because the British had not then and still have not really mastered plumbing) and pretensions of being more than it was. Although it was clearly on Bayswater Road, its official address was 11 Palace Court Road, an address that was clearly around the corner and nearer a pretty part of Hyde Park in a higher-rent area. The 88 bus took us down Bayswater Road to Marble Arch and then down Oxford to Piccadilly Circus, the Haymarket, Leicester Square, and Trafalgar Square, and then down Fleet Street to Ludgate Circus and our office in *The Times.* Knowing your way around a foreign city and being able to display your knowledge is one of life's most delightful small pleasures—although it's often a bore to anyone else.

I don't know what I did all day those first weeks in London while I was trying desperately to hang onto my job with the paper before I knew how to do it, but shortly after my stop-the-presses bowling story hit the back page, I was given another assignment commensurate with my ability.

One day in November, the desk got a memo from Maj. Gen. John C. H. Lee recommending that we do a story about a unit citation award he was giving to a Negro quartermaster supply battalion in the south of England. Lee was a pompous little martinet, but he must also have been competent because Ike gave him the major job of being quartermaster general in charge of all supply. Obviously he thought it would be good for the morale of all Negro troops if one unit got some recognition.

There were not many black units in the British Isles and I don't recall that we ever had a story that specifically mentioned one of them. If we had, we would have referred to them as Negro, not black. I wouldn't be surprised if we went back to "Negro" someday because it has more substance than "black."

It's hard to make a Pulitzer Prize winner out of a general pinning a medal on someone but I traveled by train to their base twenty miles outside London with Dick Koenig as the photographer. Dick snapped away while General Lee posed pinning unit-citation medals on proud chests that didn't understand they were being used for public-relations purposes.

Back at the office I wrote the story and anguished over how to refer to the unit. I would not, I thought to myself, have referred to the battalion as "white quartermaster corps troops" and I decided it would be wrong for me to say "Negro quartermaster corps troops." I wrote, simply, "quartermaster corps troops." And, anyway, I thought, the pictures would say what I was not saying.

Editors are notorious for not knowing or caring about the nuances of feelings or public relations. Moora or Hutton decided the story was not worth the space a dull picture would take up and they did not run Dick's picture with my story.

The day the brief item appeared, I got an angry call from General Lee's aide. The general wouldn't have stooped to complain to a private and I was recently enough out from under the heel of superior officers to be nervous. It was one of many times that General Lee was angry with *The Stars and Stripes* and one of the times we were lucky to have General Eisenhower's protective arm around our shoulders. No one had to go to him on my behalf on this occasion but he was there and someone could have gone to him.

My friends Charles Kiley, Ben Price, and Joe Fleming had a spacious suite of rooms in Clifford's Inn on Fetter Lane just off Fleet Street, three blocks from the office at *The Times.* Charley and Ben spent most of their professional lives after the war with the *Herald Tribune* and Joe joined the United Press and stayed in Germany. Years later, when people asked Joe how long he'd been in Berlin, he'd always say "Since D-Day. I was the youngest American soldier to land on Omaha Beach." He'd pause. "I understand there was one German soldier who was younger, fourteen. He lied about his age to get in the Wehrmacht."

None of that was true, of course. It just amused Joe to say it. He had a great ear for clichés and liked to deflate anyone overstating his war experience. Newsmen had a tendency to overstate the proximity of their arrival on the beaches to D–Day. If all the reporters I've heard about or read about being on the beaches on D–Day were actually there, we wouldn't have needed an army.

I had an argument with Stephen Ambrose, author of the first-rate book *D-Day June 6, 1944.* Steve said that Ernest Hemingway was there D–Day and I insisted he was not. Steve quoted from an article he said Hemingway had written for the *Saturday Evening Post* about coming into the beach that day.

If we had bet, I'm not sure who an impartial arbiter would say won it. I was more wrong than right. I looked up the article Hemingway wrote. It was in *Collier's,* not the *Saturday Evening Post,* one for me; but, while Hemingway came toward the beach in an LCI (landing craft, infantry), he did not disembark and actually come onto Omaha Beach. I was technically right, but I think Professor Ambrose wins that one and I apologize to the memory of Hemingway for suspecting him of being one of those who said they were there when they were not.

When Joe Fleming was living in Berlin after the war, I made a trip there with a group of journalists, and William Randolph Hearst, Jr., was among them. Hearst and several others wandered into East Germany while the Wall was still serious business and they were briefly detained by the police. Hearst and Frank Conniff, who often wrote the things with Bill's byline on them, made a major story out of being "held" by the communist East German police. Joe had heard the same story too often from other reporters.

In his office at UPI, Joe typed out a story that he had no intention of sending out, and pinned it to the bulletin board. It began:

"William Randolph Hearst, Jr., was taken hostage earlier today by East German police. He was brutally detained and held for ten minutes without food or water."

News was big business in London those days and the news community had a world of its own. CBS was building its reputation on the work of Edward R. Murrow and the city was filled with people whose names were legend in the upper regions of journalism. I think offhand of people like Jock Whitney, who later bought the *New York Herald Tribune,* Elmer Davis, who had replaced H. V. Kaltenborn as a commentator on CBS and then became head of the Office of War Information, Hugh Baillie, head of the United Press, Rex Smith, editor of *Newsweek* and later the *Chicago Sun,* and William Shirer, author of the best-selling *Berlin Diary.*

I got to know a lot of the working news men and women and was mildly starstruck to be working next to them on many stories.

The Stars and Stripes itself had a staff of about 110 people, including editorial, business, and circulation. We were blessedly free of space salesmen and an advertising department.

The staff of the Army magazine, *YANK,* was in more or less the same position we were in. They put out what was called a London edition even though their upper echelon editorial and business staff operated out of New York under Col. Frank Forsberg and Sgt. Joe McCarthy, who had captured a huge audience in Boston with the stories of his early adventures in the Army with a company equipped with mules.

I got to know Joe a lot better after the war than I had during it. In the late 1940s, when he was the postwar editor of *Cosmopolitan* magazine and I was trying to make a living as a freelance magazine writer, he gave me some great advice.

"Read the magazine," he said. "Find out what the editor wants, how long he wants it, and then get it to him the day he has to have it. It doesn't have to be very good."

The editor of the London edition of *YANK* was a tall, effete, dirty blond fellow named Bill Richardson who wore a large handlebar mustache and an imperious air. For no reason I can recall other than that, those of us on *The Stars and Stripes* disliked him. We considered *YANK* to be an amusing little magazine with literary pretensions that had nothing to do with news and not much to do with the war. The staff at *YANK* held an equally high opinion of those of us on *The Stars and Stripes.* At this distance, it's safe to say we were both wrong. *YANK* had some of the best young writers to come out of the war and, in spite of my generally negative attitude toward the magazine, I was pleased when they accepted and printed two short stories of mine during the time I was in London.

There was only one occasion when the arm's-length relationship between the two publications got nasty. *The Stars and Stripes* was printed five days a week. We had no weekend edition even though the Army was a seven-day-a-week organization. Every Monday Ben Price, the picture editor, got together the best photos from all the agencies in London and New York and made up a full page of pictures. My memory of it is that Rita Hayworth was there most weeks sitting on her heels on the bed just barely wearing that shimmering black-lace negligee. It has never been clear to me what the difference is between a negligee and a nightgown but I am clear that what Rita was wearing was a negligee in that famous wartime picture of her. If Benny didn't have a picture of Rita, he found a Wampus Baby Star to feature. Toby Wing, perhaps, or Toni Seven.

One Monday Ben was putting the page together and a picture of Bill Richardson, the *YANK* editor, turned up in his file. Bill was news that week because he had married a British girl. Among the other pictures Ben chose that week was one of a young woman in overalls who had gained considerable fame in the United States by winning a competition as the best female riveter working in a Navy shipyard. She became well known as "Rosie the Riveter" and bore no resemblance whatever to Rita Hayworth.

The pictures of Bill Richardson and Rosie the Riveter were among those on the picture page that day and under each was a caption. Below the picture of Rosie, in her overalls and holding a jackhammer, was the line YANK EDITOR WEDS!

Under the photo of Bill Richardson, the *YANK* editor, the line was WORLD'S FASTEST RIVETER.

Benny Price swore the mixup was an honest mistake but no one believed him, most noticeably Bill Richardson, who was furious.

There was not much of anything daring printed in *YANK* but a good writer named Debs Meyers was asked to write a review of the runaway best seller of 1943, the romantic *Forever Amber.*

"*Forever Amber,*" Debs wrote as his lead, "is the story of a girl laid in the 18th century." The report of the mildly bawdy joke spread through the troops and *YANK* never sold so well.

I'd often stop by Clifford's Inn to have dinner or just talk and I was there about ten one night when the air-raid sirens sounded. They

produced a haunting wail and sent people on the street scurrying
down into the Underground. We sat and waited to see whether the
attack was from the old V1s, the newer V2s, or Luftwaffe bombs. The
V1 was more like a high-flying torpedo than an artillery shell or a
bomb. It was self-propelled and, because it had a top speed of only
about 175mph, it could be heard coming from a distance so you had
time to dread it. The engine was timed to cut off so the explosive cap-
sule could start its descent to its target but no one on the ground
could anticipate when it was timed to cut out and drop. The very
slowness of its approach multiplied the degree of terror it generated
in the civilian population. Within minutes we heard small explosions
in the street below and light from flames danced in all the windows.
We were being bombed by aircraft.

The Luftwaffe was dropping thousands of its insidious incendiary
bombs. The mother bombs were timed to explode in the air a few
hundred feet off the ground, like fireworks. Each one contained clus-
ters of smaller chunks of white-hot phosphorus that spewed over
rooftops and into the streets, setting fire to anything they landed on.

I ran down into Fleet Street and a distraught woman came running by in tears. "St. Martin-in-the-Fields is burning," she cried. "St.
Martin-in-the-Fields is burning."

I walked several blocks and the little church placed immediately
above Fleet Street in an elbow of the Strand known as the Aldwych
was glowing from within. I could see the flames inside burning the
wood pews of the magnificent little Sir Christopher Wren church, its
stained-glass windows never more beautiful than they were that
night, lit from within by the flickering light of the fire started by
bombs that had dropped through the roof to the floor of the nave.

That church, which I thought at the time was St. Martin-in-the-
Fields, was actually a lesser Christopher Wren church called St.
Clement Danes. St. Martin is several blocks further up Fleet Street on
one side of Trafalgar Square and I didn't walk to it that night, but
whenever I go past it now in a taxi on a visit to London I always con-
found the cab driver by muttering to myself "St. Martin-in-the-Fields
is burning, St. Martin-in-the-Fields is burning."

After seeing where the bombs had hit along Fleet Street, I raced
back to Clifford's Inn and took the elevator, which was still running,

to the top floor. This was in spite of the traditional IN CASE OF AIR RAID DO NOT USE ELEVATOR sign.

There were a dozen small fragments of four firebombs burning their way down through the roof when I got there. Tony Cordero, a *Stars and Stripes* photographer built like Chernokowski who had been with the *Des Moines Register,* was already up there. There were a dozen red buckets filled with sand in the hallway and on the roof meant for such an emergency. We didn't know whether the firebombs were inert or whether they were likely to explode again into smaller pieces as fancy fireworks sometimes do as they fall to earth. We took the risk anyway and approached the glowing bomb fragments and put them out by dumping the buckets of sand on them. From the rooftop we could look out over much of London and see hundreds of burning buildings. Something perverse in our nature makes a catastrophe compelling to watch.

Over the next few months I learned enough about writing for a newspaper to get by. Little by little, Moora and Hutton started to trust me with stories of more significance than the outcome of a bowling match.

One of my early stories of the Eighth Air Force was on the occasion of the award of the Distinguished Flying Cross to Jimmy Stewart, the actor who was already famous for parts in *The Philadelphia Story* and *Mr. Smith Goes to Washington.* It was hard to look at Stewart standing there in line in his uniform without thinking, "Those don't look like lips that have kissed Lana Turner's." It was the last thing he wanted anyone to be thinking about him, I suppose—although, come to think of it, the thought of kissing Lana Turner must have come to him, unbidden, a few times during the war.

Stewart was one of the very best pilots and leaders in the Air Force and the kind of American that Americans like to think of as typical even though he was better than that. It's an indication of how many great stories there were to tell about the Eighth Air Force that his story is not better known to his fans. The word "fan" itself is wrong to mention because he did everything he could to lose them and to, temporarily at least, set aside his image as a Hollywood star. He enlisted as a private and, because he had taken flying lessons as a civilian, finally made his way into pilot training school. It was a long and tortuous route up through the ranks for him before he finally became commander of the Second Bomb Wing at Alconbury. In the intervening months he had been lead pilot in the 445th Bomb Group, operations officer for the 453rd Bomb Group, and then operations officer and chief of staff for the Second Bomb Wing.

It's quite clear from every Air Force record that Stewart was a superior flier. He was originally disappointed to be assigned several different jobs as a training instructor. It was apparent that the Air Force didn't think it needed a headline saying this popular actor had been shot down over Germany.

He was determined to get into combat though, and if he used his celebrity status at all to improve his position, it was to have himself transferred away from the field where he had a safe instructor's job to a bomb group going to Great Britain.

As an instructor, Stewart had flown everything the Air Force had. His first four-engine plane was the B-17, but he was sent to England with the 445th Bomb Group stationed at Tibenham, which flew B-24s. The men who flew with him knew he wanted to avoid any kind of publicity related to his Hollywood persona but they liked the idea of his being one of them. He had as high a reputation among other fliers as any pilot in the Air Force and he rose to the rank of colonel not because he was Jimmy Stewart but because he was good. When it comes to Jimmy Stewart, I'm the kind of sycophant I dislike.

I was reluctant to send a cameraman out in front of the line of men receiving awards and singling out Jimmy Stewart to photograph but I suspect that, in this case, he must have been a little proud and only tentatively reluctant to have his picture in *The Stars and Stripes*. He had a right to be proud. I shook hands with him that day but we haven't maintained that close relationship.

I don't know whether Stewart and Clark Gable had been friends back home, and I don't know whether they ever saw each other in England, but Gable was at First Wing headquarters at Cheltenham and, while he never did what Jimmy Stewart did, I saw him several times and always got the impression that he wanted to do his job without a lot of fanfare. I have a clear impression of how good he looked in his pinks and it didn't occur to me at the time but I suppose they were tailor-made for him in London. Everyone who could afford to had shoes made by Peels on Jermyn Street and uniforms tailored by Moss Brothers in Covent Garden, known to one and all simply as "Moss Bross."

I look at the years that have gone by and there are long periods of my life that are blank in my memory. I couldn't tell you anything that I accomplished some years but the years 1942, 1943, 1944, and 1945 are the ones I remember best. Some of those memories are indelible. If I've done too little some years, I did a lot those years, and there were millions of Americans who would say the same thing. Less than two years after I left college at the end of my junior year, I had not only learned to type but Bud Hutton and I had written a book together called *Air Gunner* and had it published by Farrar and Rinehart.

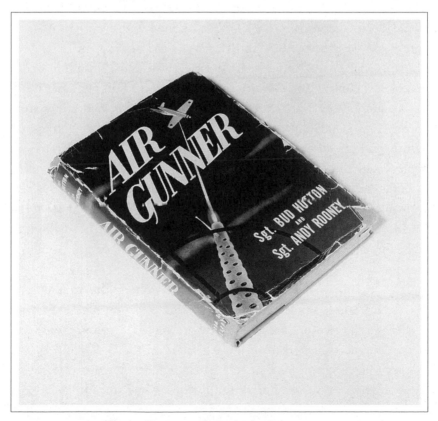

The jacket of the first book I wrote with Bud Hutton.

The book was a series of vignettes of gunners on the B-17s and B-24s. They were hungry for that sort of firsthand account back home and we got very good reviews.

The New York office sent us a telegram with one review that referred to *Air Gunner* as "One of the best books of the war."

Hutton had a tantrum and it seemed real but he must have been putting us on.

" 'One of the best.' Goddamnit! What does he mean 'One of'? Which the hell were the others?"

THE BEST STORY in the British Isles for a reporter was the air war against Germany. There were, altogether, sixty-eight U.S. Air Force bases in the British Isles, divided between the Eighth and Ninth Air Forces. The Royal Air Force had roughly the same number of fighter plane and bomber bases as we did but *The Stars and Stripes* had all it could do to cover the great number of men and events in its own forces and we gave the RAF little space in the newspaper.

My assignments took me to both Eighth and Ninth Air Force bases but I concentrated on the Eighth Air Force bomber bases nearest London. They were easiest to get to and after a raid, there were more stories at any one base than a newspaper could use. Each story I wrote about heroism, mess sergeants, mascot dogs, or death in the air represented a hundred stories just like those at another base.

The Eighth Air Force was one of the great fighting forces in all the history of warfare. It had the best equipment and the best men, all but a handful of whom were civilian Americans, educated and willing to fight for their country and a cause they understood was in danger— freedom.

The Eighth had most of the heavy bombers, the four-engine B-17s and B-24s. The Ninth had more fighter groups, the P-51s and P-47s and the two-engine B-26 bombers, but the truth is, there were better stories to be had from the ten men on the B-17s and B-24s. Before I left England for France, I had flown, in the course of covering the air war, on three bombing missions over France in B-26s and two raids on Germany with the B-17s.

A B-17 group had 2,260 men, somewhat fewer than half of whom were flight-crew members. Ideally, on the charts, there were ninety-six crews for the seventy-two bombers on a base. A crew was a close-knit unit because the men lived together and shared the fear of dying together—and often did die together. In the air, each depended on the others for his survival. Everything one man did made a difference to the whole crew.

On every bomber there was a pilot and a copilot, a bombardier, and a navigator. Five enlisted men manned the guns, one in the top turret above the cockpit, two waist gunners, the ball-turret gunner crammed into the tiny, rotating Plexiglas sphere that hung below the plane just behind the bomb-bay doors, and the tail gunner looking to the rear. Another man was on the radio.

I never cared much for nicknames for the planes of World War II. It seemed best to call the B-17 the B-17 and not a Flying Fortress, although I notice that in my stories at the time I often called them "Forts." Similarly, I preferred "B-24" to "Liberator." I was surprised in looking back to note how often in my stories they were referred to simply as "the heavies." I can't imagine using that term now but it came easily then.

The B-17 did more than any other airplane to win the war. The B-17—like the great troop and cargo carrier, the DC-3, Dakota—was not statistically exceptional. It wasn't fast, it wasn't maneuverable. It didn't carry the heaviest bomb load. What it was, was almost inde-structible. Thousands of times during the three years B-17s dropped bombs in Europe, they were riddled with flak (Fliegerabwehr-kanonen) and 50mm machine-gun bullets from Focke Wulfe 190s and Messerschmitt 109s. With three engines gone, with hydraulic sys-tems drained of fluid, with wounded crewmen onboard, the aircraft, time after time, hauled everyone back home to safety. If airplanes had human qualities, the B-17s would be called valiant.

The people who flew the B-24 Liberators were fiercely loyal to their aircraft and always argued that it was the better of the two. I don't like further angering them here now but it wasn't. The B-24 was never the bomber the B-17 was. The B-24 people argued speed, ease of handling, and bomb load, and if all you looked at were these characteristics, the B-24 was the better airplane. If you had to go to Berlin or Schweinfurt, take a B-17 and your chances of getting home were vastly improved. The B-17 could take a punch like no other aircraft ever built.

Although the men who flew it liked it and were loyal, the B-24 could be hard to handle until a pilot was thoroughly familiar with it. Training accidents were common. During 1943 alone, 850 airmen died in 298 training crack-ups in the United States and a disproportionate number of those were in B-24s. This is a lot of planes and a lot of people to lose before you get to the war.

The Luftwaffe fighter pilots, always referred to as "Jerries," had learned that the big bombers were most vulnerable if they were attacked head-on because it was the fastest way through the formation and the top-turret gunner was the only man who had a good shot at them as they made their pass. In the Boeing plants in the State of Washington, they quickly corrected the plane's front-end vulnerability by adding a chin turret, below the bombardier in the nose of the plane, with a machine gunner in another Plexiglas compartment facing forward. It gave the nose gunner a long look and a good shot at any German fighter plane coming straight into the formation. The Luftwaffe began losing so many fighter planes that they gave up the tactic and started diving at the bombers again. These were strange things for someone like myself, little more than a year away from Andy Kerr and Byron's *Don Juan,* to be learning.

The bomber crew was a tight unit and, although enlisted men and officers lived apart, the officers were generally closer to the enlisted men on their plane than they were to the officers from another. What made it so unsettling an existence was the proximity of death. Unlike the infantry, the fliers lived a civilized and pleasant life on the bases. They could go into London almost at will. They mingled at the village pubs with the friendly British townspeople but death was no less imminent to them than it was to the dogfaces in the infantry. (The term "dogface" sounds harsh and not quite right now but it was used so universally, casually and without malice at the time that it is right.)

In the early days, when the Eighth started going after targets deep into Germany during the daylight hours so they could see what they were bombing, loss rates were high. Overall we were losing about

5 percent of our planes every time they went out. You lose the plane, you lose the crew. A crew was committed to twenty-five raids before it was retired and sent home or reassigned to a safe job on the ground. It didn't take any mathematical genius to understand that if you flew twenty-five raids in a few months, and the loss rate was 5 percent, that's a loss of the equivalent of every crewman in the bomber group plus a quarter of the new replacements. I say equivalent because what happened was that, through luck or skill, some of the older crewman made it through twenty-five missions and some of the younger ones were shot down after two or three raids and so were their replacements.

It was like a death in the family every time a crew returned and found that friends in another B-17 or B-24 hadn't made it. Back in their Nissen hut, they found empty bunks and silence where friends had been that morning. The wife, the girlfriend, the mother stared out from the picture next to the bunk. The guys were gone. In all probability dead or, at very best, prisoners. No one mentioned the empty spaces at the breakfast table next morning. Some of the men survived being shot down by parachuting to earth and avoiding capture by the Germans. Many of the best and most heroic stories of the war were told afterward by men who were lucky enough to avoid being captured when they landed in France and were absorbed into the French underground. Some of those even got back to England and others lived a secret life in hiding for the rest of the war. The French who helped them were heroes beyond compare because the Germans peremptorily shot anyone caught hiding a U.S. airmen. If they were lucky they were shot. Some of these incredibly brave French heroes were tortured by the Germans trying to extract from them the names of others in the underground.

One downed pilot borrowed a French farmer's old clothes and posed as a babbling idiot as he hobbled along the back roads, mumbling incoherently when approached by anyone, and made it safely all the way to Spain.

Usually the crews knew who'd gone down by the time they got back. They'd seen the bomber on their wing take a flak hit and spin out in flames or they'd seen eight or nine men bail out of their disabled B-17 and watched with relief as their billowing parachutes dropped them to the ground alive. The assumption always was when you saw nine 'chutes that one man had been killed on board or was too badly wounded to haul himself to the door and get out.

MacKinlay Kantor, a talented writer for the *Saturday Evening Post,* wrote a poem about a B-17 mission, and the only fragment of the poem I remember still stirs me. It was written from the point of view of one of the gunners in a B-17 whose best friend, Bailey, was a waist gunner on the plane flying on their wing in the formation. When that bomber was hit, fire erupted onboard and one by one the crew bailed out. Nine billowing white silk parachutes hung in the air, floating toward the ground.

There was a gray wisp of smoke above the tenth parachute with a man below swinging from the shrouds. The wisp of smoke changed into a trail and finally the silk broke into flames. Fire crept down the shrouds toward the helpless gunner, and as air rushed faster and faster through the expanding holes in the cloth, the man, engulfed in flames now, plummeted faster toward the ground.

In Kantor's words, in the mouth of the waist gunner witnessing the fire, the haunting refrain that kept reappearing in the poem— haunting to me, anyway—was:

> *Who burned, Bailey . . .*
> *Was it you?*

It was difficult to get accurate statistics on losses from the Eighth Air Force at the time. They weren't interested in letting the Germans know how effective their flak and fighter planes were in shooting down our bombers nor did the Air Force brass want to discourage the crews with accurate details of the carnage. The crews, of course, knew in a general way what had happened and who had been lost at their own base but they didn't know specifically what was going on else- where. Even today the figures are meaningless. Air Force records list 3,030 Eighth Air Force men killed in action, 1,984 seriously wounded, and 41,552 missing in action. Missing? Fifty years later?

The 306th Bomb Group's own records show that 177 of its B-17s were shot down or lost in some other manner, with ten men on each plane. When you have seventy-two aircraft assigned to each bomb group at any one time and 177 of them are shot down—a great number of them in a one-year period—that points to a very high replacement rate.

Even with ninety-six crews for the seventy-two bombers, crews became scarce during the terrible winter of 1943. Base commanders were trying to recruit flight-crew gunners anywhere they could find them—from among the kitchen staff or the supply units. The only group relatively safe from being proselytized were the enlisted mechanics. They knew how to do something that was too valuable to risk in combat; they knew how to fix the planes and get them back in the air.

Seven hundred thirty-eight men of the 306th were killed and 305 listed as missing. In this case, as with most military lists of the "missing," it meant killed. "Missing" was simply a word that held out false hope to friends and relatives. Records show that only 885 crew members were taken prisoner after being shot down.

During World War II all units of the U.S. Army Air Forces lost, in approximate figures, 52,000 of the 290,000 Americans killed. The Air Force had about 25 percent of all service personnel so the death figure is actually a bit lower in proportion to its numbers than other forces. That's deceptive because, while Air Force ground personnel suffered almost no casualties, the casualties among the men who flew in combat were astronomically worse than those of any other service.

The Air Force casualty rate was markedly different for officers than it was for the infantry, too. Officers were killed in far greater proportion to their total number in the Air Force than in the infantry. Even though the Air Force represented only a quarter of our armed services, twice as many officers who were fliers died than officers who were in the infantry.

Those statistics were true for the whole Air Force. If you were assigned to an airplane in the British Isles, your chances of meeting a girl in London were better than those of a grunt in the ground forces but your chance of seeing her again in a month were worse. The average number of missions completed by bomber-crew members was fifteen. Only about 25 percent of all the men on B-17 or B-24 crews completed the twenty-five missions they were asked to fly. If you hear of someone who flew thirty-five or forty missions in a bomber, it was not from a base in the British Isles before D–Day. No one made it that far.

With these losses raid after raid and with no letup, you can imagine there might be a morale problem.

It was terrifying for crewmen to lie in bed at night and consider their slight chance of getting through the war alive, free and whole. There were a great many breakdowns suffered by crew members. "Gone yellow" was the phrase but it would have taken a man protected by some special kind of insensitivity in his nature not to have been afraid. It was also said, more kindly, that a man who left a crew before his tour was over had become "flak happy." There was remarkably little resentment of those who couldn't take it by those who stuck it out. They understood.

The RAF had been bombing Germany at night since April of 1940. It was still not certain who was winning the war and there was always talk of an invasion of the British Isles by the Germans, but I didn't feel any more fear in England than I had at Fort Bragg.

The Royal Air Force heavy bombers were going out several nights a week to bomb industrial targets in Germany. There was an ominous quality to the sustained rumble from 2,800 engines pulling 700 bombers out to the Channel as they headed for we-knew-not-where. Berlin, perhaps. I was usually in bed when they went out but everyone always knew they were on their way. The sound had a unifying effect on everyone. You'd look up into the darkness, unbroken by so much as a crack of light, and know that a lot of the men sitting up there where the noise was coming from wouldn't be coming home tonight. They knew it, too. Walking along the street toward the flat at eleven o'clock I'd hear them going out, and when I passed an Englishman who would not normally have recognized my existence, we'd nod. We were all in the war together and it produced a feeling of warmth between unlikely comrades.

The British had an effective although not sophisticated way of confusing German radar that was trying to locate the bombers for their antiaircraft gunners. They dropped strips of metal foil which they called "glitter" or "window" and, if they were lucky, German radar fixed on it instead of on them.

The RAF also had some radar triangulation system that was supposed to give pilots information about where they were in relation to the target. But for all their attempt at precision, what the RAF did at night was called area bombing or saturation bombing. It was close-your-eyes-and-bombs-away bombing, although the RAF didn't like to admit it. They destroyed a lot of cities and killed a lot of German civilians to get one important military target. Or sometimes no military target. The RAF bombed a lot of open fields and a lot of women and children in their homes. We did too, of course. The eyewitness reports of what was hit were seldom borne out by the photoreconnaissance pictures. Not many bomber crews returned and said they risked their lives to drop their bombs on a cabbage patch, but that's what they did very often. The fact of the matter is, most bullets don't hit anyone and neither do most artillery shells or bombs. It's why we have to pay for so many of them.

Cologne was the first German city hit in a nighttime raid by 1,050 RAF bombers on May 30, 1942. It was the British "take that" response to the raid on Coventry on November 15, 1940, in which 1,000 civilians were killed and the ancient cathedral destroyed by 550 Luftwaffe bombers. It must have been a terrifying experience to be down there in either Coventry or Cologne, huddled in the rubble of some cellar as wave after wave of bombers opened their bellies and dropped their bombs. The British were absolutely deaf to any criticism that their air force was killing too many German civilians. Their attitude was that the Germans started this war and nothing that could happen to them was bad enough. I was on their side.

The Germans started it but they got the worst of it in the end. The Luftwaffe never had the equivalent of the RAF's 1,500 four-engine Lancasters and Halifaxes and two-engine Wellingtons. The size of the German target, the British Isles, was perfect for a defense by one of the greatest aircraft of all time, the Spitfire. There was a drama about those small fighter aircraft defending their island from this monster on the Continent that has seldom been matched in warfare.

The British would probably argue that if any airplane won the war it was the Spitfire. It, more than anything else, turned back the German attacks on Great Britain during what was known as the Blitz.

The Spit was a small and wonderfully maneuverable fighter plane with gracefully elliptical wings. RAF pilots downed hundreds of Luftwaffe planes with it and more than 300 V1 buzz bombs.

Because of the Spitfire's limited range, its usefulness ended when the war was no longer a defensive one being fought over the British Isles but an offensive one over a Germany beyond the Spitfire's range. It didn't have the fuel capacity to accompany the bombers on the long runs into Germany, fight, and return home. They tried equipping it with wing tanks that were dropped when they got over Germany but it never worked out. So the RAF continued to bomb Germany at night without the benefit of fighter-plane protection. Toward the end of the war, in February 1945, the magnificent old German city of Dresden was almost pulverized by RAF and Eighth Air Force bombers. There was little military purpose to the attacks although it was what the RAF called "a center of communications for Germany's Eastern Front." The British then and now shrugged off any sense of guilt anyone tried to lay on them for the Dresden raid by pointing to what the Germans had done to Winchester and Coventry or even to the center of London.

Even now you hear reasonable Germans—Germans who assure you they don't approve of what Hitler did—refer to Dresden as though its destruction was a crime against humanity committed by the British. I heard a bright young lawyer from Cologne mention Dresden in this way fifty years after it took place. Some of them still don't get it. I would merely concede that it wasn't a nice thing for the British to do—and I can understand perfectly well why they did it.

Winston Churchill had some hand in getting the RAF to back off bombing civilian targets, although hardly out of the goodness of his heart. "If we come into an entirely ruined land," he said, "there will be a great shortage of accommodation for ourselves and our allies."

It's impossible to live a long life without acquiring prejudices based on experience with people. The best thing to do with prejudice you wish you didn't have is to understand it's wrong to have it, keep it to yourself and make sure it doesn't alter your conviction that everyone is equal before the law and god, if you believe in one. To the extent that I'd rather be in Paris surrounded by French people than in Berlin surrounded by Germans, I am prejudiced.

There is no question my feelings about the Germans was influenced by World War II. The German people are endowed with many great characteristics that are considered admirable by most people but that I, so lacking in those qualities myself, don't always admire. The average German young man made a better soldier, in the traditional sense of what a soldier is, than the average American. Primary among the characteristics that made Germans good soldiers in the eyes of all the world's military leaders was their lack of resistance to the idea of taking orders without questioning them.

There are millions of descendants of German immigrants in America who have contributed, not only their share, but more than their share of what has made our nation great. As my friend Joe Fleming said, "They make wonderful Americans but lousy Germans."

I don't feel any necessity for being an expert in these matters to write about them. What expertise I have comes from having observed a lot of people. It just seems to me that Germans have more good characteristics and more bad ones than most nationalities. These thoughts rush to my head when the name Dresden is mentioned in relation to the war the Eighth and Ninth Air Forces and the Royal Air Force fought with Germany.

A REPORTER COVERED the air war by traveling from London to one of the hundreds of air bases to interview the crews of the bombers that had been out that day over France or Germany. The Eighth Air Force went out two or three times a week in 1943, depending on weather conditions and depending on the bombs and equipment that were available. It wasn't an airline operation where they were cleaning out the debris left by previous passengers and bringing on fresh containers of coffee. When 600 planes go out, each carrying 8,000 pounds of bombs and tons of .50-caliber ammunition for each ship's ten machine guns and 2,300 gallons of gas, there's a huge resupply problem the next day for ground crews.

There were always a few bombers on every raid that got in the air and then, because of some engine problem, had to return to their base. As a safety precaution they usually went out over the English Channel and dropped their bombs and all but emptied their fuel tanks

Getting on board a 385th Bombardment Group B-17 before a trip over Saint-Nazaire, France. With the doors open at the gun positions, it was cold and drafty up there. The sheepskin jacket was a prized possession that I lost on the way home from China a year later.

to reduce the chance of fire if they crashed on landing. Even during the war it was impossible for me not to think of 2,300 gallons of gas in terms of how many times I could have driven the 100 miles between college and home with it.

It was hard to translate the money being spent in a way that meant anything to people. I was always impressed with the idea that each .50-caliber bullet cost about $1 then and when all ten guns were firing away over a target with German fighter planes diving in on the formation, the air gunners could fire away $10,000 worth of ammunition in a few minutes. The tail gunner's position was so cramped that his machine gun had to be fed by a track that led from a storage magazine amidships. The ammunition on his track alone probably would have sent him to college. The ball turret rotated and revolved on a complicated set of geared wheels inside a piece of equipment worth five times as much as any car the gunner ever owned.

When the planes were ready to go, the Eighth Air Force public-relations office, under the direction of Col. John Hay (Jock) Whitney, got the signal from bomber headquarters that there was to be a raid the following day. Col. Jack Redding, Maj. Hal Leyshon, Capt. Tex McCrary, or Cpl. Jimmy Dugan called the dozen reporters covering the Eighth Air Force as late as 2 A.M. with a cryptic message.

The phone calls we got were wonderfully mysterious. The phrase from the other end was always something like "There will be a mail delivery tomorrow" or "Travel arrangements have been made for 8 A.M." No matter what the voice said, we knew what it meant. The calls gave me the feeling that I was part of a great conspiracy to save the world.

But the pride I felt being an Army newspaperman was diminished whenever I went to one of the airfields to meet the returning B-17s whose crews risked their lives while I was so safe from danger myself. They were doing it, I was watching from a distance. It seemed unfair that I could go back to my snug apartment in London when a dozen of my friends who flew had to stay close to their bases and wait for the dreaded words "We're going out in the morning."

It was important that the Germans not know the bombers were coming and the phone calls we got telling us of the impending raid would be considered a security leak of major proportions today.

Imagine reporters in Saudi Arabia during the 1991 war with Iraq being given information about a military operation that was to take place any time in the future! The American public is lucky now if it's told what the military has done after it's done it.

Early the following morning, a group of reporters would meet at St. Pancras station and board a train for Bedford. Among the friends I made on those trips were the legendary Homer Bigart, then of the *Herald Tribune,* Walter Cronkite with United Press, and Gladwin Hill, who was with the Associated Press and later *The New York Times.*

Cronkite had escaped being drafted because he was color-blind. People are proud of being color-blind and The Most Trusted Man in America is no exception. I've mentioned this to Walter, who remains one of my best friends. I rank the color-blind diagnosis along with reports that "Doctors said he would never walk again" as being very difficult to pin down. It's my feeling that people aren't actually blind to color but when they were young someone gave them the wrong name for a color they were looking at and they've been confused about the colors they've been seeing ever since.

These reporters were my teachers although they didn't know it. While I tried to act more like one of them than a student, I watched and listened carefully. Anyone who thinks of Walter Cronkite today as the authoritative father figure of television news would be surprised to know what a tough, competitive scrambler he was in the old *Front Page* tradition of newspaper reporting. He became the best anchorman there ever was in television because he knew news when he saw it and cared about it. He was relentlessly inquisitive. The subject of his interview always sensed that Cronkite was interested in what he had to say and knew a great deal about the issue himself.

Homer Bigart had a serious speech defect. He stammered but he had a great knack for getting stories out of people who might have been reluctant to talk to someone else. When I first heard Homer interviewing someone, he sounded so dumb and uninformed about the subject that I thought he'd lose the interest of the person he was talking to.

"And then what happened?" Homer would ask, a cigarette dribbling ashes down the front of his khaki necktie.

It doesn't seem like much of a question but first thing you know, the person being interviewed would take this poor sap of a reporter by the hand and lead him, step by step, though the whole story in detail that it might not have occurred to him to give a more knowledgeable newspaperman.

"Boy!" one waist gunner said to me after he'd been interviewed by Homer, "that guy don't know anything, does he? I about had to tell him what an airplane was."

Homer didn't know anything—like a fox.

The Eighth Air Force press group was the first of a great many newspaper men and women I met during the war, and I realized then that I preferred the company of reporters to the company of most people I met. Hal Boyle, of the Associated Press, became a good friend, and when people, making small talk with Hal, said, "You must meet a lot of interesting people in your business," Hal would say, "Yeah, I do. And most of them are other newspapermen."

Life was great for me at this point. I had stopped worrying about being shipped back to the Seventeenth Field Artillery. I was getting stories in the paper several times a week.

When there were no bombing missions, I was often given another assignment, and several times I went to 20 Grosvenor Square to attend a press conference by General Eisenhower. I realized, at my first press conference, that my education as a reporter was not yet complete.

Sometime during the early winter of 1943, SHAEF announced a press conference and I was assigned to attend it. About twelve reporters assembled around a large, boardroom type desk in a meeting room near Eisenhower's office. He came in the room promptly at the announced hour. I had a pencil and a reporter's notebook. I knew how I should look and what the tools of the trade were but I didn't know what to listen for.

Eisenhower spoke for about ten minutes. He began by announcing several appointments to important jobs. I wrote them down. He told us about a new plan for cooperation between the British and the Americans and I wrote it down. He made half a dozen statements that didn't mean much to me but I made careful notes about everything. Gladwin Hill of the AP asked Eisenhower whether there was any schedule for the invasion of France. Eisenhower was vague and talked all around the question, but toward the end of his answer he said, "Within the year."

I went back to the office and, almost literally, started to transcribe the notes I'd taken, in the order in which I'd taken them. Before I'd finished, Gladwin Hill's story came tapping in on the AP wire.

"General Dwight Eisenhower announced today that the Allied invasion of France will take place within the year." The story said nothing about new appointments or cooperation with the British. I had taken for granted that the invasion would be within the year, and it hadn't occurred to me that Eisenhower's saying so made it a story.

That was the day I learned you don't report statements made at press conferences in the order in which they were given or in the order of importance assigned to them by the person holding the press conference. I wouldn't want anyone to think everything went smoothly in my new career as a journalist. I think I probably understated the trouble I got into on one occasion in a letter to Margie dated January 18, 1944. The letter was inadvertently dated "1943" but there's no question it was 1944.

Yesterday morning I went to an Eisenhower press conference. I don't usually do anything like that but Charley Kiley, who does, was out of town and I was glad of the chance to do the story. Eisenhower announced Omar Bradley as U.S. ground forces chief. That was the big news but mostly I was just interested to see what kind of a man Ike is.

Everyone was sorry to see the 8th Air Force commander, Ira Eaker, leave. I guess he got fired. I was particularly sorry because he was always decent to me, often giving me half an hour of his time. Out of one of those interviews I got a story that caused more trouble than any I've done before or since. He told me, casually, that we'd soon be taking off and landing from English bases in the dark. Well, one of the things you learn is that you always pick something out of the middle of an interview and use that for the lead of your story. It's amazing to me how often ten newspapermen will pick up the same statement, casually made, and play that.

Like a good newsman with an eye toward something sensational, I quoted General Eaker as saying the 8th Air Force would be operating at night before long.

When we ran the story the next morning every American news agency here called and wanted more dope from me. Eaker wouldn't give them any time and they wanted to know where I got my information. I told them about my interview, still innocent of what turned out to be a blunder I made, and it was played big in stories home. The headlines read: U.S. TO BOMB AT NIGHT!

Eaker never did call to bawl me out although I don't know why. He meant to say, or said and I misinterpreted him, that our bombers would take off in the dark but just in time to be able to reach enemy targets in daylight. Or that they would bomb late in the afternoon and return in the dark. The whole thing wouldn't have caused so much trouble if there wasn't a big political thing between us and the British about night bombing. It was a great beat for me—while it lasted.

I found myself liking generals better than colonels and majors. I interviewed Lt. Gen. Frank M. Andrews in April of 1943 when he was the first commanding general of all forces in the ETO. He was killed ten days after this picture was taken when the B-24 he was flying back to the U.S. hit a mountain in Iceland.

I was surprised to find myself liking many of the high-ranking officers I met. It was the majors and the colonels who were more apt to give me trouble. In the three years I spent with *The Stars and Stripes,* I came to have great respect and affection—if a sergeant can feel affection for a general—for Dwight Eisenhower. He was somehow lovable, being, at the same time, competent and bumbling.

It was the strength Ike gave us, with his edict declaring our independence from interference by officers of other commands, that made it possible to publish an honest newspaper in the military. Under ordinary circumstances the two are incompatible, in the same sense that once led someone to say of Army bands, "Military music is a contradiction in terms."

Winston Churchill, in his World War II book *Triumph and Tragedy,* wrote of Ike, "No one knew better than he how to stay close to a tremendous event without impairing the authority he had delegated to others."

Churchill wouldn't have known how accurately that statement reflected the opinion those of us on *The Stars and Stripes* had of Eisenhower. He knew what we were doing at the paper but never stepped in to impair the authority he had given the editors.

It's always a pleasant surprise to find that an opinion you have of someone, which you think of as exclusively your own, is the same opinion everyone else has of that person. It accounts for why Eisenhower was elected president after the war. Americans saw the same general qualities in him that we saw in specific detail on *The Stars and Stripes.*

SOMETIMES DAYS WENT by when there were no bombing missions, either because the weather was bad or the B-17s and B-24s were short of bombs or replacement crews. On those days I stayed in London, and I spent most of my free time alone. I was lonely when alone but discontented when I was with someone. I went to several concerts at the Royal Albert Hall, more to have something to write home to Margie about than because I liked the music, and I went to the White City greyhound racetrack every once in a while when I wasn't working.

I was uneasy about going to the greyhound races at White City. It didn't seem like a classy thing to be doing—but the races were a diversion from the horror stories I was writing several times a week and they passed the time. It was one of the few times in my life I've wanted time to pass. As eventful as my life was as a reporter, I still thought of it as an interim occupation. The end of the war was always on my mind. I was not waking every morning thinking to myself "Wow! This is some experience I'm having." No event in our lives is so great that, halfway through it, we don't start looking forward to the day it will be over.

On the days we were alerted to a raid, I usually joined the other reporters for the train ride to Bedford but occasionally I could borrow a jeep from the circulation department. (I'm going to call them jeeps, not Jeeps. The jeep was one of the great inventions of the war and, while its name has been expropriated—legally I'm sure—by the Chrysler Corporation, the word "jeep" has a meaning that exceeds the corporation's proprietary right to it. It was made initially, I think, by the Kaiser-Frazer Automobile Company. It was one of the best pieces of equipment any army ever had. I've never understood why an exact replica made today and sold cheaply wouldn't find a big market. The little wartime jeep had almost nothing in common with the Chrysler Jeep of today except its square look and four wheels. I think you might be able to get the World War II jeep in the back of a modern Jeep if you folded down the seat of the new version.

One day after I'd been lucky enough to get a car, I drove to a B-24 base up north near Birmingham. I'd heard that the Wedgwood china factory was in the nearby town of Stone and the following day, after I'd written my story, I drove there. In peacetime it must have been a tourist attraction, but this day I was the lone visitor and I was surprised to find elderly artisans still putting the garlands of white clay flowers around the edges of the traditional blue Wedgwood dinner plates before the plates were fired. I spent the equivalent of almost $200 on china cups, saucers, and dinner plates. The freighters going back to the States were empty and it was easy to have the Wedgwood packed and shipped home to my mother. There were few things I did for Mother in her life that she liked as much as she liked those plates. She cherished them to the day she died.

After the war we were at dinner at Mother and Dad's house at Lake George. Mom didn't like unpleasantness of any kind. She wouldn't watch a sad movie or read a depressing book. She even disliked family arguments at the dinner table and always avoided any conversation about an unhappy event. One of the guests that night, carrying a Wedgwood plate to the kitchen, dropped it and it crashed to the floor and scattered its blue and white pieces over the kitchen floor.

"It's only a plate," my mother said to the guest, dismissing it as if it meant nothing to her.

Later, just before going to bed, I went to the kitchen for a drink of water. Mother was there sweeping a few remaining fragments of the Wedgwood from under the stove into a dustpan. There were tears in her eyes.

SOMETIME IN APRIL 1944, a great change came over my writing career. I became "Andy Rooney." The byline "Andrew A. Rooney" was gone. I objected but Hutton summed up his argument by saying, "Andrew A. Rooney don't mean sweet fuckall."

There's no doubt "Andy Rooney" is catchier, and the fact that I'd always disliked the name Andy didn't matter to Bud. He made me Andy for life. I couldn't argue much about it because I've always felt that no one gets to choose the name by which he or she is called. People ought to be able to call you by the name they feel fits. It's been a lifelong source of disappointment to me that people think Andy fits me.

Some weeks I'd have three bylines in the paper and then ten days would pass when I'd have none. There were times when the desk decided not to use a byline on my story and other times when what I wrote was folded into a bigger story and became part of that. It was a different kind of journalism in the Army because, while you were an observer, you were not a neutral observer. You were a cheerleader. *The Stars and Stripes* was a good newspaper but, looking at my files of it fifty years later, I'm struck by how often stories were written with an artificial kind of optimism about the progress of the war. And if the stories themselves were objective, the headlines often had a jingoistic quality.

GI'S SHOW JERRY
HOW IT'S DONE

We did not run stories that showed the Germans in a favorable light. We weren't alone. Most U.S. newspapers did the same thing. American newsmen, without meaning to be propagandists, filed stories about hospitals, churches, and schools in England that were bombed. Women, children, and the sick were always killed in those stories. The stories were true if sometimes exaggerated, and they carried with them the implication that our bombers never hit a hospital, a church, or a school and did not kill women, children, or the sick.

While the paper was written and edited primarily by enlisted men, Bob Moora accepted a commission as a lieutenant halfway through the war, and a major named Arthur Goodfriend started writing heavy-handed editorials, which I assume now we were ordered to run by some higher authority.

"HAVE YOU KILLED YOUR GERMAN TODAY!" a headline on one of the Goodfriend articles, became a permanent joke among the writers and editors.

The Stars and Stripes would not have been much more than a house organ had it not been for Eisenhower's noninterference edict and the collection of experienced and independent newspapermen on its staff who fought any tendency on the part of Army brass to dominate us.

There were very few stories that were put off-limits to us by the two military censors who were always in *The Stars and Stripes* office. For one thing, we all knew what the rules were as well as they did and, for the most part, the rules made sense. No one wanted to give information to the Germans that would have helped them. The Office of Censorship in Washington was under the intelligent direction of Byron Price, former executive editor of the Associated Press.

The worst kind of censorship has always been the kind that newspaper people impose on themselves. I was not aware of being in any way a propagandist as a reporter for *The Stars and Stripes,* but there were stories I didn't write because I didn't like to think of the bomber crews with whom I spent so much time talking reading them. Too sad. During the two years I covered the air war, there were half a dozen stories I couldn't bring myself to write even though it would have been more honest if I had. I remember one in particular.

The Eighth Air Force had a disastrous day when it bombed Regensburg deep inside Germany, and I was at a base waiting to interview some of the fliers when they came back.

It was the custom for concerned ground crews and flight crews that hadn't been assigned to go out that day to gather in front of the control tower shortly before the bombers' ETA. (Another good time-saving acronym produced during the war: Estimated Time of Arrival. Most acronyms are used by people who think they make them sound knowledgeable when they use them, but there are some that are useful. The British were good at both acronyms and code names. They were responsible for popularizing the use of such words as "Overlord" for D-Day, "Cobra" for a strike to the south after the breakout at Saint-Lô, "Mulberry," the name for the prefabricated docks towed across the English Channel to the beaches. I wouldn't be surprised, in spite of their American sound, if the D-Day beaches Juno, Gold, Sword, Omaha, Utah were named by the British. Winston Churchill was referred to cryptically in top-secret memos as "Colonel Warden.")

All of us on the ground that day were relieved as specks appeared in the sky over the Channel. As the specks became dots and the dots grew to spots, radio reports started coming through and it became certain the ordeal wasn't over. There were dead and dying men on board half a dozen of the group's bombers. There was a frantic call from one radio operator. The ball-turret gunner was trapped in the plastic bubble hanging beneath the B-17. The gears that rotated the ball to put the gunner in position to shoot and then returned him to the position that enabled him to climb out and back up into the aircraft had been hit and were jammed. The ball-turret gunner was caught in a plastic cage.

Two of the engines of the B-17 were stopped, about 3,000 pounds of dead weight hanging from the wings. The plane was losing altitude fast and flying at barely 135 miles an hour, close to stall-out speed. The pilot ordered the crew to unload everything on board.

"Everything!" he yelled in a command that reached the control tower over the radioman's open microphone. The crew started pitching out machine guns, .50-caliber ammunition tracks, oxygen tanks, and every instrument they could tear loose in an attempt to lighten the load and keep the foundering plane in the air.

The pilot opened the petcocks on the fuel tanks to drain them down to the last few gallons. This was common practice when a plane was about to crash because it lessened the chance of fire. I think the gas evaporated before it rained to the ground because I never heard of anything catching fire on being dampened by any of it.

The hydraulic system was spewing fluid where the tubing that conveyed it was shot full of holes. The gas tanks were leaking. Nothing worked. The wheels, folded up into the bomber, could not be brought down without its hydraulic system and a belly landing was inevitable.

There were eight minutes of gut-wrenching talk among the tower, the pilot, and the man trapped in the ball turret. He knew what comes down first when there are no wheels. We all watched in horror as it happened. We watched as this man's life ended, mashed between the concrete pavement of the runway and the belly of the bomber.

I returned to London that night, shaken and unable to write the most dramatic, the most gruesome, the most heart-wrenching story I had ever witnessed. Some reporter.

The incident has been fictionalized in half a dozen different ways over the years. President Reagan, in one of his speeches, told the story of a gunner trapped in the ball turret. After the rest of the crew had bailed out of the fatally damaged aircraft, the pilot was said to have left the cockpit and gone back to reach down into the ball to take the gunner's hand in his. As the plane plummeted toward the ground, according to Reagan's speech, the pilot said, "Don't worry. We'll ride this one out together."

The story seems to have come, not from an actual incident, but from an old black-and-white movie called *A Wing and a Prayer,* starring Dana Andrews.

IT WAS A terrifying life the bomber crews lived, always so close to death. In the days before the invasion when a tour of duty was twenty-five missions, everyone kept track. In the Nissen huts where the bunks were up against the wall, most crew members marked each mission with a single vertical line. It was four lines and a horizontal slash for the fifth. One gunner at Chelveston had meticulously carved his marks in the pine wall behind his bunk with a jackknife—probably a Boy Scout knife he got as a Christmas present from an uncle three years before.

I talked one day to the young man sitting on the bunk in front of that set of marks, indicating missions completed.

卌   卌   卌 ||

"You've flown seventeen missions," I said. "You're practically done."

"No," he said. "Those aren't mine. Today was my third."

I didn't have to ask about the man who had carved the seventeen marks. He never got back to carve the eighteenth. A great number of American boys had their last night's sleep in a Nissen hut in England.

The bomber crews were only aware of their own statistics. They knew when thirty of their planes went out and only twenty-six came home. They had known all forty of the men who were gone as well as you'd know a classmate in a small school.

BETWEEN HIGH-SCHOOL friends from The Albany Academy and classmates at Colgate, I knew a lot of fliers. Obie Slingerland, Phil Greene, Bob Freihofer, Bill Judson, Charley Wood, Bob O'Connor were not acquaintances, they were close friends. Three of them, Obie, Charley, and Bob O'Connor, were pilots who were killed in their airplanes. Obie and I were cocaptains of the Academy football team. He was—I have never used the word to describe anyone—a sweet boy. He died in a flight off the aircraft carrier *Saratoga*.

Charley Wood was shot down by small-arms fire that hit his Piper Grasshopper artillery observation plane. The Army bought thousands of these useful little adaptations of the Piper Cub and paid just $800 each for them. Bob O'Connor was shot down in his B-17 over France.

Some of those friends had seemed capable in school but some of them had not. It never occurred to me when I was with them all those years that they had within themselves the ability to fly an airplane in combat. At six feet two and 210 pounds when he was fifteen years old, Bill Judson, for example, was a graceful athlete, but he was also a charming, inept oaf. He played football next to me all through high school. Once we were huddled around Obie, our quarterback, on the high-school fifteen-yard line in a crucial situation for us during the biggest game of the year, listening intently for the play call from Obie, when Jud leaned over and picked up something glittering in the grass.

"Hey look!" he said. "A nickel!" But Jud ended up as the pilot of a B-17. I never flew with him but I'd guess he did it gracefully.

Obie Slingerland's parents were victims of the Great Depression of the 1930s to a greater extent than most of his friends at The Academy. Obie never went to the movies with us Saturday night. He just didn't want to go, he'd tell us. Obie's older brother, Henry, is a successful rancher in Wyoming.

In addition to being the cocaptain and quarterback of our football team, Obie was the best pitcher on the baseball team. He'd pitch a nine-inning game and then trot over to the small, wooden field house where the track team was competing and win the mile run in his baseball shoes. On one such occasion, Charley Weaver, the wise and wizened old caretaker of our track and our football and baseball fields, complained to "Country" Morris about how his cinder track had been torn up. After that, Obie changed into track shoes.

Before he went into the Navy, Obie had been the quarterback for the Amherst College football team. We didn't stay in touch much in college but I could have been away from Obie for fifty years and known him as well as I did the day we parted. I remember this minute, as I write, how he tied his shoes.

There were two or three friends of mine at The Academy whom my mother invited to come to our cottage at Lake George with us every year and Obie was always one of them. We were close friends. Of all the deaths of all the friends I've mourned over the years, none was so sad as Obie's because he was so promising—so young, so good, so sweet. I have awakened in the middle of the night a thousand times and thought about the life I've had—am having—that Obie never got to have.

Charley Wood wrote like an adult in grade school. His poem, "The Miloserdnaya," won all the awards at graduation although it was beyond the understanding of some of us. It was, he explained, "the begging song of Siberian exiles" and it was pure invention on his part, composed after he'd read a news story from Russia. This is part of it, taken from an old copy of our school magazine:

> *O our fathers, pity our journey dreary!*
> *Mercy on us, the travelers weary!*
> *Forget us not, who in the cell*
> *Dream of those we love so well.*
> *Feed us, O our fathers, feed us*
> *We the doomed are crying, heed us!*
> *We, like you, have fathers, mothers*
> *Somewhere—far away—our brothers*
> *Pray for us and think in pain*
> *Of those they'll never see again!*
> *Mercy in the name of Jesus*
> *For the sake of Christ, appease us!*
> *We have prayed, like you, to God.*
> *Even on the frozen sod*
> *Even mid the ice and snow—*
> *He would have you pity so*
> *We have watched the summer die;*
> *Pity us; the walls around us*
> *Gratings, padlocks, stones surround us*
> *Shadow, substance, oaken doorways*
> *Iron bars that branch in four ways!*
> *Bunkers we have slept in, cried in*
> *Caves that some of us have died in*
> *Those we loved were not to cheer us*
> *O our fathers, pity, hear us!*
> *We have known no food nor bed—*
> *Pity on the walking dead!*

Charley Wood, writing poetry like that at age fifteen and dead at twenty-two.

One of his short stories was called "The Devil's Dinner at Shantung."

In reading of the recent diplomatic crisis caused by the bombing of the American boat "Panay" by a renegade Japanese colonel, I was reminded forcibly of a similar incident in 1932, to which my good friend Laughlin of *The Times* attributed my immediate assignment to the Obituary Department. "It seems," said he at the time, "that your singular penchant for depicting violent death with such vivid flashes of imagination would adapt you admirably for your work. Give you an hour in the morgue and there wouldn't be room in the paper for anything but your articles."

He went on to weave a mystery story of Oriental intrigue that amazed his classmates and his teachers. What might Charley Wood have written if he'd lived to be thirty?

When I get to thinking that perhaps there is a balance between the good things and the bad things about war, I think of Obie and Charley and I know there is nothing so good about war that it isn't overwhelmed by the death of young men like them.

Bob O'Connor was a fraternity brother and the best friend I had in the class ahead of me in college. That's always a special friend. The memories you have of someone are not always the ones you'd choose to recall. I always think of Bob playing bridge one night in the fraternity house when the four players got talking about drinking. None of them drank much except beer. Hub Stephenson bet Bob $5 he could drink a bottle of whiskey in an hour and keep playing bridge. He finished the bottle in fifty minutes, still bidding reasonably well, but suddenly he keeled over and passed out on the floor with convulsions. Bob called the town ambulance and the medics pumped the liquor out of Hub's stomach. Hub's still alive and well. Bob died when his B-17 was shot down over France.

Bob Freihofer was stationed at Basingbourne with the Ninety-first Bomb Group. Reporters tended to go back to the same base because they were familiar with it and they knew and liked the public-relations officer. There was no compelling reason to move around unless a reporter was thinking of the morale at the bases that were being ignored in his stories. I was most comfortable with the 306th Bomb Group at Thurleigh, but I often went to the 303rd at Molesworth and the 305th at Chelveston. I went to Basingbourne occasionally to see Bob Freihofer. I went there one day when a mission was scheduled because I had a clipping from the *Knickerbocker Press,* the Albany newspaper, that I wanted to show Bob.

Bob flew as copilot with Oscar O'Neill. Oscar, whom Bob called "Ox," was also in our class at Colgate although I didn't know him well in college. Oscar's postwar claim to fame was as the father of the actress Jennifer O'Neill. I never got to show the newspaper clipping to Bob that day because they'd left by the time I got to Basingbourne and they didn't come back. The good news was the other crews counted ten 'chutes opening over Germany so they were certain the downed crewmen were alive even if they were prisoners. Years later Bob would often get telling stories about his two years in the POW camp. It sounded surprisingly like *Hogan's Heroes,* although Bob told the funny stories and left out the grim part of imprisonment. The crewchief and turret gunner in Bob's crew, a boy named Larry Goldberg, refused to wear his parachute. Bob and Oscar pleaded with him and ordered the gunner to wear the parachute but nothing worked. The 'chute gave him claustrophobia, Goldberg said.

When Bob and the others hit the ground, they were surrounded almost immediately by German soldiers. It was always preferable to be taken prisoner by soldiers instead of civilians because a mob of angry civilians were less predictable and their knowledge of the Geneva Convention nonexistent.

Nine men in the crew got to camp. Everyone felt too bad about their missing friend to do any we-told-him-so about his refusal to wear a parachute but they were certain he'd died when the plane crashed to the ground.

The following morning the new POWs were trying to get used to confinement when who walked into the compound accompanied by a guard on either side of him but Larry Goldberg.

His nose and eyes were purple from having been hit with something. The black and blue ran down his shoulders all the way to his forearms.

Bob said he and the other crew members, with guards all around, started a low rumble of complaint as they saw him coming. They were all thinking the same thing—Goldberg was Jewish.

"The dirty sonsofbitches," someone said hoarsely, "they held him and beat him to get information."

They were ready to riot when Goldberg joined them.

"Jesus, kid, what did they do to you?"

"Naw, nothin'," he said. "I grabbed my 'chute but I didn't have time to put it on so I hooked my legs through the cords at the knees. I come down nice but upside down and landed on my head." Bob laughed until tears came to his eyes when he told the story.

After the war, Bob often spoke of his time as a prisoner of war and, in a strange way, I think he enjoyed life more for having had that experience. One night after we'd had dinner with Bob and his wife, Terri, I was reminded of something from *War and Peace* by what Bob had said that evening.

Back home, I found the passage and was struck by how close the reaction of Tolstoy's hero, Peter, was to Bob Freihofer's attitude when he spoke of captivity.

Peter was supposed to be the richest man in Russia, but when the French invaded Russia Peter was taken prisoner. The French dragged him along with them through the bitter winter as they were being driven back out of Russia. Peter had a terrible time. He was always hungry, often sick, and, on several occasions, he almost froze to death.

After Peter was freed, he never looked at his life the same again.

"Here only for the first time," Tolstoy wrote,

Peter appreciated, because he was deprived of it, the happiness of eating when he was hungry, of drinking when he was thirsty, of sleeping when he was sleepy and of talking when he felt the desire to exchange some words. . . . Later in life he always recurred with joy to this month of captivity and never failed to speak with enthusiasm of the powerful and ineffaceable sensations and especially of the moral calm which he experienced.

Bob died in 1992, after a notably successful career as president of the Freihofer Baking Company, and before I ever told him he reminded me of a character in Tolstoy's *War and Peace*. Bob would have dismissed it with a laugh but he and Peter had something in common.

HEROISM AND HEARTBREAK in the air were commonplace and usually more clearly defined than anyplace else at war. There were a thousand ways to die. It's a popular misconception of war, often promoted by veterans organizations, that everyone who goes to war and everyone who dies in one fights in danger of his life and is, to some extent, a hero. There are no more heroes in war than in peace. It's just that in peacetime heroism is not so dramatic, is not apt to be life-threatening, and so doesn't call as much attention to itself. Stories of bravery and heroism are important to a nation trying to propagandize its citizens to participate in the conduct of a war. There is an unlikely line I recall from A. A. Milne (unlikely from him because he was also the author of the Winnie-the-Pooh books):

"If war is to be made tolerable, the romantic tradition must be handed on. 'Madam, I took away your son, but I give you back the memory of a hero. Each year we will celebrate together his immortal passing.' "

Patriotism and war go together. Anytime anyone gets thinking patriotism is one of the supreme virtues, it would be a good idea to remember that there was never any group of people more patriotic than the Nazi Germans. It's strange that love of country brings out the vicious character in so many people. In that respect, it's a lot like religion. Here are two things that almost everyone agrees are good, patriotism and religion, but between them they account for almost all the people who ever died in a war.

It was to promote the patriotic spirit that the United States gave out 4 million medals during the Persian Gulf War even though there were never more than 570,000 servicemen and women in the war zone. The National Defense Service Medal was given to everyone in the service at that time, whether or not he or she served in the Middle East.

Bravery in war is different and separate from bravado or foolishly dangerous behavior undertaken without much thought about consequences. It's also true though that bravado can't be dismissed as unimportant. It's good to have some of the swashbucklers on your side even though, strictly speaking, their actions are something other than brave.

In July 1943 we got word that Secretary of War Henry L. Stimson was coming to the 306th Bomb Group at Thurleigh to pin the first Medal of Honor given in the European Theater of Operations on an air gunner who had saved the lives of several crew members. (I find it interesting that what we now call "Secretary of Defense" was known then as "Secretary of War." Political correctness must have set in. We should have known the image-conscious people in postwar Washington wouldn't let it stand. The fact is, it might not be a bad idea to have two cabinet posts, a Secretary of Defense and a Secretary of War.)

The sergeant gunner to be honored that day was a man named Maynard Smith. Maynard was known to one and all as "Snuffy" and I knew a lot about him because I'd written the original story of his heroic acts the day he returned from the raid on which he performed them. In addition to being known as "Snuffy," he was known to everyone as a moderately pompous little fellow with the belligerent attitude of a man trying to make up with attitude what his five-foot-four, 130-pound body left him wanting. He posed part-time as an intellectual and loved to go to the British pubs in Thurleigh, the small town near the base, to argue with and lecture to the British civilians who frequented them. From the time he entered the Air Force he had been in some kind of trouble over one petty matter or another. "Snuffy" was, in fact, known by the fourteen other inhabitants of his Nissen hut by an Army phrase for which there's no socially acceptable replacement. He was a real fuckup.

The incident occurred on Snuffy's first raid, on May 1, 1943. The mission was to try and destroy the German submarine landing and repair docks at Saint-Nazaire. German U-boats were doing a great deal of damage sinking troop and supply ships in the Atlantic on their way from the United States to Great Britain. It was never a well-known part of the war because the tragedies—the drowning of several hundred men in a sinking ship in the frigid waters of the North Atlantic—occurred without public notice. Our War Department knew but would not give the Germans confirmation of the success of their torpedoes by announcing it, so no sinking ever made the news. The men drowned or froze to death anonymously. "Missing in action" was their only epitaph.

The raid was intended to damage the twenty-foot-thick concrete U-boat pens at Saint-Nazaire. While it was one of the most heavily defended places in all of Europe, it was considered a better place to go than deep into Germany because it was close and got relatively little help from the Luftwaffe.

Seventy-eight planes of four bomb groups took off that day. Eleven of these came back to their bases with mechanical trouble. The pilots of thirty-eight decided the weather was so bad that they should turn back and they did turn back. That happened a lot. In the end, only twenty-nine of the original seventy-eight bombers reached the target and dropped their bombs on Saint-Nazaire that day.

It was not the easy target the 306th expected it to be. There were no ME-109s or FW-190s from the Luftwaffe but there was a heavy concentration of flak batteries. By this time the Germans had 900,000 men assigned to antiaircraft guns, and they were everywhere. Seven B-17s were shot down that day, a high percentage of twenty-nine, and seventy-three men were killed or taken prisoner. Eighteen were wounded and two returned dead onboard. It was hardly a milk run.

Snuffy Smith was on a B-17 piloted by 1/Lt. L. P. Johnson. I knew Hutton was going to be angry at me for leaving out L. P. Johnson's full name but that's all I had in my notes and that's probably what he liked to be called. When someone prefers initials, it almost always turns out his given name is something fancy that he hates or his mother's maiden name, which makes an improbable first name for a man.

Snuffy Smith was told he'd be manning Johnson's ball turret. Snuffy wasn't happy with his assignment because he'd never flown in the bubble even in practice runs.

"I knew we'd been hit," Johnson said to me in the briefing room after the raid. "The plane was on fire and it wasn't flying well."

Johnson told Sgt. William Fahrenhold, the engineer, to go back and check out the midsection, but Fahrenhold was stopped when he met a wall of flame as he opened the door from the bomb bay to the midsection of the plane.

"I can't go back there," Fahrenhold told Johnson on his intercom. Meanwhile, in the ball turret, Snuffy Smith behaved with rare understanding for a rookie gunner.

"My intercom was out and all my hydraulic lines were broken," he told me. "I hated the sound of little pieces of flak sort of raining on the ball turret. I hand-cranked the ball into position so I could get out and crawled into the waist. I saw a sheet of flame coming out of the radio room and another fire up where the wheels fold up into the fuselage," he said.

"Suddenly," Snuffy said, "the radio operator came staggering out of the flames. He made a run for the left waist door and dove out. Dove right out. He hit the horizontal stabilizer but he bounced off and his 'chute opened. The right waist gunner had already bailed out and the left waist gunner was trying to jump but the straps of his chute were hung up on some strut or something and he was stuck half in and half out. I pulled him back in," Snuffy said, "and asked him if the heat was too much for him."

This was Snuffy at his best and worst and it's exactly what he would have said.

"He just stared at me for a minute," Snuffy continued. He was wound up. "He didn't say a thing and then he jumped. His 'chute opened okay.

"The smoke and gas were really thick in there. I wrapped a sweater around my face so I could breathe, then I grabbed another extinguisher and started on the fire in the radio room.

"I looked back at the tail fire and I thought I saw someone crawling toward me. I ran back and it was Roy Gibson, the tail gunner. Roy had blood all over him—his face, his hands, and everything.

"I looked him over and it seemed as if he'd been hit in the back and the bullet had gone through his left lung. I laid him down on that side so the blood wouldn't drain into his other lung, then I gave him a shot of morphine from the medicine kit and went back to the fire.

"I just got started on the fire when an FW came in at us from eleven o'clock, so I used the waist gun and then went back at the fire in the radio room.

"I got into the room this time and started throwing out some of the junk that was burning. The fire had burned holes in the side of the ship so big that I just threw the stuff out the hole.

"I went back to the tail fire, but it was so hard getting around that I took off my 'chute. I was glad I hadn't taken it off sooner because I found a fifty-caliber bullet halfway through it. It would have gone all the way through me.

"I was plenty mad. I pissed on the fire and beat on it with my hands and feet until my clothes began to smoke."

At the controls, L. P. Johnson knew the B-17 was in bad shape but he didn't know how bad until he landed it. He was afraid from what he knew that it didn't have enough strength left in its frame to withstand the stress of any maneuvers, so he came straight in to an emergency landing field near the Channel coast. As he put the tail wheel down, the fuselage cracked in the middle and came to a stop in two pieces as it crumpled in half and settled on the runway. The engine were salvaged but the rest of that riddled B-17 was junked. It was Snuffy Smith who had enabled everyone left onboard to get back alive.

In looking at the story I wrote that day, I recall worrying, for the first time, about how to quote people I was writing about. I didn't have a tape recorder and my notes were fairly good but sketchy and I was uncertain about how literal the quotes should be. It's an old question for reporters. For example, I'm sure Snuffy said "My hydraulic system was broke." He did not say "My hydraulic system was broken." Reading that now, I think it would have been better if I'd quoted him more literally instead of trying to clean up the natural flow of his speech. That's a problem that never goes away for a reporter. There's a wide gap between the way we talk and the way we write and either style seems out of place in the other medium.

While Snuffy Smith's acts in the air were genuinely heroic, the decision to give him the medal was more a public-relations decision than a real desire to recognize his heroism. Most awards are given by someone whose purpose in bestowing them is to borrow glory or prestige from the honoree. The secretary needed a hero to honor by way of calling the attention of everyone back in the United States to his presence in the ETO. Snuffy Smith was the designated hero.

I wasn't enthusiastic about the ceremonial medal-awarding story but there was no bombing mission scheduled and it seemed worth a few paragraphs. Snuffy was unpopular with most of the crews on the base and their attitude was that there were probably thirty or forty other crewmen just as worthy of the Medal of Honor and a lot more likable than Snuffy. But it was Snuffy who was selected for the award although it didn't come through until almost six weeks after his heroic flight.

When Henry Stimson's entourage arrived, the eight-car caravan was welcomed to the base by a band from wing headquarters and a full-dress assemblage of most of the enlisted men and officers on the base. It was a command performance. Leaves had been canceled for the day, and even the flight officers were ordered to appear for the ceremony. The event was supposed to begin at one o'clock sharp because it was being broadcast back to the United States live on radio.

Everything had been carefully arranged except for one thing. No one had told Snuffy Smith where he was supposed to be. When the time came for Sgt. Maynard Smith to take his place of honor on the temporarily erected stand on the edge of the airstrip, he was nowhere in the vicinity. A hasty search was started and Snuffy was located in a most unlikely place for someone about to be honored with his nation's highest award for valor. He was in the kitchen of his squadron's mess hall, washing the divided stainless steel trays from which everyone had eaten breakfast that morning. He'd been put on KP for having—well, fucked up. He had missed a briefing for a raid.

The event was a serious embarrassment for the base commander. They got Snuffy out of the kitchen, into his best uniform, which wasn't very good, and lined him up so the secretary of war could march up and have the base photographers take pictures of him looping the baby-blue ribbon holding the Medal of Honor around Snuffy's neck. The Medal of Honor isn't pinned on.

It was a better story than I'd dreamed of getting and the headline in *The Stars and Stripes* the next day read:

MEDAL OF HONOR WINNER SNUFFY SMITH FOUND!
ON KP!

Snuffy never let up, either at the ceremony or in the months thereafter. At the press conference held after the ceremony, one of the reporters asked a question.

"Isn't meeting the Secretary of War and facing all the reporters' questions worse than the experience you had putting out the fire on board the Flying Fortress?"

I loved Snuffy for his answer. He looked at the reporter silently for a moment and then said simply "No."

His answer evoked a great deal of laughter because it was a smart response to a dumb question.

From that day on Snuffy gloried in living the life of a hero. If you've heard of modest heroes who didn't want to talk about their exploits, Snuffy wasn't one of those. Photographers came to the base and posed him for pictures peeling potatoes. In town he handed out autographs, and at the pub he held forth almost nightly and his monologues on such matters as relativity, theocracy, and pragmatism, about which he'd recently read in the base library, got the rapt attention of his British audience.

Back at the base, Snuffy got a $2-a-month increase in pay. He was allowed to stay in bed after reveille and no longer had to go to the mail room to pick up his mail because it was delivered to him.

Snuffy Smith was living proof that greatness may be found in unlikely places; what he did on board the B-17 that day was great.

There were more heroes in flight than will ever be known to anyone but themselves. The circumstances were right for heroism in a bomber. Ten men, all well known to each other, were fighting for their lives, in close proximity, in a situation that demanded physical and technical skill. It is those elements that most often produce heroism. Heroism is risking your life to save someone else's. There were gunners who stayed with dying friends who were too badly wounded to jump until the plane crashed to the ground. They didn't so much

Maynard H. (Snuffy) Smith about to get his Medal of Honor from Secretary of War Henry L. Stimson after being found on KP.

refuse the captain's order to jump as they waited. I don't think they thought about dying. They just put off jumping. They were thinking not about themselves but about their friend, and that is heroic.

Pilots were heroic out of proportion to their numbers. They were almost always the most capable, most intelligent, and most determined to accomplish their mission of anyone on board. They were in charge for good reason. Unlike so much authority in the military that is based on nothing but rank however attained, the pilot was in charge because he was the natural leader onboard. Many of them continued to be in charge after they were wounded in flight and when it would have been easier to set aside willpower and die quietly as blood drained from their wounds.

There were a lot of pilots and crew members of the Eighth Air Force who did very brave things. Bravery is closely associated with death because, without the possibility of it, bravery is less extreme.

When I was twelve, I read about one of the legendary heroes of World War I, Sgt. Alvin York. Sergeant York was the prototype of the hero who, single-handed, wipes out a German machine-gun nest by racing across an open field, bayonet at the ready, kills twenty of the enemy, takes 132 prisoners, and captures the hill, thus saving his company. They make movies starring Gary Cooper or John Wayne out of these stories.

There's no question that Sergeant York's action was heroic, but it was a more visceral and less cerebral kind of heroism than that of the wounded pilot. It came more from the balls than the brain. It occurred to me, writing here, that I must have written dozens of stories that illustrated that thought about bravery and heroism, and I found one printed in *The Stars and Stripes* in the summer of 1943.

FORT PILOT KILLED
IN 25TH RAID BUT
CREW GOT HOME
Airmen Beat Flames, Flak
And Nazi Fighters
Over France

A USAAF BOMBER STATION, July 2—Men of this station paid a final tribute to Capt. Raymond J. Check, "the finest pilot and the greatest guy on the field," when Capt. Check, who was killed on the raid over France last Saturday, was buried, with full honors, at the Army cemetery at Brookwood.

The men who returned with Capt. Check's ship, *Chennault's Pappy III,* wrote another story of heroism into Eighth Air Force annals.

It was Capt. Check's 25th raid and it was to be his last. With him in *Chennault's Pappy III* were Lt. Col. James W. Wilson, of Bowling Green, Ohio, station air executive, who flew as copilot, and Maj. George L. Peck, of Denver, a flight surgeon. The regular copilot of the ship, 2/Lt. William P. Cassedy, of Brookhaven, Miss., was flying as right waist gunner.

"We were hit by ME 109s just as we released our bombs," said 1/Lt. Milton P. Blanchette Jr., of Abbeville, S.C. "They came out of the sun and we didn't see them until they hit us."

GUNNER ON FIRE

"I heard a shell hit the plane," the navigator continued, "and the top turret gunner (S/Sgt. James A. Bobbett, of Burkley, Ky.) came running into the nose with his clothes and hair on fire. I smothered out the fire with my hands."

A 20mm shell hit the oxygen system and Capt. Check was killed instantly when another shell hit him in the neck and exploded. Fire started in the cockpit and oxygen leaking from their punctured tanks turned the compartment into an inferno.

Col. Wilson kept control of the plane and tried to put the fire out with his hands.

"About this time, the colonel hollered that the cockpit was on fire," Lt. Blanchette said. "I grabbed a fire extinguisher, ran back there, got the fire under control, then went back to the nose and told the Doc and the bombardier to go up to the pilot's cockpit."

Col. Wilson had been seriously burned trying to put the fire out but he was still flying the plane, controlling the Fort with his arms above the elbow.

BOMBARDIER BAILED OUT

Meanwhile, someone had rung the alarm bell, signaling the crew to bail out.

"I turned to put on my earphones and just then, I heard the hatch open behind me. I looked around and saw someone bailing out. All I could see was his boots and I didn't know until later that it was the bombardier," Lt. Blanchette said.

In the waist of the ship, Lt. Cassedy, an experienced flier, could feel that the ship was still under control and he told the crew not to bail out. He did not know yet that Capt. Check had been killed and Col. Wilson was flying the ship severely burned. The doctor, Maj. Peck, had gone from the nose to the pilot's compartment and was trying to help Col. Wilson.

"It was a wonder a man could stand the pain and fly a plane at the same time," Maj. Peck said.

Disregarding the possibility that he might have to bail out, Maj. Peck, who was on his first mission, had taken off his parachute so that he could move freely around the plane where he was needed.

SHELL-SPLINTERED SHIP

The tail gunner, S/Sgt. Milton B. Edwards, of Laurel, Md., was wounded in the arm. The radio operator, T/Sgt. William T. Johnson, of Wellsburg, W. Va., had been hit in the leg with flak, and Bobbett, the top turret gunner, was burned. None of the guns was being manned. There were flak holes in the right elevator and the leading edge of the right wing as well as through the fuselage. A 20mm shell blasted a hole through the dorsal fin.

Lt. Cassedy went forward from the waist, and standing between the body of Capt. Check, one of his best friends, and Col. Wilson, who was in agony, he flew the ship.

When Maj. Peck had dressed the wounds of some of the gunners he went forward again and took Col. Wilson from the cockpit to the nose of the Fort. He dressed the colonel's burns and bandaged his hands. The colonel insisted on going back to the pilot's compartment to help Lt. Cassedy fly the ship but with his hands bandaged heavily with gauze, there wasn't much he could do. Lt. Blanchette, who was also flying on his 25th operation over Europe, helped Lt. Cassedy bring the ship home. Maj. Peck continued to help wounded members of the crew.

Other members of the crew were 1/Lt. Lionel F. Drew, of Oneco, Fla., the bombardier; S/Sgt. Jerry O. Hooks, Clermont, Fla.; and Sgt. Archie H. Garrett, Evansville, Ind.

When I read that story fifty years after I'd written it, it seemed to me that I'd done a competent job. Everything was there and it was a moving story of bravery and death that I had told directly without embellishing it with many adjectives.

I was impressed with how right Hutton had been as the editor in insisting that, without exception, we had to include the full name and hometown of any soldier mentioned in a story. Hometowns were more interesting to soldiers than the stories they appeared in.

Most bombardment groups, like most infantry divisions, fighter groups, and major Navy units, have someone who tries to maintain a directory of living members. Russell Strong of Charlotte, North Carolina, wrote about the 306th in his book *First Over Germany* and has done a remarkable job keeping his directory up to date.

It seemed as though it might be worthwhile to see how many of the crew of *Chennault's Pappy* I could track down today. I found three, and it was from one of them that I learned, fifty years too late, that I had missed one of the most dramatic stories relating to the sad flight of *Chennault's Pappy*.

James Wilson, the visiting copilot who was so badly burned on the hands and arms, stayed in the Air Force and became a general. Either his memory of the event is dim or he's an unusually taciturn man. He spoke matter-of-factly about the trip from his retirement home in Palm Springs and told me that the reason he was burned so badly was that he'd taken his gloves off.

"Damn supercharger on those 17s," he said. "You had to keep adjusting them every time you changed altitude. We dropped two thousand feet over the target and I made the mistake of taking my gloves off while I tried to adjust the supercharger."

When I started looking for the navigator, Milton Blanchette, in a small town in South Carolina, the operator told me there were four Blanchettes, no Milton. I later found out he was usually called Prue. The man who answered the first number I called was laconic, a word I don't have occasion to use often.

"You know a Milton Blanchette?" I asked.

"Yup," he said.

"Is he there?" I asked.

"Nope," he said, and I began to fear Milton was no longer living.

"You know where he lives?" I persisted.

"Yup," he said, but he didn't offer to tell me where Milton lived.

"Where does he live?"

"Lives over in Columbia."

I found Prue Blanchette and talked to him at great length. It was he who let me know the story I'd missed that day fifty years ago.

"Know why we landed with the wind on our tail?" he asked me.

I told him I recall hearing someone say that they were afraid the B-17 wouldn't make a turn around the field so it would be headed the right way, into the wind.

"Nope," he said.

"Pappy Check was gonna marry that pretty nurse on the base next day after he'd finished all his missions. They were havin' a party for the two of them and she was waitin' in a jeep at the end of the run-way for him.

"We couldn't bring him up to her that way with his head blown off so we come in with the wind on our tail. She never saw him. Good thing."

In the year and a half I covered the Eighth Air Force, I came on more gut-wrenching stories than I could write. I was at Chelveston one afternoon when the bombers came home and after the debrief-ing, I approached some crew members I knew. They seemed remote and strange and I couldn't understand their reluctance to talk to me. Several hours later I found out why they were reluctant. Their top turret gunner had his right arm blown off at the shoulder over Bre-men. He was spouting blood and they knew he had no chance of liv-ing on the three-hour trip back to their base in England so they wrapped him tightly in one parachute and pulled the rip cord on the second 'chute strapped to his back as they dumped him overboard. They knew he had to get lucky. His only hope was to be picked up quickly and cared for by a German doctor on the ground.

They had walked away from me in silence because they knew how slim the chances were that their friend was still alive. They didn't feel like talking to anyone about anything.

IT SEEMED WRONG but after several months covering the air war I stopped writing some of the stories of bravery and heroism I saw or heard about because they were commonplace. I was afraid readers would become inured to them. More and more I wrote frothy feature stories that had less tragedy and more human interest or stories of heroism with happy endings.

▪ Harold Rogers used to be a Hollywood stunt man before he was a waist gunner on a B-17. Rogers loved dogs. He found Mister when it was an abandoned puppy in a town near the base. Rogers taught Mister to wear an oxygen mask and then took it on eight missions with him. *The Stars and Stripes* ran a picture of Rogers at his machine gun in the waist of his B-17 with Mister, in its oxygen mask, looking perky at his side.

▪ Capt. Arthur Isaac was Jewish and from Brooklyn. Nervous about being shot down and landing in Germany, Isaacs had dog tags made that gave his name as "Otto McIsaac." He always swore that if he had to parachute into Germany, the first thing he was going to do was demand to be taken to a Catholic church so he could attend mass.

▪ Top-turret gunner Clifford Erickson of Fond du Lac, Wisconsin, brought back the B-17 *Dangerous Dan* after his pilot and copilot were hurt even though he'd never flown before.

▪ A fighter pilot, blinded when bullets shattered his Plexiglas cockpit hood, was brought down safely by a friend flying on his wing and giving instructions.

▪ Capt. Purvis Youree and his copilot, Leroy Sugg, were coming home in a B-17 riddled with flak. I described the plane after it landed as "looking like a colander." The B-17 had been hit so many times that Youree had little control over it. The cables running to the wing flaps were gone and the ship was in immediate danger of spinning out. Disregarding his personal safety in what seemed to be the likely event he'd have to bail out, Sugg took off his parachute, cut off pieces of the long cords, and tied one to the broken end of a control cable. He gave the other end to Youree and the pilot brought the ship in, using the flaps pulled by the pieces of harness from Sugg's parachute.

THROUGH ALL THIS, I had the companionship of my friends on *The Stars and Stripes* of the newspapermen I traveled with, and letters from Margie. In the midst of so much sadness, there was plenty of warmth and some humor.

On one memorable occasion half a dozen reporters were flown to Oran in North Africa for the occasion of King George VI's visit to the troops in North Africa. We were all assembled, about sixteen of us, at a British officers club in Oran where we were to meet the king.

One of the reporters who had flown down was the incomparable Homer Bigart. It is important to this story to remind you that both King George and Homer stammered badly. Both of them had great difficulty getting out their words.

In the lineup of reporters, I stood to Homer's right and, as the king started down the receiving line, I heard his greeting to Bob Considine of International News Service.

"How . . . how . . . how . . . da . . . da . . . do you . . . you do?" the king stammered. "Who . . . who . . . whom . . . da . . . da . . . do you . . . rep . . . rep . . . repre. . . . represent?"

"The International News Service, sir," Bob said.

The king moved on to the next reporter and repeated his question.

After having spoken to seven or eight people, he came to the ninth man and said simply "How . . . how do . . . do you do" and moved on without asking a question.

The next two people were asked their affiliations and then it was my turn.

"The U.S. Army newspaper," I said in answer to his hesitating question, "*The Stars and Stripes.*" Next man was Homer.

"How . . . how . . . are . . . are ya . . . ya . . . you?" the king said to Homer and moved on.

Later, Homer, who always put everyone listening to him at ease with his sense of humor, said, "It's a ga . . . it's a ga . . . goddamn . . . good thing, ta too. There ca . . . could . . . ha . . . have . . . ba been . . . an inter . . . international . . . in . . . incident."

I DON'T KNOW whose idea it was but someone decided the reporters covering the Eighth Air Force ought to go on a mission themselves. It probably grew out of that uneasy feeling we all had that we were watching too many young men our age die while we were writing stories about them and then going back to London for dinner.

As correspondents we were not supposed to be armed or fire weapons of any kind. This allowed for better treatment in the event we were captured by the enemy, although my position as an Army sergeant with a correspondent's credentials was unusual. I don't know whether I'd have been considered a correspondent or a soldier.

In spite of the rule against weapons for reporters, the two officers charged with preparing us for the trip decided that if we were going on a raid we'd have to go to gunnery school and learn how to shoot a .50-caliber machine gun. It didn't make a lot of sense but we did it.

It was their argument that in a life-or-death situation we might be faced with the choice of shooting or dying, and it would be better if we were prepared to shoot.

There were eight of us: Walter Cronkite, United Press; Homer Bigart, *New York Herald Tribune;* Paul Manning, MBS (Mutual Broadcasting System); Jack Denton Scott, *YANK* magazine; Gladwin Hill, the Associated Press; Bill Wade, International News Service; Bob Post, *The New York Times;* and myself. We were sent to some kind of training camp for a week and we learned a little about parachutes, life rafts, and the .50-caliber machine gun. There was some talk of learning to pack a parachute and several demonstration classes were held but, in the belief that there was no chance that someone who couldn't make a bed would ever learn how to pack a parachute, I did not attend.

I don't recall ever pulling the trigger on a machine gun, either. The closest we got to any death-dealing weapon was a shotgun we were asked to learn how to use on a skeet-shooting range. Bob Post had obviously grown up in more advantageous circumstances than most of us because he was the only one who had ever done it before. On a skeet range, they released clay dishes from stage left and stage right with some kind of spring-activated sling that, at timed intervals, tossed them in an arc 100 feet in front of the gunners. Bob was the only one of us who ever hit one of the clay pigeons.

It was a good week we spent together partly because of the excitement of imminent danger and partly because it was generally good company. At the time, the other reporters seemed much older than I was, but today those of them who are left are my contemporaries. It's like a brother who was twelve when you were seven.

When the time came for us to join a bomb squadron and wait for word of a mission, we each went our separate ways. I went to Thurleigh where the 306th Bomb Group was based. Cronkite went to Molesworth with the 303rd Bomb Group, which was commanded by Brig. Gen. Curtis LeMay, easily the most visible group leader. It was LeMay who had changed the way the bombers flew. Even after they put the chin turret on later models, they were losing too many B–17s to the Luftwaffe, whose fliers were coming through the formations from front to rear with guns blazing. The chin turret helped, but LeMay thought the answer was to fly tight formations that left no room for intruders.

Day after day, LeMay took his group up to practice formation flying. He made Blue Angels of all his pilots by making them fly wing tip to wing tip. LeMay made his men put in so many practice hours in the air that he was getting regular complaints from wing headquarters about the huge amount of fuel he was burning compared with other groups.

LeMay ended up as a caricature of himself after the war, running as he did for vice president as a far-right candidate on a ticket with the segregationist governor of Alabama, George Wallace, but during 1943 and 1944 he was the best bomb-group commander we had. We grow up with the illusion that there are men with all the virtues and others with none and it's not true. LeMay was the first general I ever heard called "Old Iron Pants" and, while the name was used more by newspapermen than by anyone in his outfit, the name fit his personality. He had suffered some kind of stroke at an early age and the right side of his face was paralyzed and thus expressionless, but to hear him talk you might have guessed that he wouldn't have had any expression on his face if he hadn't suffered the stroke.

Years later, when I was writing for the radio and television personality Arthur Godfrey, I met LeMay again. Arthur was making a speech in Detroit one night to an assembly that General Motors had put together, comprising every important U.S. military man in the Army, Navy, and Air Force. It was a little gift to them from GM.

I came to Godfrey's hotel room early in the evening with a handful of papers on which I'd prepared opening remarks for Arthur to use as well as notes for his use as toastmaster at the dinner. LeMay was sitting in a big chair and Godfrey was lying on the bed. The room was blue with smoke from the huge Cuban cigars they were puffing.

It struck me as funny that the life of this really good World War II warrior was so changed since the days when I'd known him that he was reduced to sitting in a hotel room, smoking a cigar and talking to an entertainer for whom I'd just written a sheaf of jokes.

The morning of the mission, February 3, 1943, we were up in the dark at 5:30. There weren't many secrets kept from reporters in the war we were watching, but I'd never been included before in a briefing at which the details of the mission were laid out. Inasmuch as I was going on the raid myself, I was allowed into the briefing that day.

It had apparently occurred to someone that I could hardly be considered a security risk who might reveal the target to the Germans in advance of my arriving over it.

I went to the Nissen hut where the officers were assembling. It's hard to understand why the enlisted men and the officers going on a mission weren't all told about it at once in the same room but they were not. I suppose it was for the same reason a coach doesn't meet with his wide receivers and his linebackers at the same time. They have different jobs.

The briefing was dramatic. I guess they always were. The G2 (Intelligence) officer stood with a long pointer in his hand in front of a wall with what was obviously a map covered with a blanket-sized piece of blue cloth. Sometimes I can't remember my own name but I remember, fifty years later, that the cloth was blue.

I remember thinking how good, how all-American, the young fliers looked in their leather jackets, open shirt collars, and jaunty, leather-peaked caps set on their heads at a casually rakish angle. There were a few who wore neckties. Yale, perhaps.

When everyone was seated, the G2 officer with the pointer stepped up to the map, paused briefly as he scanned the room, and then grasped the lower right-hand corner of the cloth and threw it back. There was a hush at first as the fliers stared intently at the map. Gradually a murmur developed and then gasps as they realized it was a large-scale map of a western sector of Germany. Our destination was—Wilhelmshaven!

Targets for the first year had been exclusively in France or Holland, where the Eighth Air Force had bombed U-boat pens and railroad yards where cars were loaded with supplies for the Wehrmacht defending the French coast.

The map revealed was six feet wide with colored tape three quarters of an inch wide crisscrossing it to indicate our route in and out. The tapes had fat arrows at their ends that told us precisely what we were to hit.

Wilhelmshaven was a port city heavily defended by antiaircraft batteries and well within range of several Luftwaffe fighter squadrons.

February 26, 1943, was the first time I'd seriously considered my own death. Until then, when the thought of death occurred to me, it was someone else's, not my own. From the time I was six, it had seemed to me that people got slowly old, lost track of time and feeling, and faded away until one night they died in their sleep. They always died at night in their sleep. It never hurt. They had finished life and were unaware of going. They weren't frightened by the thought of never anything ever again.

I remember thinking that maybe my mother, my English bulldog, Spike, and I would be the first people not to die. I included Spike as one of us people. This may have been because my mother tended to treat him that way. Once at the lake, she had baked a cake and put it on a low shelf in the woodshed to cool. It was a handy height for Spike standing on his hind legs with his paws on the shelf, but Mother refused to indict him on such flimsy circumstantial evidence.

"I don't think he'd eat it," she said. "It must have been some animal."

This was to be only the second Eighth Air Force raid into Germany. The dangers were as yet largely unknown except that they were considerable and the feeling among the officers on the base was that the second raid would be even tougher than the first because they knew we'd be coming.

A thousand things went through my mind. I wondered what I was doing there. Was it really necessary for me to volunteer for a mission that could easily cost me my life simply to get a story for the newspaper or to appear more legitimate in the eyes of the crewmen I was covering on a daily basis?

Obviously it was too late to pull out and I never seriously considered it. I did think of Margie and Mother and Dad and all the people I'd left at home and wondered if I'd ever see them again. I don't recall being so much afraid as introspective. I suppose I felt the way a lot of infantrymen feel in the front lines. If they were alone they'd run, but they can't because they feel an obligation to the people all around them who are doing the same thing. And then I had the same feeling everyone who ever fought a war has. I heard it expressed a thousand times. "The guy next to me may get it but I think I'll be okay."

The crew of the *Banshee* got out to the hardstand an hour before takeoff. I suppose there may have been a lot of small jokes, but if there

were I've forgotten them. The chance of being shot down was estimated to be something like one in five or six. About as good as Russian roulette with a six-shooter—which isn't very good.

On the day of the mission, two of the eight reporters who were to
have gone on the raid came up lame and decided they weren't well
enough to go. Listen, it happens. The thought crossed my mind that I
didn't feel too well myself.

You got in a B-17 through the waist opening on the right side.
There was no door because the machine guns were permanently
installed and their muzzles protruded enough to give the gunner full
range up, down, forward, and backward when he was aiming at an
attacking Luftwaffe fighter plane. (It was simple enough, but I never
got thoroughly easy with the direction of an approaching enemy
fighter. When someone yelled "Boogie! Eleven o'clock high!" meaning there was an Me-109 or an FW-190 bearing in from that direction, I was slow to know where to look. It was not a situation in
which visualizing a clock came readily to my mind.)

There was no access from the left side of the plane because the
gunner's opening didn't go down to the floor. The open sides made
the B-17 slower than it otherwise would have been—and colder, too.
Cold was a bitter factor on many missions when men were wounded.
It was colder than traveling at eighty miles an hour in a convertible
with the top down in below-zero weather, with the added inconvenience of having people shooting at you from the ground and from
other aircraft.

To get forward on the B-17, you went from the midsection
through the bomb bay, walking on a narrow steel (or perhaps aluminum) beam with the bombs hanging on either side below you. It
was easy to get snagged on something as you came through the bomb
bay wearing all your equipment because it was narrow and there were
wires and jagged spurs of electrical connectors protruding from it on
all sides that grabbed at you.

We were given flak jackets, but there was a difference of opinion
about the advisability of wearing one. Being lead-lined canvas, they
were heavy and bulky and I already had my parachute. The 'chute
alone was more than I was comfortable carrying and it was cumber-

Smelling the roses while leaning against a pile of bombs headed for Germany in the belly of a B-17 must have seemed like an amusing picture to send home when I posed for this. The camouflage nets have been thrown back.

some. I'd been given the choice between wearing it on my chest and wearing it on my back and I'd chosen to wear it on my chest. That way, I knew where it was.

I made the decision to stand on my flak jacket instead of wearing it for several faulty reasons. I felt that if we had to bail out, my chances would be better if I didn't have to get it off first and, second, I had this natural apprehension about being castrated by a flak burst underneath the aircraft.

The cockpit, half a level up, was immediately ahead of the bomb bay. The top-turret gunner was behind the cockpit, and to get to the nose area you bent down and went under the pilot and the copilot and past the radioman's position. Among other discomforts, I felt claustrophobic.

The nose, from the bombardier up front to the navigator, who was actually under the pilot, was about twelve feet long.

As I sat, considering my circumstance, on the small, makeshift seat behind the bombardier and opposite the navigator, Casey revved the engines to give the propellers enough spin to pull us out off the hard-stand and onto the runway.

"It's perfectly possible I'll never come back," I thought. "There's a good chance we'll be shot down or that I'll be seriously wounded." Thousands of crewmen who were not killed were seriously wounded by the shards of shrapnel that cut through the fuselage of the aircraft when a German shell exploded in the midst of a formation. We didn't know it at the time but the Luftwaffe was already planning to drop bombs from fighter planes above our formations that would explode in the middle of them. "Young to die," I thought that day at twenty-four. "This is a silly, fake brave gesture I'm making considering the high risk it involves. Nothing I have to do. Not fair, really, to my wife at home or to my father and mother." In 1943 I thought only of the possibility I was seeing my last day on earth.

It would be a great convenience if we were allowed to know, sometime in our early teens, the occasion of our demise. There could be great parties for those of us who drew a lucky, faraway date. If I knew now, or had known in all the years I've considered the thought of my own last day, what day that would be, it would have saved me uncounted sleepless nights.

In recent years, because I'm finally resigned to its inevitability, I think of death as frequently but with somewhat less terror and more thoughtful consideration for what it will mean to the family and friends I leave alive behind me. It seems like an acceptable degree of ego to think that their lives will be, to a small degree at least, different.

There were a lot of hard things to do onboard a B-17. I was nervous about everything because I didn't know how to do anything. I was uneasy with my oxygen connections and considered the possibility that I'd be asphyxiated in flight because I didn't know how to work a valve on my tank. You begin to need oxygen anywhere above 12,000 feet and we were going to be in the air at 24,000 feet for five hours. Had I known what I was about to go through, I might have thrown pride to the wind and climbed out.

The trip over the Channel was dull. When we started in over France I was impressed with the regularity of the patterns of the small farms. I thought of myself as going to a war zone and was mildly surprised to see farmers working their fields with horse-drawn plows. It seemed strange that anyone was doing anything so normal as farming.

There were fifty-three bombers in our formation, a relatively small group. No fighter cover. We were ten minutes from Wilhelmshaven when we encountered the first bursts of flak from perimeter antiaircraft artillery. Looking forward over the bombardier's head, I could see the mushroomlike puffs of smoke that marked the shells exploding around the lead planes. When a shell burst, it sent thousands of bulletlike shards of metal in every direction. It was more like a shotgun than a rifle because it released a lethal spray of deadly missiles. Whether you were hit or not was a matter of luck. Direct hits, when the shell actually hit and exploded inside a plane, were relatively rare and, of course, always fatal.

We dropped our bombs—I never saw them hit—and the pilot, Bill Casey, wheeled *Banshee* around and the bombers regrouped and headed home. Some of the B-17s had been hit and were unable to stay with the formation. They were in the most trouble. Like the old wildebeests in the African herd trying to outrun the lions, it was the bombers that dropped back, with one or two engines knocked out, that were most vulnerable to being shot down by the ME-109s and FW-190s. The raid was before our own fighter planes, the P-51s and P-47s, were flying cover for the bombers.

It was on the way out from the target that we took direct fire from the Luftwaffe, which by now had about 100 planes in the air attacking our relatively small formation of fifty-three bombers. They had stayed clear of the target area because they were as vulnerable to their own antiaircraft shells as we were, but once we'd left the target, the German fighter planes dove through our riddled formation and swished through it head-on with guns firing. I couldn't see anything but a flash of glistening metal in the sunlight because they were flying at 450mph and we were flying at 250 in the other direction. That was 700mph, and at that speed the gunners had a hard time sighting the approaching Jerries far enough in advance to aim and get a burst off.

Several B-17s around us were hit. Three in the formation went down. The long, slow, death spiral of a bomber with its crew on board is a terrible thing to see. It was worse for the crew because they knew all thirty men as friends. Ten 'chutes came from one, three emerged from the second. The third exploded into fragments in the air leaving behind nothing but a small cloud of dirty smoke, and it was impossible to tell the parts of machinery from the bodies of men as they all tumbled toward earth. I don't know what happens inside the brain but I was no longer nervous.

Suddenly there was an explosion six feet in front of me in *Banshee's* nose compartment where the bombardier sat hunched over his bombsight. A shell or fragment of one had clipped off the tip of the plastic nose of *Banshee,* leaving a jagged hole not much bigger than a man's fist. The Intelligence reports later said that, for the first time, the Germans were using parachute bombs. These were explosives equipped with parachutes that were shot up 25,000 feet by artillery. When the parachute opened, the explosive package was designed to drift down and explode in the middle of one of the bomber formations. I never saw one and I don't know for sure what hit us, but at 200 miles an hour, four miles above the earth, it's a viciously cold gale that rushes in a hole that big. It was the navigator's first mission and, in a moment of panic, he tore off his gloves and tried to stuff them in the gaping hole. Within minutes his hands had frozen and chips of flesh broke off his fingers as they caught on the jagged edges of the plastic.

I had taken as many steps forward as my oxygen tubes allowed but there wasn't anything I could have done even if I'd known how. I looked over at the navigator, Lt. Bill Owens, and saw that he was slumped over his desk, unconscious, with his oxygen mask supply line dangling free where it had been cut.

"Casey," I called to the pilot. "Bill's out. I think he's lost his oxygen."

Casey had his hands full flying evasive action trying to give the German fighter planes a moving target. He didn't hesitate though.

"There are four oxygen bottles up here behind me," he said matter-of-factly. "Take some deep breaths, take your mask off, and get back up here and grab a bottle for him."

It was unsettling to be pressed into service doing a real job. I felt inadequate. They'd forgotten I was a reporter.

I expected I'd collapse after ten seconds without oxygen but it doesn't happen quite that way or so fast and the bottles were very close. With my parachute dangling from me, I made the trip back up the narrow passage behind the pilot and copilot. Casey saw me out of the corner of his eye but never said a word. He just wanted to make sure I'd done it.

I took the oxygen tank and another mask and tried to remember a few things I'd been taught about how to use one. I was afraid Owens would be dead before I could hook him into the emergency supply. I didn't know. I took off his useless mask, fitted him with the emergency one, and turned on the valve in the air bottle. Within minutes he was conscious again. He looked over at me. I don't know whether he realized what I'd done or not. It was as if he'd awakened from a nap. Owens got the bombardier quieted down and then went back to his position with some maps across from me. (The copilot that day was also named Owens. He wrote to me in 1994 with kind words about my going on the raid but with a complaint about a negative comment I'd made on *60 Minutes* about people who keep trailers or mobile homes in their driveways. He now sells them.)

All I could see from my place at the rear of the nose of the plane was straight ahead and a little to either side. My back was up against the metal sheath of the aircraft before it became Plexiglas a few feet forward. The only reason I knew we were being attacked from the side was the sound of .50-caliber machine-gun fire from the two waist gunners and from the gunner in the top-turret bubble, above and behind the pilot's cockpit.

It was a grim and silent trip back across the English Channel. Not a lot of fun, and it was not clear to any of us that we'd hit much of anything with our bombs. No one spoke on the intercom of seeing the B-17s on our wing go down but everyone must have been thinking about it.

Several years ago a publication for a veteran bombardiers association called *Crosshairs* attacked me for saying that most bombardiers didn't have much to do on a mission. I had said that most bombardiers and navigators didn't do much bombing or navigating because the bombardiers dropped on cue from the lead bomber and the planes flew together and no one but the navigator in the lead plane had to know where they were going. The rest played follow-the-leader.

It wasn't kind of me but I repeat it here. The B-17s and B-24s flew as tight together as the Blue Angels because it gave them more collective firepower against Luftwaffe fighter pilots and made it difficult for them to dive through the bomber formation.

When the sophisticated Norden bombsight was installed in the B-17s and B-24s, it was supposed to revolutionize high-altitude, daylight bombing. Fifty years later the Pentagon was still talking about "pinpoint" accuracy when it launched a missile in the direction of a Saudi nuclear plant, but the word "pinpoint" doesn't often apply to bombing when the missile is dropped from an airplane. "Close" would be a better word.

The Norden bombsight was good but hard to use. Not what they'd call these days user-friendly. It was a complex instrument that figured in, among other things, height, lateral distance from the target, wind speed, wind direction, air speed, and bomb weight. It took the brightest kid in the class to do the necessary mathematical calculations. The average bombardier was not capable of executing these in a hurry and under fire. There was no reason to expect he would be. It made more sense, with the bombers flying wing on wing and nose overlapping the tail of the bomber below, to have the best bombardier in the lead plane make the calculations. When he released his bombs, everyone following would release theirs. It was easy to plan out brief delays for trailing planes if that seemed necessary to hit the target. The lead bombardier always had a backup, the next plane in the formation, in case he was shot down, killed, or wounded.

The six correspondents who went out that day were to meet after the raid at Molesworth, where facilities had been set up for us to write our stories and transmit them back to London. Five of us straggled into the temporary pressroom at intervals over a period of half an hour, and then the word came that we had dreaded. There would never be more than five of us. Bob Post, the friendly and able young reporter for *The New York Times,* was missing. Bob was thirty-two, a Harvard graduate with a bright future ahead of him at the *Times.* Others in the formation reported seeing parachutes open before his B-17 crashed into the ground, but Bob was never heard from again. He went down with the plane.

Most of us writing our stories used the word "missing" in refer-ring to Bob because it held out hope that he was still alive and allowed us to be more enthusiastic about our own stories. With the dangerous assignment behind us, we were all high with the relief of having the job over with and it led to a display of exuberance in our stories that was, in retrospect, not very becoming of journalists. I think most of us would be embarrassed to see those stories in print today.

As good as he was as a reporter, Cronkite was never a great writer. He never got over the wire-service style he was brought up on. Homer Bigart, on the other hand, was one of the best writing reporters there ever was.

When I want to remind Cronkite that he is mortal man, I quote him a few sentences from his United Press story that day. I've been pleased, over the years, that he hasn't been able to find a copy of mine.

Walter tells the story of riding back to the debriefing hut after the raid in a jeep with Homer. He says Homer told him he wasn't sure how to start his story of the raid.

"I told him I already had my lead," Walter says.

"Wha. . . . wha . . . what is . . . is it?" Homer asked, haltingly.

"I have just returned from a mission to hell!"

Walter says Homer looked at him for a minute and finally said, "You . . . you . . . wou . . . wou . . . wouldn't!"

One of Walter's endearing traits is his ability to tell better stories about himself than anyone else tells.

The fact was, I ended up with the best story of the day because of the hit we took on board *Banshee* from a German antiaircraft gun.

The following morning, my story was played on page one of both *The Stars and Stripes* and my hometown newspaper, the *Times Union* in Albany, New York. It was a HOMETOWN BOY BOMBS GERMANY kind of story. I was pleased to have Margie and my family and friends know where I was and what I was doing, but not so pleased at the suggestion I was some kind of hero for doing once what thousands of young men were doing three days a week.

The following day, I read the official report on the raid. We had not won the war with it.

"Both the B-17s of the 1st Bombardment Wing and the B-24s of the 2nd Bombardment Wing stirred up a sizable force of enemy fighters, estimated at more than 100 aircraft."

As a result of the raid I got my first taste of a kind of celebrity that I've grown to detest although I haven't had the courage to cut it off by refusing to participate in the sort of thing that perpetuates it.

Ben Lyon and Bebe Daniels, sometime Hollywood movie stars, were living in London and had a regular BBC radio show called *Lon-*

don Calling. It was sent to the States for broadcast, and I was asked to be on it to describe my experiences on the raid. One of my least-prized mementoes of the war is a copy of the script for that program. Not a word of it was ad lib. I must have given them some information before I came into the studio, I don't recall, but when I got there I was simply handed a script and asked to read it.

> LYON: HELLO, AMERICA! THIS IS BEN LYON TO BRING YOU ONCE AGAIN MEN AND WOMEN OF THE U.S.A. SERVING IN THE FORCES ON THIS SIDE OF THE ATLANTIC. WE OFTEN HEAR OF OUR MEN BEING DECORATED FOR FEATS OF COURAGE. NOT QUITE SO OFTEN DO WE HEAR OF THOSE PERSONALITIES BEHIND THE SCENES WHOSE BROAD EXPERIENCE, GOOD LEADERSHIP AND LONG HARD WORK ENSURE THE SUCCESS OF SOME OF OUR GIGANTIC OPERATIONS. TODAY I WANT YOU TO MEET SGT. ANDREW A. ROONEY OF ALBANY, N.Y. I'M NOT JUST CERTAIN WHAT SGT. ROONEY'S JOB IS BUT WE'LL SOON FIND THAT OUT. WHAT IS IT, ANDY?
>
> ROONEY: I WRITE REGULAR FEATURES FOR *STARS AND STRIPES* AND DO NEWS STORIES.
>
> LYON: DO YOU COVER ANY MISSIONS TO ENEMY TERRITORY? [I should have said "no."]
>
> ROONEY: YES, I WENT OVER ON THE RAID ON WILHELMS-HAVEN.
>
> LYON: WELL, ANDY [All the "wells" are in the script and suddenly we were best friends. I was no longer "Sgt. Rooney." I was "Andy."] WELL, ANDY, SUPPOSE YOU GIVE US SOME LOW-DOWN ON ONE OF THOSE RAIDS?

Those were some of the best parts of my very first broadcasting experience. It's hard to believe I was so young and impressed with being on the BBC that I didn't say "Hey, what is this crap anyway?" The BBC show is the last time I ever read something for broadcast I had not written myself.

In spite of my broadcasting debut being such a dismal event, two good things came out of it. First, the BBC gave me a formal-looking contract to sign which I've kept all these years as a memento, and £12 in cash, which was somewhat more than my week's pay.

THERE WAS A great deal of pressure from the PROs (public-relations officers) for reporters to come to their bases. I don't know how the PROs were selected for the job but most of them were pretty good. Morale was such a problem that any recognition they could get in print for their fliers was welcome encouragement. The crews wanted someone to know they were fighting and dying, and it was the PROs' job to get their names in a newspaper somewhere, anywhere.

Some of the PROs had more to work with than others. At a fighter base, hot aces like Don Gentile or the Eagle Squadron leader Chesley Peterson brought the newspeople. The Eagle Squadron was a group of Americans flying Spitfires for the RAF before they changed over to the Ninth Air Force, where they were given P-47s to fly.

Reporters were keeping track of who shot down the most Luftwaffe fighter planes as if the statistics were batting averages. A fighter pilot with a large number of "kills" was always suspect because he was the only one who could verify his claims, but neither other pilots nor reporters mentioned that there was ever any doubt when a pilot said he had shot down two enemy planes to bring his total to nineteen. It made too good a headline, and most of the claims were true.

At a bomber base, a colorful commander or a gunner like T/Sgt. Michael Roskovich attracted coverage. Roskovich was a carefree spirit known as "the Mad Russian" who shocked several high-ranking officers who boarded his B-17 by cutting off their neckties below the knot.

Dramas seldom played themselves out in a satisfactory way at the bases though. Heroes, in real life, are not immortal and happy endings were rare. Rosky was immortalized when he became the first enlisted man to complete twenty-five missions. He was grounded and then commissioned and became a gunnery officer. Dissatisfied with his dull job after a few months, he joined another flight crew and was killed when the pilot, attempting to return to their home base, foolishly tried to take off from an airfield in Scotland with three engines and crashed, killing all nine men on board, including Roskovich.

One especially good and colorful P-47 group commander was Hubert Zemke from Missoula, Montana. I must have written "Missoula, Montana" for *The Stars and Stripes* 500 times with his name ahead of it. Zemke was commander of the Fifty-sixth Fighter Group, a leader independent of that, and an ace who ended up shooting down seventeen German fighter planes. He was shot down himself on October 30, 1944, after he'd switched from P-47s, first to the twin-tailed P-38 and then to the P-51 Mustang. He may have been the best fighter pilot the Ninth Air Force had. Certainly he was the best group commander.

Zemke's Fifty-sixth had five of the top ten aces in Europe—Francis Gabreski, the leader with twenty-eight; Robert Johnson with twenty-seven; David Schilling, twenty-two; Walker Mahurin, twenty; and Zemke himself with seventeen.

I wrote several long stories about Zemke and they were fun for me to do because he was genuinely disinterested in seeing his name in the paper. I don't think he cared one way or the other. On one occasion Zemke reported that he'd been on the tail of an ME-109 when a P-51 came in on the German pilot from an angle and hit him with machine-gun fire. The pilot jumped with his clothes in flames. Zemke saw the writhing body of his enemy slowly being burned to death as the flames were fanned to white heat by the rush of air flowing around the parachute. "I fixed him in my sights and fired to put him out of his misery," Zemke reported.

No one who knew Zemke's sense of honor would doubt that he'd kill a man under those circumstances for any other reason but to save him from the agony of burning to death. He was of the old school of gentlemen warriors. Eddie Rickenbacker and the Red Baron, von Richthofen.

By the time Zemke started flying into Germany accompanying the heavy bombers, he had already spent a year in Russia teaching Soviet pilots how to fly our P-40s and, as a test pilot, he'd had a hand in the design of the P-47. It was 47s the Fifty-sixth Fighter Group flew so successfully. The P-38 group he went to was having a lot of trouble being effective, and I suppose he was transferred there to help with the problem. I don't know why he then transferred to P-51s. His aircraft was the P-47 Thunderbolt. He and that aircraft grew up together.

The public-relations man at Zemke's base asked me to come into the control tower one day, normally off-limits, as the P-47s were returning from a mission accompanying the B-17s into Germany.

As the fighters got close to home, the tower started picking up their radio conversations and one man, Lt. Ralph Johnson of Pikeville, Kentucky, was in trouble. He'd been shot at and hit. He could get only one wheel down for landing and, now that it was down, he couldn't get it back up. A belly landing was an option but a one-wheel landing was suicide.

Zemke had already landed and was taking off his flight gear when he heard Johnson's problem. Without a second thought, Zemke strapped himself in again and took off to get a better look at the underside of Johnson's plane. As he drew up alongside the damaged P-47, I took down the following notes of the tense conversation between Johnson and Hub Zemke:

ZEMKE: Have you tried to shake it down?

JOHNSON: Yes.

ZEMKE: Get way up and try it again. If you can't shake it down, you'll have to jump. Go over to that lake there straight ahead. Put your landing-gear handle in the down position, do a bank on your left wing, and snap it over to the right. Let me get a little ahead.

JOHNSON: Okay. (Long pause.)

ZEMKE: That hasn't done it. Do some violent weaving back and forth.

JOHNSON: Sir, my landing-gear handle is stuck.

ZEMKE: Is it stuck down?

JOHNSON: Yes, sir.

ZEMKE: Let's go upstairs. Follow me. (Pause.) Do you want to try one wheel?

JOHNSON: I certainly do, sir.

ZEMKE: Let me take a good look at you. (Pause.) You don't have any flaps and you're gonna need plenty of field.

JOHNSON: Whatever you say, sir.

ZEMKE: Better bail out. How much gas have you got?

JOHNSON: Thirty gallons. He never hit my tank. That fellow didn't do a very good job gunning on me.

ZEMKE: I'm afraid of a landing.

JOHNSON: You aren't half as scared as I am, sir.

(At this point Zemke cut out transmission to Johnson and spoke directly to the tower.)

ZEMKE: His plane's in bad shape. I'm going to have him bail out northeast of here. (And then to Johnson): Did you come back alone?

JOHNSON: No, sir. One of the boys came back with me.

ZEMKE: Be sure to hold your legs together when you go over and count ten. Try shaking it once more.

JOHNSON: Yes, sir.

ZEMKE: You don't have to sir me up here. Head her out to sea.

JOHNSON: Yes, sir.

ZEMKE: Open up the canopy.

JOHNSON: It is open, sir. It's been open a long time.

ZEMKE: Okay. The crate's headed out to sea. Go.

Johnson turned his P-47 over, dumped himself out, and parachuted safely to the ground. The plane landed in the water.

Hub Zemke got most of the awards available to fighter pilots but because it was such a lonely war they fought, their bravery was not in relation to each other. Mustang ace Col. James Howard was the only fighter pilot to win the Medal of Honor.

For what they were doing, the B-24 Liberators were losing more planes than the B-17 Flying Fortress groups. The B-24 handled like a car with mushy steering and, because of that, it was more difficult to fly a group of them in a tight formation.

I spent less time with the B-24s of the Third Wing than with the B-17s of the First Wing, but I did have a favorite group among them. Brig. Gen. Leon W. Johnson commanded the first operational B-24 group, the Forty-fourth, and I often went there. The Forty-fourth was having a terrible time.

During the spring of 1943, the Forty-fourth lost twenty of its original force of twenty-seven Liberators and another seven were so badly damaged that they couldn't fly. Of the ninety crewmen who arrived in England in the fall of 1943, with the Sixty-seventh Bomb Squadron, for example, fewer than ten were still there by the end of May. The twenty aircraft and the men lost were replaced, but everyone knew the record. Bomber bases were depressing places much of the time in spite of what was often a warm and gay air created by bright people trying to laugh off their troubles. Frequently a crew member would have dinner after a raid and then go back to his bunk and sit there, staring at nothing. Many of the bomber crews were always on the ragged edge of breaking down mentally. It was a combination of the fear of death and the relentlessness of the loss of friends.

Typical notations from Air Force records of late 1943 read:

"243 HB [heavy bombers] hit rubber factory, synthetic oil plant Gelsenkirchen. 25 HB lost."

"315 HB hit Regensburg Messerschmitt plant. Good results. 60 HB lost."

"320 HB strike ball bearing production Schweinfurt. Strong fighter opposition. 60 HB lost." HB referred to heavy bombers.

The fliers in the officers club at a bomber base and the enlisted men in the mess hall usually sat in the same places every night at dinner. I often had dinner in both places and at the meal after a raid or at breakfast the following morning it could be a bad experience.

There were gaps at the table where familiar faces had been, and it was hardly conducive to happy dinner-table conversation. Within a few days the empty seats were filled with replacement fliers fresh from training stations in the United States but it took a while to get used to the idea that friends were gone forever whether they were dead or captured. More often than not, no one was certain. If someone had seen the plane go down in a smoking spiral from which no parachutes emerged, they knew. In many cases, the centrifugal force of a spin made it impossible for crew members to get themselves out of a plummeting plane.

No matter how many losses a group had, the crews always thought their group, their squadron, their pilot was the best in the Air Force.

That was true at the Forty-fourth Bombardment Group and part of it came from the fact that Brig. Gen. Leon W. Johnson was such a good commander, good pilot, and all-around regular guy. The uniform I wore didn't make my rank as sergeant apparent. I wore no stripes and that called attention to the black-and-gold oval correspondent's patch on my shoulder. As a sergeant, I was partial to high-ranking officers who treated me as a newspaperman and not as an enlisted man. Johnson was great in that respect, and he flattered me by engaging in long conversations in his office about Franklin Roosevelt as a President, about whether West Point was a good educational institution, and about the quality of the doughnuts the Red Cross truck on his field served.

I don't know where he got it but General Johnson had this big, seven-passenger 1936 Packard touring car that he tooled around in, and it was a beauty. He drove it himself, he didn't have a driver. He often went down to London in it and he'd amaze the enlisted men hitchhiking along the road by stopping to pick them up until he had a full load.

I WAS AT the Forty-fourth in late July when they took off for North Africa in preparation for the momentous raid on Ploesti starting from there.

Because the emotional stress on fliers was so great, the Air Force was always trying to find ways to make their situation less fearsome— and of course, the Air Force almost always failed at it.

Before the Ploesti mission, Tex McCrary, one of the great public-relations experts and con artists of all time, was given the job of quelling the fears of the crews that were to make the fearsome trip to Ploesti. We were all in awe of Tex because he was married to one of the world's most fascinating beauties, Jinx Falkenberg.

Before the raid, I watched the film he'd made to show the crews. It was called *Soapsuds,* the original code name for the mission that later became Tidal Wave. The film began with a picture of a nude woman. In a soothing voice, McCrary tried to make the picture a plausible opening shot by announcing that Ploesti was "a virgin target," one that had never been bombed before.

"The defenses are nothing like as strong here as they are on the Western Front," he told the fliers. "The fighter defenses at Ploesti are not strong and anyway, the majority of fighter planes will be flown by Romanian pilots who are thoroughly bored by the war. The heavy antiaircraft should not bother you at low altitude. All the antiaircraft guns are manned by Romanians so there's a pretty good chance there may be incidents like there were in Italy at the beginning of the war when civilians could not get into the shelters because they were filled with antiaircraft gunners. The defenses at Ploesti," he concluded, "may look formidable on paper but remember, they are manned by Romanians."

No one headed for Ploesti on a B-24 the next day slept any better because of having seen that film.

The raid took place on August 1, 1943, on the biggest oil refinery and storage plant in Europe. Ploesti produced 2 million metric tons of oil a year. I have no idea how much 2 million metric tons is but I have those figures in the notes I took at the time and it must have been a lot because Churchill referred to Ploesti as "the taproot of German power." Less literary leaders called it "the single most important target of the war."

Ploesti was different from any target the bombers had previously attacked. For one thing, it was in distant Romania (which we were spelling "Roumania" at the time). It may have been the single most heavily defended place on earth. The Germans had thousands of anti-aircraft guns surrounding the oil fields, and four wings of Messerschmitt 109s were based on the airfield at Mizil, twenty miles from Ploesti.

Maj. Gen. Uzal Ent asked the Eighth Air Force commander, Gen. Ira Eaker, that they be allowed to go into Ploesti at high altitude but Eaker refused. Ent felt that with so many antiaircraft guns and that much fighter power, it would have been suicide for the bombers to make a long run at normal altitude where they'd have been target practice for the unopposed Luftwaffe and ground gunners. The Germans even had antiaircraft guns mounted on railway cars that ran through the refinery at almost the same speed as the bombers overhead so they could keep firing away at them.

The decision was made for the Liberators to go in "on the ground," no more than 100 feet in the air, fifty if possible. Keep in mind, some of the smokestacks were 200 feet tall, so the planes had to weave through those or go up to 300 feet where they were more vulnerable. It wasn't suicide but it was close.

The first wave of bombers dropped their loads on the oil tanks, sending flames and thick black smoke billowing into the path of the bombers that followed.

As Capt. Harold James flew away from the flaming refinery, his radioman reported that he could see only one other Liberator going out with them.

"His bomb bay doors are open," he said, "and his number three engine is stopped." Zimmerman, the radioman, recognized the B-24 as Capt. Bob Mooney's. They'd often flown wing on wing. There was a flashing light. It was the ship's emergency Aldis lamp, sending its signal. "Pilot dead" was the message. "Wounded aboard. Trying for Turkey."

Zimmerman blinked back: "We're short on gas. Will join you for Turkey."

Bob Mooney's head had been shot off by a 20mm shell. The co-pilot, Henry Gerrits, was trying to wrestle Mooney's body out of the pilot's seat, and five of the gunners were lying around the interior of the plane, bleeding.

There were dozens of aircraft in the same condition and some of them in conditions so much worse that their stories will never be told because every man onboard died.

By the time all the B-24s had passed over the target at low level, not many had four working engines left and more than half had serious structural damage. There were dead or dying onboard most of the aircraft. The problem of helping the wounded was always complicated by the lack of oxygen when the bombers resumed normal altitude.

Of the 177 B-24s that started for the target, 160 got over Ploesti. Seventy-three were shot down and fifty-five others were badly damaged. Five hundred and thirty-two crew members were killed or wounded that day and another 100 were taken prisoner.

Well after they'd left the target and headed home, they were still in danger. A squadron of ME-109s attacked what was left of a formation over the Ionian Sea and took down four more B-24s.

I don't know why they chose the B-24s for the Ploesti raid. I hate to think so but Bomber Command probably thought they were the most expendable. More B-24s were built than any other warplane the United States had. In 1942 alone, the War Department ordered 10,000 Liberators. The B-17 was being phased out in favor of the B-29 even before it saw combat but it ended up being the B-17 that did the heavy-duty bombing in Europe anyway. It was my opinion at the time that if 160 B-17s had gone into Ploesti, seventy-three of them would not have been lost. They weren't asking for my advice.

When General Johnson returned to his base in England after the Ploesti raid, I interviewed him and he made a charming, offhand remark in the quiet of his office that I've thought of ten thousand times over the years:

"I just had the feeling," he said softly, "that I'd make it back safely." He paused. "You know how that is sometimes?" He paused again, fiddled with a pencil in his hand and then looked back at me. "Of course," he said, "I suppose a lot of people had that same feeling who *didn't* make it."

That's been on my list of True Things About Life ever since.

Several months later Leon W. Johnson became one of three men awarded the Medal of Honor for their bravery in the air over Ploesti. No infantryman ever deserved it more than this good and brave Air Force general.

THE BRITISH ISLES were overrun with American soldiers by the end of 1943. It doesn't much matter whether an occupying army is friend or enemy, it's still uncomfortable for the country being occupied. For all that and all the problems, the British and the Americans got along well. Letters that soldiers wrote home were filled with stories of warm beer, driving on the "wrong" side of the road, and new words like "lorry" for truck and "bonnet" for hood.

The language was close enough to be easy and different enough to be fun. GIs were amused that, in a British hotel, "knocked up" meant to be awakened. There were a lot of barroom brawls, quite a few robberies, a few murders, and a handful of rapes, but hundreds of thousands of Americans behaved like guests and the British, though sometimes resentful of their affluence and brashness, liked the Americans. Elsie Armitage, the woman who rented the room to Dick Koenig and me on Bayswater Road for £5 a week, would often see us walk in the hall door, singly or together, and call out for us to come in and have a spot of tea and some cake she had made. She was puzzled and embarrassed that her fifteen-year-old nephew, who often visited her from Yorkshire, detested Americans. We would occasionally meet him in the hall and his wordless attitude was obvious. I've often thought it would be fun to go over and find him and see how he feels now, in his sixties.

The British are more persistently British than the people of most countries are what *they* are, but the British and the Americans were amused by their differences. And then, at the bottom of it all, the British knew we were there to give them help they desperately needed.

In late May of 1944—I do not know the exact date—I was taken off my Eighth Air Force beat and sent to Bristol, a port city on the side of England away from the English Channel to await taking part in the invasion of France. I didn't know what my part would be. Phil Bucknell had been practicing with the Eighty-second Airborne and G. K. Hodenfield was set to go in on the first wave with the Rangers of the First Infantry Division. I don't think Hod knew when he accepted the assignment that he was going to be climbing Pointe-du-Hoc in the face of enemy fire. My friend Charley Kiley and I were billeted—it's surprising the words you find yourself using in the Army—in the modest home of a childless young British couple. We didn't have to be told why we had been sent there but neither did we know the date of the impending event.

The man had been exempt from service in His Majesty's armed forces because he was building Rolls-Royce engines for British bombers and U.S. fighters. I asked a little about where he was on the production line and he didn't seem to understand.

"Me and my two buddies are buildin' an engine," he said. He hadn't understood my question because there *was* no production line. It may have accounted for why the Rolls-Royce engines were so good.

The couple tried to be hospitable to us but generally failed hospitality. I don't know what the monetary arrangement for housing us was between them and the Army nor do I know who made the arrangement for us to stay there. On the second morning the woman, knowing we liked coffee for breakfast and not tea, had managed to get some coffee. She had heard that most Americans liked it for breakfast and she had brewed it, not with water but with milk.

We were there about five days and it's frustrating not to be able to recall any of the details of so important a week in my life but I cannot. I'm pleased that Charley Kiley can't either. I don't remember when, in relation to our presence there, we first learned that the Invasion had taken place. There had been such an obsession with secrecy—and for good reason—about the Invasion that the communication barriers came down slowly.

By that time you didn't have to be a German spy to know there was going to be an invasion. SHAEF, that most important acronym of the war, meaning Supreme Headquarters Allied Expeditionary Force, had sent a memo to newspeople asking them to be careful with information. It was an extraordinarily friendly and plaintive memo. Nothing threatening. It assumed we knew a lot and Eisenhower was simply reminding us to be careful. It also assumed, which is what made it friendly, that we were all on the same side. The relationship was not an adversarial one as it so often is now between reporters and the Pentagon.

Even so, there *were* German spies in England and British Intelligence did a good job of finding them and then of using them to our advantage. The British are best at the spy game—and it *is* a game—even though they have also had more spy disasters than successes over the years. Almost nothing any spy has ever done has given his country much really useful information. The most damaging information most spies get is the names of other spies.

British Intelligence operated from a charming thatched-roof country home called Bletchley Park that couldn't have been improved on for mysterious atmosphere by a spy novelist. It was at Bletchley Park where the German code was broken, enabling the British to decipher and read many German communiqués during the war. It was good intelligence work but it was not accomplished by a spy.

Ultra was the top-secret name given material decoded by an enciphering device called Enigma.

Enigma was invented by the Germans after World War I and used commercially for a time before World War II. A couple of Polish cryptologists copied the German computer and gave two of their copies to the British and two to the French. It's easy to forget that, before the Germans got at them, the Poles were world leaders in science and culture. This casual gift may have changed the course of events for the next four years because getting hold of the machine was the most important intelligence coup of the war.

Enigma took an ordinary sentence and translated it into what looked like gobbledegook. If the operator pressed the "B" key, it might type "G," but the second time the "B" key was struck it would type "R." Unless you knew the pattern, it was impossible to read, and the formula was too complex for any expert to decipher. Enigma not only enciphered messages but it helped in the deciphering process, too.

After the war I talked to a British colonel who had worked in Bletchley Park. He said that the way they cracked the German code, using Enigma as an aid, wasn't really very strange or unusual. The Germans made the mistake, in their communiqués, of repeating phrases like "Nothing to report today" in code. It was simple sentences that recurred frequently in predictable places in a message that led to the breaking of the German code.

British sophistication in the art of deceit reached its high point in the way they manipulated the spies they knew were in their midst. Axis Sally used to do regular radio reports in English in an effort to undermine the morale of American soldiers who listened to her. Someone high up in the U.S. command had the good sense not to forbid GIs from listening to her.

Sometimes Axis Sally did seem to have tidbits of information that suggested she—and the German high command, of course—had an inside track to all our secrets. Her broadcasts were intended to make American soldiers think the Germans were watching and knew every move they were about to make. Axis Sally did have some amazing information but what she had was the result of a British Intelligence trick of the trickiest kind. The British knew who the spies were and allowed them to operate and get limited kinds of information but under close surveillance. Every piece of information they got and passed on to their superiors in Germany was either too old to be of any help or worthless even if it was accurate and not out of date.

On one occasion, Axis Sally broadcast an item directed at one of our bomb groups. She suggested that the boys get town officials to fix the clock in the church steeple because it was three minutes fast. Americans at the bomber base were amazed because she was right, and they were puzzled about what spy in their midst could have given her such specific information. What they didn't understand was that the harmless information about the clock was provided to the spy in London by an informer working for British Intelligence.

It gave the German spy confidence in the informer, setting up the spy to be provided with false information about the invasion later on.

It was a miserably foggy night when Jimmy Stewart arrived in England, and his group landed at the first airfield they could find open. It turned out to be six miles from Tibenham, where they were supposed to be stationed.

Later that evening Stewart and his crew were sitting around a Nissen hut listening to the radio and the notorious if somewhat heavy-handed German propagandist, Lord Haw Haw, came on the air. He had an exaggerated British accent that amused Americans.

"Good evening," Lord Haw Haw began. "Allow me to be the first to welcome the Four Hundred and Forty-fifth Bomb Group to England."

I wasn't there but it seems safe to say that Jimmy Stewart's jaw dropped.

Arthur Hadley says in his book *The Straw Giant,* "The possession of secrets enhances the power of those who know them. Intelligence information is often unnecessarily restricted for reasons of bureaucratic prestige rather than national security."

What was called the Green Door Problem was typical of the convoluted workings of spy organizations. The Green Door Problem referred to information the British or Americans had that they didn't release to units whose safety would have been improved by possessing that information. The theory was that the unit's action would make it apparent to the enemy that the unit had information it could only have obtained from a spy or from a secret message it intercepted and was able to decode. That would have told the Germans that the Allies had cracked their code. It was a uniquely wartime dilemma, and some British and American men went to their certain deaths—deaths that could have been avoided if they'd been given the information their Intelligence people had—because their high command decided they had to be sacrificed to protect the biggest secret of all: we knew how to decipher the Germans' coded messages.

Time and time again we had information obtained by deciphering the German code that we did not use because that would have alerted the enemy and they'd have stopped using the code. It was later revealed that the British had been using the Enigma machine before the 1940 raid on Coventry and could have warned that city but did not because of the fear it would tip off the Germans to the fact that the British were reading their messages. This was big-time deceit and an indication of the complexity of war.

My old outfit, the Seventeenth Field Artillery Regiment, ran into trouble in North Africa as a result of information gleaned from the Germans by a spy we had in their midst. The problem appeared when Field Marshal Erwin Rommel, one of the few military geniuses of the war, decided not to follow a preconceived plan that had been laid out for him by the German high command. There was no evidence in the decoded messages that his forces would stop running, turn around, and counterattack in the narrow Kasserine Pass through which they had recently fled. The reason there was no such information in the coded messages was simple: Rommel ignored the orders in those messages that the British had read.

While I never understood the exact nature of what happened, my 17th F.A. friend Phil Tranchina told me after the war that 400 of the 500 men in the First Battalion of the Seventeenth were taken prisoner in Kasserine Pass. My battalion.

As an artillery outfit, the Seventeenth wasn't equipped or trained to fight like an infantry regiment, and the Germans simply walked over them, taking all their equipment, 155mm howitzers and trucks, and capturing most of the men. The Seventeenth offered so little resistance in the ground fighting that not many of them were killed.

If I hadn't been transferred to *The Stars and Stripes,* there's a good possibility I would have spent all of 1943, 1944, and six months of 1945 in a German prison camp in North Africa.

So much for the sneaky stuff. There's certainly a case to be made for collecting and interpreting information about other countries but not much of a case to be made for coming by the information surreptitiously. It seems to me that today's CIA should be left with 25 percent of its secret budget for legitimate purposes but with none of it for its spies. They should all retire and write books about their escapades. "Escapades" is a false and superficial word that fits a spy's work. The novelists of the future should have to go it alone and we should all be aware that the course of events in the world has been little changed by anything spies ever came up with. They make good movies and good novels but they aren't good for much else. The legendary Mata Hari of literature was a fabulously brave and beautiful woman. In the books she is sentenced to death as a spy and, standing in front of a French firing squad, bares her breasts in the hope that the French soldiers will be distracted. In actual fact, Mata Hari was a pretty unattractive prostitute who never got any useful information out of anyone.

Intelligence agencies of every country work the same way. They convince citizens that they're about to be attacked by another country and, because of the threat, there's a need for all sorts of spy and intelligence activity. When the threat doesn't materialize, the intelligence agency doesn't admit it was wrong—it takes credit. It says the enemy didn't attack because we built up our defenses. The enemy knew we were prepared so, the argument goes, they changed their minds.

There's no evidence spying did us much good in World War II, and the faulty intelligence provided us by the CIA about the Soviet Union in the postwar years cost us billions of dollars.

After the war one of the top German spies was asked how he managed to get hold of the formula for one of the deadly gases we had developed. He said he found out the name of the company that made it and wrote a letter to the president asking for the formula. They sent it to him.

Spies are, generally speaking, maladjusted, double-dealing misfits who can't make a living at anything else. The spies of our country and the spies of their country are the same people. They're interchangeable. When you hear of defectors, it's almost always spies who defect, not other government officials. Spies defect because they're frequently congenitally dishonest and get their kicks out of deception.

Intelligence agencies are impervious to the kind of inspection or criticism that other agencies of a democratic government are subjected to. When the CIA is questioned about anything, they have a standard answer:

"Sorry. Torture us, but we're patriotic Americans. That's a secret that would compromise the security of the United States."

Spy agencies spend half their time trying to catch other spies. British Intelligence is divided into two sections. One half does the spying and the other half tries to catch spies in their midst. There is nothing of value to a nation in catching a spy. The course of very few historical events has been altered by their work.

The World War II stories about Ultra and Enigma are fascinating to read, and the decoding machine had some effect on shortening the war, but Enigma was a machine, not a spy.

IV

THE LAND WAR

T HERE HAVE BEEN only a handful of days since the beginning of time on which the direction the world was taking has been changed for the better in one twenty-four-hour period by an act of man. June 6, 1944, was one of them.

What the Americans, the British, and the Canadians were trying to do was get back a whole continent that had been taken from its rightful owners and whose citizens had been taken captive by Adolf Hitler's German army. It was one of the most monumentally unselfish things one group of people ever did for another.

In answer to the standard questions, do I know where I was when John F. Kennedy was shot or do I know where I was when I heard that Franklin D. Roosevelt had died, the answers are yes. But, for some reason, I can't remember where I was or when I heard that the Allied Invasion of France had finally taken place.

It seems most likely that when the announcement of the Invasion was made, Charley Kiley and I were already onboard the small ship that was to take us around the end of England, past Cornwall, which Mother's father had left when he was sixteen, and across the Channel to France. I looked forward to getting to France because I hoped to determine, once and for all, whether Mr. Sharp was right when he failed me for two successive years in the French course he taught at The Academy.

The whole world knew that the Invasion was taking place about the time we were midway between Bristol and the French coast alongside the Cotentin Peninsula, but we didn't know. Not knowing was a familiar condition that soldiers found themselves in all the time during the process of fighting a war—theirs not to reason why, theirs but to do or die or, in my case, try to find out. They were always the last to know what they were doing and the last to know what they had done when it was over. There had been rumors of television before the war but it was not yet a fact. Radio was not part of our lives once we were shipped out of the United States and they weren't delivering newspapers to us onboard our invasion craft. We were part of a vast armada moving toward the action along those narrow strips of beach that the first waves had already landed on.

There were ships and smaller vessels everywhere. The operation was more than I could think about and I didn't do much on the trip across except hope I wouldn't be seasick. Some of the guys played cards or wrote letters but I didn't feel like doing anything but stare at the Channel waters. Someone had organized this great seaborne movement of men—built the ships that managed to float and not tip over after being crammed with men and materiel. They had arranged to clothe everyone, to put weapons in their hands, to supply them with food, to put toilet paper in their backpacks, and I was staring out at the rough waters of the Channel and idly considering that Gertrude Ederle had once swum across it. Far from thoughts of the magnitude of the adventure was I. It's hard to see the big picture and especially hard if you're in the picture.

We all have days of our lives that stand out from the blur of days that have gone by, and the day I came ashore on Utah Beach is one of mine.

As we approached the French coast, there were small clouds of smoke and sudden eruptions behind the small, weed-covered hills bordering Utah Beach. German artillery was lobbing shells, blindly now, hoping to hit U.S. troops or some of the massive amount of equipment piled up on the shore.

The French call D-Day "J-Jour" and I don't have a lot of complaints with the French but it was our day and I think they ought to call it by our name, D-Day.

If you're young, and not really clear what D-Day was, let me tell you, it was a day unlike any other.

I landed on Utah Beach several days after the first assault waves went in on the morning of June 6. I am uncertain of the day. When I came in, row on row of dead American soldiers were laid out on the sand just above the high-tide mark where the beach turned into weedy clumps of grass. They were covered with olive-drab blankets, just their feet sticking out at the bottom, their GI boots sticking out. I remember their boots—all the same on such different boys.

They had been dead several days and some of them had been killed, not on the beaches, but inland.

No one can tell the whole story of D-Day because no one knows it. Each of the 60,000 men who waded ashore that day knew a little part of the story too well.

To them, the landing looked like a catastrophe. Each knew a friend shot through the throat, shot through the knee. Each knew the names of five hanging dead on the barbed wire in the water twenty yards off-shore, three who lay unattended on the stony beach as the blood drained from holes in their bodies.

They saw whole tank crews drowned when the tanks rumbled off the ramps of their landing craft and dropped into twenty feet of water.

There were heroes here no one will ever know because they're dead. The heroism of others is known only to themselves.

Across the Channel in Allied headquarters in England, the war directors, remote from the details of tragedy, were exultant. They saw no blood, no dead, no dying. From the statisticians' point of view, the invasion was a great success. The statisticians were right. They always are—that's the damned thing about it.

It's not possible for anyone who's been in a war to describe the terror of it to anyone who hasn't. I wrote a poem the day I came ashore, writing in my jeep with a pad on my knee. I thought it was a poem.

> *"Here" the battleground guide will say when the tourists come,*
> *"They fought the bloody battle for the beach."*
> *They'll talk on with pointers in their hands*
> *To a bus-load of people*
> *About events that never happened*
> *In a place they never were.*

How would anyone know that John Lacey died
In that clump of weeds by the wagon path
As he looked to the left toward Simpson . . .
And caught a bullet behind the ear?
And if there had been a picture of it
It wouldn't show the snapshot in his breast pocket
Of his girlfriend with his mom and dad
At Christmas.

I sound young and I didn't have any experience punctuating poetry but on five subsequent visits to the beaches over the years, I've been pleased to find how accurate I was with the observations about the battleground guides. The buses dump crowds on the bluffs above the beaches and twenty-five-year-old French guides, speaking a variety of languages, tell the tourists what happened down there on the sand.

On each visit, I've wept. It's almost impossible to keep back the tears as you look across the rows of crosses and think of the boys under them who died that day.

Even if you didn't know anyone who died, the heart knows something the brain does not—and you weep. If you think the world is selfish and rotten go to the cemetery at Colleville overlooking Omaha Beach. See what one group of men did for another on D-Day, June 6, 1944.

MY TEARS DRIED up on the fiftieth anniversary visit to Omaha when I got thinking of how presumptuous it was of some Army authority to have put nothing but crosses or Stars of David over the graves, as though there was no room in the cemetery for anyone who held beliefs other than those represented by two religious symbols.

Normandy after our landing was a crash course in land warfare for me. It didn't have any relationship to what we'd been taught on maneuvers with the Seventeenth Field Artillery in North Carolina. One of the things I was learning was that the reason everyone in a war doesn't get killed is that most bullets, most artillery shells, and most bombs don't hit anything. The world would be out of trouble if it had all the money to spend on poverty that it has spent during its history on ammunition that failed to serve its purpose—to kill. How slow does a bullet go before it falls? It's strange that, for all the millions of rounds of ammunition that came toward U.S. forces from the Germans, I never saw a bullet fall, spent. Uncle Bill used to take me to the Saratoga battlefield where the British general Burgoyne had enlisted Indian troops to help fight American soldiers, and in the 1930s, 150 years after the battle, we used to find arrowheads. I should think French farmers would be tilling metal bullet fragments from their soil for a thousand years.

I landed in France near the inner elbow of the Cotentin Peninsula at the end of which, twenty-five miles out, is the port of Cherbourg. It had not been as rough for the men who came in at Utah as it had been at Juno, Gold, Sword, or Omaha. Omaha was closest to Utah and the worst. The two beaches were separated by several miles and the promontory known as Pointe-du-Hoc.

The war was still close to the beaches when I came ashore and I waited to be raked with machine-gun fire but there were no German soldiers within two miles of where I was. There were none because the areas immediately behind Utah had been cleared out by paratroopers. The Eighty-second and 101st Airborne Divisions had cut off the only main road leading from the mainland out the thick, thumblike Cotentin Peninsula to Cherbourg. Their mission was to interrupt German supply columns feeding their tank and infantry divisions that were isolated from the main body of their troops but were still ferociously defending the port. The Fourth Infantry Division had sliced clear across to the other side of the peninsula before turning and heading out toward Cherbourg, away from the main lines of the war behind the beaches. When I came in, the Fourth, Ninth, and Seventy-ninth Divisions, a formidable force of about 50,000 men, were stretched across the peninsula from one side to the other and moving on Cherbourg in a solid phalanx.

The German lines were intact on the mainland behind Omaha Beach, twenty miles away, around the elbow formed by the peninsula. The Germans, under do-or-die orders from Hitler, were desperately trying to push the British, Canadians, and Americans back into the Channel where bodies still floated facedown in the water lapping the shore. Bodies always floated facedown.

The major German forces defending the Cotentin Peninsula had all run toward Cherbourg to form a defensive line in front of it, so the area behind our beaches, leading out to the peninsula itself, was relatively safe. The enemy meant to save the port for themselves or destroy it so we couldn't use it.

In Bristol, I had spent some of the time waterproofing my jeep with the help of mechanics who supervised those of us who didn't know how. I covered all the electrical connectors, the generator, and the ignition with a thick, greasy coating to enable the jeep to wade, in two or three feet of water, without stalling. When Army rifles were shipped in boxes, they were coated with something called Cosmoline to prevent rust. One of the things first sergeants liked to do best was supervise the removal of Cosmoline from a private's rifle. The stuff I put on my jeep was not Cosmoline, but Not Cosmoline is as close as I can come to a name for it.

The exhaust pipe had been disconnected, and in its place I attached an L-shaped pipe to the manifold that came up alongside the driver's seat and stuck a foot above the top of the jeep's windshield. The theory was that the jeep would actually have to run a short distance from the ramp of the landing craft, through several feet of water offshore, and to dry sand on the beach without having its engine sputter to a stop.

When I came ashore, I was wearing an Army olive-green wool uniform that had been impregnated with some kind of greasy wax intended to protect the skin in case of a mustard-gas attack by the Germans. Just the threat of gas had cost Allied forces thousands of hours of time and millions of dollars. The uniforms were very uncomfortable and the jeeps didn't like what had been done to them any better than we liked our uniforms. Our orders were to get the coating off the jeep engine as soon after landing as possible.

I got the waterproofing off my jeep and headed out to the peninsula toward Cherbourg, trying to make heads or tails of a battle I didn't understand. The geography of Normandy on a map is easy for me to understand now, but I didn't comprehend it at the time. By the time you're familiar enough with territory to understand a map, you no longer need it.

THERE WERE TWO large towns on the peninsula before Cherbourg, Montebourg and Valognes. It would be more accurate to say, they *had been* towns. I've seen hundreds since, but then I had never seen a town that had been leveled. Our bombers must have destroyed the towns in an effort to cut the German supply lines to Cherbourg and it was the first time it had occurred to me that the French people of Normandy must have felt some ambivalence about the Invasion. It was true they were being freed but at the cost of the total destruction of everything they had. And there's no question that many of the people of Normandy were sullen in their attitude toward the Americans.

There have been half a dozen times in my life that I'd like to live over so that I could improve on my performance and the next few weeks are foremost in my memory among those times. My output as a reporter was small and the stories I wrote for the paper were petty. I was not experienced enough to understand that everything I saw was a story. I was witness to one of the most monumental operations ever staged by man, and I was writing pieces about a Fourth Division infantryman from Texas who adopted a lost and bewildered Morgan stallion and rode the horse for several days as the division moved on Cherbourg. It was a good feature piece but it seemed to me I should have been providing readers who weren't there details of how our effort to capture the port was going. The problem was, I didn't know how it was going. I was too close to the battle to see the war. That was the first of a lot of times that was true in the following months.

Within a few days after the invasion, a *Stars and Stripes* headquarters had been established at a small printing plant in Carentan, not far from Omaha Beach. The infantry was still unable to break out of that narrow strip of coast where it was being contained by German forces behind a low range of hills running parallel to the beach. The landing infantry had forced its way ashore in the face of terrible fire from the bluffs above the beaches but had been able to push inland and break through the main line of German resistance containing them.

Night and day German artillery poured shells into the thin strip of land we held. Ships offshore were dumping supplies on the beaches and it got so the area we'd taken was so constricted that there was no place to pile them. Carentan and *The Stars and Stripes* printing plant were part of that narrow strip. The paper was printed there for just two days before being forced to move back up the Cotentin Peninsula and eventually to Sainte-Mère-Église.

At some point, date unknown to me, I left the Cherbourg area and drove back down the peninsula to *The Stars and Stripes* headquarters that had been established in Sainte-Mère-Église. The staff had taken over two attached stone houses to live in on the main street. Most war buffs know the town because it was from the church steeple there that the American paratrooper, John Steele, hung all night from the cords of his parachute, wounded but not daring to make a sound. There were German soldiers in the streets below when he first drifted down and they would have riddled his body with bullets.

One paratrooper who made it told me about his commander.

"Colonel Wolverton got hung up in a tree," he said. "He was killed in his parachute."

"The Germans shot him as he hung there?" I asked.

"Everyone come along shot him," he said.

Every trooper had a story if he was lucky enough to have lived through the night. Months later when the men from one battalion of the Eighty-second Airborne reassembled in England, there were only 114 of the original 800 left.

Several *Stars and Stripes* editors were living in an old stone house on the main street in Sainte-Mère-Église. Two Frenchwomen lived in adjoining houses and someone on the newspaper struck a great deal with them. It was my first exposure to the genius of French cooking.

The basic Army field ration was called ten-in-one. It came in a heavy, waxed cardboard carton weighing about forty-five pounds. I think ten-in-one meant it served ten men for one day. *Stars and Stripes* people roamed freely, and all it took was a stop at a quartermaster depot to pick up as many ten-in-ones as a jeep would carry. There were no tight controls so soon after the Invasion. The newspaper staff people in Sainte-Mère (we dropped the *Église* soon after we got there) simply gave the ten-in-one boxes to the two women and they worked their French magic on them.

Sainte-Mère was surrounded by the lush Norman countryside and, while many of the farmers had fled, and the bloated carcasses of dead cows were everywhere, there were still chickens laying eggs and cows giving milk. The ten-in-one contained, among other things, a two–pound tin of bacon.

The following morning I headed back out the Cotentin Peninsula toward Cherbourg and again drove through Montebourg and Valognes. On the fiftieth anniversary of D-Day, I arrived in Cherbourg on the *Queen Mary* and drove down the peninsula, through those restored towns, to where I'd come ashore on Utah Beach. It's hard to describe how I felt. I kept looking at the people living there in 1994, young people mostly, and I wanted to stop every one of them and tell them what their town looked like in June of 1944. I suppose it interested me more than it would have interested them. They'd read about it and seen pictures and anyway, they had cows to milk or chores to do.

It was my real first look at war on the ground. The closest I'd been previously was 25,000 feet above Germany in a B-17 or 12,000 in a B-26 and I realize, in retrospect, that I was more a tourist than a reporter.

The three infantry divisions were too late reaching Cherbourg. The port had been totally destroyed and rendered unusable as a landing place for Allied ships carrying men and equipment. I suppose it had taken thirty years to construct the port facilities because they were among the best in Europe, but the Germans had made them useless with demolition charges in three days. A masterful job of deconstruction.

Just outside Cherbourg, railroad tracks disappeared into a hillside and, although the railroad was no longer operative, I saw a small group of American soldiers crowding into the tunnel. I thought perhaps some German soldiers who'd been hiding in there had come out to surrender. As I came up to the mouth of the tunnel, I saw that the point of interest was not the enemy. The German officers had used the tunnel as what was, at that time, probably the world's greatest wine cellar. The cavernous interior was stacked with thousands of cases of the best wines they could appropriate in France. There was cognac, champagne, port, and sherry enough for, literally, an army. German officers apparently lived better than our own.

Soldiers and several reporters who got there ahead of me were going in and then reappearing at the mouth of the tunnel a few minutes later, carrying cases of wine of an excellence far beyond their beer-trained taste buds' ability to appreciate. It was my first exposure to the spoils of war and to the word "loot" used as a noun. They put the loot in jeeps and trucks and drove off. It gave me a new view of looting, too.

In school I'd read how Hannibal's troops looted and plundered as they moved across the Alps and then into Rome. It was something out of the ancient past but as I watched this anthill of activity at the mouth of the tunnel, as Americans helped themselves to this great stock of wine and liquor, I realized the standards of what's right and wrong change in a war. These soldiers and the newsmen helping themselves didn't have any sense that they were stealing. Stealing suggests taking property away from someone else. They weren't taking from anyone, and it didn't seem wrong to them. It wasn't wrong, I guess. They were taking something that wasn't theirs but it wasn't anyone else's, either.

These were second-generation spoils, of course. They'd already been spoils once when the Germans took them from the French. Now they were spoils again as American soldiers helped themselves. I remember the feeling I had that I should get in on this good thing going on and take several cases back to Sainte-Mère myself. Here was something valuable absolutely free. Mine for the taking.

I didn't take any wine that day. It wasn't so much that I had any inhibitions about taking it because it wasn't mine. At that time in my life, I didn't drink wine or liquor of any kind—a personal shortcoming that I was to correct after the war when I learned what a good, wholesome, American drink bourbon is.

Cherbourg was of vital importance to the success of the Allied drive toward Germany because without a port it was difficult to bring ashore the vast quantity of supplies that a million soldiers already ashore needed. They had to be fed, moved, and stocked with ammunition, a monumental supply job.

Without Cherbourg, supply ships were coming into Mulberry, the huge code-named docking area off the landing beaches. The Mulberries had been constructed in England and then towed across the Channel and sunk to form a pier for landings. This man-made harbor was built in a top-secret operation by 19,000 British construction workers, and when they got it over to the coast of France it looked like a six-story building lying on its side. It was one of the most inventive things the Allies did in planning the Invasion. One of the good things about war is, people come up with a lot of good ideas. The bad thing about those good ideas is, half of them are ideas about how to kill people.

Two Mulberries, one off the British beach, Gold, and one off the American, Omaha, had been put in place shortly after the Invasion. The one off Omaha was destroyed a few days later by the worst storm to hit the area in fifty years and it could never be used. You can still see parts of it sticking up out of the water at low tide now, fifty years later. The one off Gold, the British beach, stood up and was an important factor in the success the Allies had in shoveling millions of tons of supplies into France.

Those Mulberries are not the only evidence left of the landings on the coast of Normandy. The French have been casual about removing or paying much attention at all to the vestiges of D-Day that are everywhere. Schoolchildren play tag amid the ruins of a massive German fortress on top of Pointe-du-Hoc. They haven't preserved it but they haven't removed it. It's just there and it's going to be there for the 100th anniversary of the landings, too.

A few French people have summer cottages just behind the beaches, and many of them live with six-foot-thick German bunkers in their front yard. They'll be there in the year 3000—if there is one.

I was wide-eyed in those first days ashore as I gaped at the land war. Everything was so different. The only similarity to a bomber base was the imminence of death. There were so many things to feel bad about that it was hard to feel as bad about all of them as you knew you should. We seem to have some built-in governor that limits our capacity for sadness.

Many French farmers, who had looked forward with great hope to the invasion, had been killed by U.S. bombs. Families had lost fathers, mothers, brothers, sisters. Every family had lost someone. Surviving farmers in Normandy often had to flee their homes and fields as they were surrounded or overrun by both German and American soldiers spraying machine-gun bullets everywhere. They returned to their homes days or weeks later to find them ruined and ransacked. Their cows were dead in the fields and, as the sun beat down on the animal carcasses, they had begun to rot. Their bellies swelled with gases trapped inside and turned them on their backs. With bodies bloated, their four feet stuck straight up, pointing to the sky in a grotesque death pose. The cows that had survived often wandered the fields in pain, their udders unmilked, distended to the bursting point.

Think of taking a drive on a maze of narrow country roads where every farmhouse is an armed fortress, every church steeple a sniper's observation post, where every stone wall conceals infantry with rifles and machine guns and where, at every curve in a road, there may be a tank with an 88mm gun trained on the curve you're coming around. That's the way it was in Normandy in June and July of 1944.

THERE WERE GOOD stories in Cherbourg and I stayed there for several days, talking with American soldiers during the day and sleeping at night in a three-story French house whose flat stone facade was separated from the cobblestone street by nothing but four feet of flagstone sidewalk.

Joe Liebling was staying in the same house, and if you don't know who Joe Liebling was I can only say you don't know much about reporting, because he is one of the patron saints of the art and one of the very best who ever lived. He and Homer Bigart would be at the top of any reporter's ten-best list. I didn't know that at the time. All I knew was that Joe had a big reputation as an eater and a writer and I was impressed that he wrote for so literary a publication as *The New Yorker* magazine.

I didn't learn as much as I should have from Joe. He had such a strange and flawed personality that it didn't occur to me at the time that he was as good as he was. We talked at night as if we were equals.

Or, at least, I talked that way. I remember arguing with him about how the quality of his magazine had deteriorated. This is something people have been saying about *The New Yorker* since the second week it was published and I don't know how I latched onto so fashionable a criticism about something I knew so little about. And, of course, I didn't read what Joe was writing about the war for *The New Yorker* at the time because the magazine was not available. All I knew about Joe was that he couldn't see very well and he was a gourmand who knew a great deal about food and boxing.

I have since read many of the articles Joe wrote when he was in Normandy, some of them while we shared a room, and I cringe with greatly delayed embarrassment at some of the things I said about writing and reporting in conversations with him.

One night in a long conversation during which Joe consumed almost a bottle of Calvados alone, he started philosophizing, and I was so young I still liked hearing people philosophize. Joe started speaking of his own mortality and even mine, although I was still twenty-four. He espoused the virtue of dying at the peak of one's obituary value. He was considering it, he said, because he felt he was close to his own peak.

After the war, Joe lived through several thousand huge lunches, and we ate about six of those together. I always felt he enjoyed the food more than my company and, while I was ambivalent about him as a friend, I never passed up the opportunity to be with him. Jap Gude, a classy agent—which may sound like a contradiction in terms—was Thurber's and E. B. White's agent. In about 1958 he invited me to have lunch with Thurber, White, and Joe Liebling.

It was a long lunch and, even though I was in awe of the company, I had a job that I had to get back to writing for Arthur Godfrey. It was inappropriate for me to leave first, so I stayed until Joe got up. I only respected Joe. I wasn't in awe of him as I was of the other two.

When we got out on the sidewalk outside Louis & Armand's Restaurant on East 52nd Street, Joe, referring to Thurber's vision, said, "The trouble with eating with Jim is, he never knows when you want to talk."

Joe's idea of a good lunch was to have everyone talk about something he'd written, and White and Thurber didn't do that.

Thurber ate scrambled eggs. Jap later told me he always did because they were easy to find on his plate. I asked Thurber—I think I had the temerity to call him "Jim"—why he wasn't writing much for *The New Yorker* anymore.

"The trouble is," he said, "if I write it they print it."

It was the most modest thing I ever heard a writer say.

It was nothing Joe Liebling would have said, but I was sad when Joe died in 1963 at age fifty-nine, so close to the peak of his obituary value.

THE STARS AND STRIPES was well established in Sainte-Mère early in July. The town was near the landing beaches and the bulk of our soldiers were still jammed up in the narrow corridor between the English Channel and the roads running parallel to the beaches. While our forces were pointed toward Saint-Lô, the British were aimed at Caen. ("Caen" has been a constant source of trouble to me because I can't pronounce it in a way that separates it from "Cannes." And neither, I might add, can anyone else who isn't French.)

There weren't many safe places for a reporter to go in that confined area and if you did go somewhere, it was hard to get back because all the traffic was coming at you from the other direction. It must have been one of the first days of July, after I came down from Cherbourg, that I picked my way up behind the depleted ranks of the Eighty-second. They were together as a unit now not far from where most of them had landed on D-Day. The men of the Eighty-second Airborne were unhappy because they felt they'd done the most dangerous job when they jumped in early D-Day morning and now they were being treated like any other infantry division. Morale was low because casualties were high. Companies that started with 200 men were down to fifty. I was writing about them but my stories did not accurately reflect their attitude at the time.

The Eighty-second was not just a good division, it was a great one. There were no foot-sloggers. Every man was an athlete and a trained fighter. They had jumped in behind German lines at the beginning, and their mission was to cut ammunition supply lines and distract the defense forces manning the guns along the beaches before the main Allied landings began around 6:30. From the German point of view, it must have been a terrible feeling to know that two elite divisions of enemy soldiers, the Eighty-second and 101st Airborne, had dropped in behind them and were moving in their direction in the dark. Every paratrooper had a dramatic story of survival against heavy odds.

Had the German soldiers known all the problems the paratroopers had on D-Day morning, they might not have been so worried. The troopers were widely separated, disorganized, and disoriented. Some had landed in fields flooded by the Germans.

Infantrymen who had crash-landed in gliders suffered heavy casualties. I wandered through the fields outside Sainte-Mère and looked at the carcasses of the gliders interspersed with the dead cows. A glider landing wasn't much different than a runway crash of a commercial airliner except that the gliders didn't even have the luxury of a runway.

The gliders that had been towed across the Channel behind Dakotas (DC-3s) were not much more than expendable piano crates with wings. They were built for just one flight and a violent end. The Germans had planted long poles in the ground ten feet apart in every empty field that might have been a landing ground. Many of the gliders were impaled on these poles when they came down, and if they weren't, they had their wings sheared off by others as they bumped and skidded to their violent stop. There were no flight attendants onboard to welcome passengers to France or to advise them to keep their seat belts firmly buckled until the glider came to a complete stop.

When I got there all this debris was right where it had dropped or crash-landed. There certainly was no evidence that the Invasion had been a success.

Each paratrooper had carried a reserve parachute, his rifle, a .45 pistol, a hunting knife, a machete, a heavy cartridge belt, two bandoliers crossed over his chest, about 700 rounds of machine-gun bullets, sixty-six rounds of pistol ammunition, a mine for blowing the tracks off a tank, four sticks of dynamite, a trenching shovel, a first-aid kit, a gas mask, a canteen of water, three days' supply of K rations, six grenades, a blanket, a raincoat, a change of socks and underwear, and two cartons of cigarettes. Even nonsmokers carried cigarettes for swapping with anyone they encountered. The total load weighed close to 100 pounds. This is a lot of dead weight to add to the soldier's own weight and then drop from a mere 700 feet. The DC-3s were supposed to slow down to make it easier on the paratroopers when they hit the wind but, under intense fire from the ground, pilots were not always inclined to slow down much. The force of the interruption of the free fall was so abrupt that many of the jumpers were seriously hurt before they hit French soil. Many of them lost hands or fingers that were caught and cut off by the strands of the parachute. Joints separated.

All around Sainte-Mère there were shells of stone French farmhouses that had been burned to the ground, and I was puzzled that either the Germans or the Americans would have had reason to set them on fire. The troopers straightened me out and I wrote about it at night after wandering among them all day. When the Germans realized paratroopers were dropping out of the sky on top of them, they set fire to the farmhouses to light the sky to give themselves a better shot at the American paratroopers hanging helplessly in the air. They made eerie targets drifting to the ground in the bright light of the fires of burning farmhouses, many of which had withstood centuries of weather and natural disasters.

By infantry standards, they were lightly armed. Some of them carried the carbine instead of the M-1 rifle, and they didn't have much of the rear-echelon support that other divisions, fighting by their side, had. They didn't have their own artillery. The original plan had been to pull these special forces out of action once they'd completed their mission behind enemy lines on D-Day, and it must have been a heartbreaking decision for Eisenhower to make when he ordered them to stay on the line. He'd asked them to do everything and now he had to ask them to do more. Too many of them had been killed or wounded and it wasn't fair, but if life seldom is, war never is.

The difference between my life and theirs was that I could walk among them crouched behind hedgerows and, with notebook and pencil in hand, get names and stories—and then leave. I had the same uncomfortable sense of copping out that I'd had covering the Eighth Air Force.

What I did was marginally dangerous because there were always artillery and mortar shells coming in, but when the dreaded whisper "Moving out" was passed down the line from one man to the man behind him, I didn't have to move out. I didn't have a gun, I had a notebook. I stayed behind in the safety of whatever nook or cranny we'd found while we talked. After I had what I knew were enough notes for a story, I'd go back to the press camp and write it.

I DIDN'T YET have credentials for the First Army press camp. The Ninth Air Force was already a presence in Normandy because engineers were laying wire mesh runways wherever they could find an open field to provide a landing area for Ninth Air Force P-47s. The Ninth Air Force's capable public-relations officer, Maj. Ben Wright, had taken over a big house on the beach at Grandcamp where he provided food, shelter, and transmission facilities for stray newspaper people who weren't accredited to anyone else in the hope of getting a few fragments of favorable comment about the Ninth. It was surprising how much every unit cared about being mentioned. At Grandcamp I shared a room looking out over the Channel waters with an Associated Press photographer named Bede Irvin. We didn't spend much time looking at Channel waters.

The Ninth was called the Tactical Air Force, meaning it supported ground troops by strafing German gun positions, troop concentrations, and caravans of vehicles. For the P-47 pilots, zooming in with their eight machine guns blazing on a line of trucks bringing up ammunition and food, it was a vicious but satisfying business. They made it impossible for the Germans to move anything on wheels in daylight hours. A P-47's firepower could turn over a heavy truck, cut a horse in half, knock the steeple off a church, or pierce the walls of a stone house and kill its occupants. If we were lucky, its occupants were German.

I talked to a pilot one day after he'd come back from a day's work. His name is blurred in my notes.

"Being in an airplane helps you do it," he said. "If I was down on the ground with a machine gun and a bunch of Germans came by, I don't think I could stand there and kill them. I can do it sitting there in the cockpit of a fighter plane."

The war didn't end on D-Day. When we got out into the French countryside, it was only beginning.

All the military genius of every West Point graduate there ever was could hardly have designed a fortress more difficult to penetrate than was the French countryside.

Each farmhouse with its stone walls and stone barns provided a place behind which German gunners could hide and shoot at approaching Americans.

It's always harder to attack than to defend. A few men behind a stone wall can hold off a company of riflemen for hours.

The church steeples in Normandy are all less than fifty years old because we destroyed the originals. The steeples had to be knocked off with fire from our howitzers and the 75mm guns of our Sherman tanks or by the P-47s because the Germans were using them for their spotters. Watching with binoculars, they radioed the location of their shell hits to their artillery commanders and that enabled them to drop their shells more accurately on the beaches where the supplies were being brought in. The beaches were dangerous for weeks because of German artillery shelling.

The fashionable word for this farm country behind the beaches now is "bocage." I'm sure the French in Paris were using it then, but the farmers of Normandy never referred to it that way and I never heard the word used at the time by any of our people. The GIs didn't use it. "Goddamn hedgerows" is what they called them—and the hedgerows were the worst. Six to ten feet high and five feet thick, made of roots twisted around dirt and stone, they were impenetrable. German gunners leaned up against them, their rifles poking over the top, their bodies protected. A tank coming down the narrow lane between two hedgerows separating fields on either side was a sitting duck for an 88mm artillery piece at the end of the lane. The fields of the Norman farmers were all divided up by those confounded hedgerows and veined with small dirt roads perhaps ten feet wide running between them. Often the small roads between the hedgerows were just wide enough for a farmer with his horse and cart. It was a tight fit for a Sherman tank making its way through that path between two hedgerows.

While our tanks often traveled between the hedgerows bordering adjacent fields, they couldn't go over them. If they tried, the nose of the tank would simply head straight for the sky and finally, if the driver gave it more power, tip over backward. The other danger for a tank exposing its underbelly that way was its vulnerability to a direct hit from an 88mm gun to that lightly armored area on its bottom between the tracks.

The armored crews learned about their inability to deal with hedgerows early and, back in England, foundries were put to work making huge, flat, four-tyned heavy steel forks that were affixed to the front of the vehicle. When a tank equipped with one of these hit a hedgerow, the forks dug in and prevented the tank from somersaulting. By repeatedly hitting the hedgerow, a tank driver was often able to batter it down and get through it.

A great many soldiers on both sides were killed behind the hedgerows, mostly by mortar fire that had dropped accurately into them. Walking down a lane with high hedgerows on each side, you often passed dead German or American soldiers. The Graves Registration units couldn't keep up with the killing.

There were some fine tank commanders in Europe, and I spent a lot of time with good armored divisions. There's no doubt they helped win the war but of all the time and money spent on weapons, it was my experience that tanks were on top of the useless list. They look so good in news pictures of them rumbling at great speed across wide, flat plains that the public perception of them is positive. In the 1990s we're still spending something like $2.5 million on each tank. We'd be better off buying enlisted men and every commissioned and noncommissioned officer in any of the services a Ford Taurus. It would be cheaper, less vulnerable, more dependable in battle, and a better all-around weapon with just one machine gun mounted on its roof with a remote-control trigger.

There are two simple facts that often make tanks worse than useless in battle:

1. Battles are no longer fought on great, wide, sweeping plains. They are fought along roads or often in narrow city streets. When a column of tanks heads for a city accompanying forces that are going to try to take it from the enemy that holds it, one tank leads the way. The instant that tank is hit by enemy fire and burns or is otherwise disabled, it's the equivalent of a tractor trailer pileup on a four-lane

highway. All traffic behind it comes to a halt. The enemy might just as well have hit all thirty tanks in the column because none can move.

2. Tanks are more vulnerable than ships at sea. The Sherman tank was a beautiful piece of machinery. It was the product of the U.S. auto industry working at full speed and at its best. It had two and a half inches of armor on its front, but the Germans knew that as well as we did so they hit them from the side or from underneath where their armor was nowhere near as thick. That it was a beautiful piece of machinery didn't make it a good weapon.

Being inside a tank when it's hit must be one of the worst ways for a soldier to die. A direct hit by a German 88mm gun didn't always penetrate the armor of one of our tanks, but even if it didn't go through, thousands of razor-sharp shards of steel, more deadly than bullets because of their jagged, irregular shape, ricocheted inside the tank, tearing up anything they hit and especially human flesh. Usually a tank that was hit caught fire. Unlike the German Tiger tank, our Shermans were gasoline-powered, not diesel, and they burned, with their five-man crew inside them, too quickly and too often. The turret allowed one man to leave a tank at a time, and if one or two got out of the inferno, the other four were often incinerated while they waited their turn.

A tank wasn't a safe place to be with the enemy close up, either. A tank gunner had no shot at anyone within a few feet of the armored vehicle and an enemy soldier with a grenade could run to the side of a stopped tank, almost up against the armor of the vehicle, and stuff an unpinned grenade in the opening around the gun position that allowed it to traverse.

There was open hostility between the infantry and the tank corps in France, too. There always is. The infantry thought that, with all that armor, tanks should go first, force the enemy out of their dug-in positions, and get them running so the infantry could move up and shoot them down.

The tank crews, on the other hand, knew better about their own vulnerability. When the tanks rolled down those narrow lanes between hedgerows, there was always the chance of a German sniper or an 88 at the end of the road. The crews kept the tanks buttoned up because it wasn't safe to get out from behind the protective steel plates on the front of the tank. When they had to make the next field and when it would have been dangerous to stop or hesitate, they kept rolling even when there were dead—or worse, badly wounded—soldiers strewn across the path between the hedgerows. No one got out to move bodies—or the wounded. They kept going. Seeing what a tank left behind after it had traversed the narrow path between two hedgerows with dead or wounded lying in it is my grimmest vision of the war.

Walking the same road a day or so after a tank had passed through, I would often come upon the gruesome sight of the whole halves of four or five men, and four or five halves of what had been men, mashed into the dirt and mud by the grinding tracks of a ten-ton tank.

"There are days," Ernie Pyle wrote to his wife, "when you see things so horrible that you wonder what it is that can make this war worthwhile." Ernie and the rest of us were still eight months from seeing the answer to his question when we got into Germany.

You didn't read a lot about that sort of thing, especially if those bodies had been American boys. You didn't see pictures of war at its worst in *Life* magazine. I've heard people accuse the Army of having censored it but I don't recall that kind of censorship if it existed. Photographers exercised their own kind of censorship. Years later, when I read about American soldiers missing in action in Vietnam, I always thought I knew what happened. Nothing mysterious or evil. The idea that their captors had held American soldiers for years after the war and that those Americans were still alive seemed ludicrous to me. Of course there were men missing in action in that jungle war. There must have been Americans killed when no other American was watching, in parts of the jungle where no human being ever passed again. Their bones must still be there. Anyone who thinks there is some mysterious enemy holding MIAs in Vietnam doesn't know what happens in a war. By the time a few dozen tanks passed over the dead, they were to dust returned.

I found early that not everything was hell at war. There were good things, high points and even fun. American soldiers were always finding something on which to take a joy ride, for instance. German soldiers who fled abandoned their own Volkswagen-made command cars and thousands of motorcycles. You saw GIs everywhere riding them for the fun of it when they weren't on the line. On one trip to the front, I found two German motorcycles and I piled both of them on the back of my jeep and took them to the *Stars and Stripes* house in Sainte-Mère Église, just as though I'd shot two deer. Like every American boy, I'd always wanted a motorcycle and having these BMW beauties was a good way to get the craving for a motorcycle out of my system.

For several days I rode the more powerful of the two motorcycles, and by the time I'd hand-wheeled that thing over a few miles of rutted and shell-pocked roads, avoiding dead bodies and areas marked DANGER: BOOBY TRAP, I was dog-tired and more grown up—at least to the extent that my fantasy of owning a motorcycle and flying up and down rolling and open highways was gone forever. Out of my system.

For some American soldiers, the horses, wandering and frightened, that had been abandoned by fleeing French farmers, were friendly toys. The boys who knew how to ride were proud to show their expertise to their friends. I don't think the horses minded, although it's hard to tell what a horse objects to. At the very least the French horses must have found it difficult to understand commands given by a Texas American.

I knew as I was thinking how sad animals were in war that it was a misplaced emotion for me to have with human beings dying in every way on every side, but nonetheless I kept feeling bad about unmilked cows, homeless horses, abandoned dogs. Occasionally a soldier who knew how would milk one of the cows wandering in the fields with distended udders, but most of them got no help from humans concerned mostly with staying alive themselves.

The French dogs did better. American soldiers love dogs like mail from home, and every wandering dog was adopted and fed by some GI.

When a GI captured a German officer it was even better than getting an enlisted man because the officer often carried something better than either a good watch or Carl Zeiss binoculars. He had a Luger, the finest pistol made. The Luger was an unusual design with an appearance unlike any other handgun because it had a sort of futuristic Buck Rogers look to it. A Luger was the ultimate war trophy for an American GI.

The Stars and Stripes ran a story about an unnamed soldier to whom a Wehrmacht captain surrendered. The soldier was determined to have his Luger intact back home when the war was over but he knew he'd have a tough time getting a pistol past the baggage inspectors so he started to carefully disassemble his prize, breaking down the Luger into fifty or sixty small parts. Several times a week he would write to his wife and every time he would include with his letter or small package one of the Luger parts. Shipped in one piece, the gun never would never have been allowed into the United States.

Finally, the soldier had sent off the whole pistol, bit by bit. He was pleased at the thought of having it when he got home.

Three weeks later a package came from his wife. He eagerly tore it open, expecting cookies. No such luck! The soldier's loving wife, wanting to please him, had taken the parts to a gunsmith in the United States. The gunsmith put the Luger back together and she proudly shipped the fully assembled pistol back to her husband in Germany.

I got more familiar with weapons than I ever thought I would. The slingshot, water pistol, and bean blower were the extent of my knowledge of lethal weapons until I was drafted. I had never shot a gun.

The 88mm gun was the smallest enemy artillery piece. The Germans had them on wheels and mounted on their heavy Tiger tanks. The 88's long barrel gave its shell a low, flat trajectory so it was ineffective against troops behind a hedgerow or in a foxhole. It was the high-flying mortars you had to watch out for in those hedgerow weeks. They went almost straight up, traveled a few hundred yards and came almost straight down.

Reporters with the press camp would drive up as close to the front as we dared and then walk up to talk to the infantrymen hunkered down behind the hedgerows, waiting for the order to move out. Soldiers who had been in the line for a long time were remarkably calm. They smoked and talked. The thought of them still comes to me sometimes in the middle of the night. The lives they led were evidence of the truth of the cliché "war is hell." The best they could hope for was a hot meal and not dying.

Those infantrymen must have been as scared as I would have been but they went, often in the face of terrible fire from the hedgerow across the field. There was nothing for them to do but run as fast as they could and hope they weren't hit.

Infantrymen are no braver than anyone else and they do what they have to do, which is often to be killed, not so much because they are ordered to but because each man feels a sense of obligation to the man next to him. It is for that man, not the officer or noncom ordering them, that they go into the face of fire. I laugh when I hear the phrase "He gave his life for his country." No one gives his life. His life is taken.

THERE ARE HALF a dozen major events that dominate my memory of the war. They divide it into sections in my mind. Each one changed the way I worked and lived. The Breakthrough at Saint-Lô was one of those. I capitalize Breakthrough because it was as important, if not quite so singularly dramatic, as D-Day, the fall of Paris, or the crossing of the Rhine.

The reporters behaved as differently in the face of danger as the soldiers themselves. Some were laid-back while others pressed forward as though the best stories were always going to be at the frontline positions. Ernie Pyle was laid-back but he got the best stories.

In view of the fact that I recognize now that it was foolish, not brave, I think it's okay for me to say that I was a reporter who pressed forward. Just outside Saint-Lô, there was a long hill that curved down into the town. There were several hills around Saint-Lô that must have had their own names, but our Army numbered them and in a situation like that it's interesting that a number can be imbued with so much meaning as "Hill 122" did outside Saint-Lô. To us its mention sounded like "Tarawa" must have sounded in the Pacific. We could not get the Germans off it, and a lot of American boys lost their lives trying to climb it in the face of withering enemy fire from bunkers at its top.

Early in the morning of July 18, I picked up Bob Casey in my jeep and together we headed for Saint-Lô. Bob, a reporter for the *Chicago Daily News,* was the oldest correspondent in Normandy and one I greatly admired because, although I had never read one of them, he had written twenty-two books. Casey was a good companion. "Casey" was like a nickname.

As we approached Saint-Lô, there were mortar shells dropping regularly within a few hundred yards of us and we could hear machine-gun fire and 88 shells whistling through the air. Sometimes there was an explosion as they stuck home but more often they disappeared into that never-never land of spent ammunition. Saint-Lô was being defended by the crack Third Parachute Division, one of Hitler's best. Our First Division, the Big Red One, was moving into town, and a fight between those two units was the Super Bowl. The Big Red One had the Third and Fourth Armored Divisions on its flanks.

We rolled slowly toward town in low gear, weaving our way down the road strewn with dead bodies and tanks, trucks, half-tracks, and German command cars that had been destroyed and abandoned.

"I think this is it," Casey said nervously.

"This is what?" I asked, although I knew what he meant.

"Let's pull over."

We got out and Casey leaned against the embankment by the side of the road and looked down into the town, from which eight or ten different plumes of smoke arose.

"I'm just going to walk down a ways," I said.

Casey laughed nervously.

"Tell me about it when you get back," he said. "If you get back," he added.

It was the mindless sort of thing you wouldn't do if you considered the risk but I was interested, curious, and somehow oblivious to danger. The thought of being hit never entered my mind.

I lucked out that day—twice. I didn't get hit and I got a story.

The attack on Saint-Lô is a long book. There were at least eight divisions I know of involved in it, and seven of them were our very best: the First Division, the Second, the Fourth and the Twenty-ninth. On the infantry flanks were the Third and Fourth Armored Divisions. The Thirty-fifth Division was relatively new to battle. Good as they were, all but the Thirty-fifth had taken terrible losses and it looked for a while as though we were going to fail to capture Saint-Lô once again. Things weren't going well.

Maj. Gen. Charles Gerhardt was a tough old buzzard who commanded the D-Day veterans of the Twenty-ninth Division, and I'd talked with him in a brief meeting one day with some other reporters and endeared myself to him by remembering that he'd been the West Point quarterback on a team that beat Notre Dame. Gerhardt finally gave the major commanding his 116th Infantry Regiment a Patton-like command to "take Saint-Lô if you have to expend the whole battalion."

The 116th was commanded by Maj. Thomas D. Howie, a natural leader who was liked and respected by his men. He had been driving them hard but he'd been with them every step of the way. Shortly after Gerhardt sent his merciless order to move out at all costs, Major Howie was killed by a German shell that landed within a few yards of him.

As I came down the hill past small farms along the road, I passed one or two American soldiers every few hundred yards who had been left behind to secure the area that had been taken. When I finally got down into the center of Saint-Lô, there was a knot of men by the side of the main church in town. The church was big but not what I'd call a cathedral. The whole side of it had been knocked out and the rubble was piled high where it had fallen. I hurried over and saw ten or fifteen soldiers lifting a flag-draped body laid out on a wooden door up the heap of stone and mortar that had been the side of the church. It would be accurate to say that Saint-Lô had been leveled and the mound of stone and brick was the highest point in town. The soldiers were placing the body at the very top of the heap. It was their leader, Tom Howie.

I spoke with some of the men from the Twenty-ninth. Soldiers at war do not display much emotion, and placing Howie's body there was an unusual thing for them to have done and they were emotional about it. My jeep must have been more than a mile back up the winding hill, and by the time I got there Bob Casey was gone. It didn't surprise or worry me. We were within ten miles of the press camp and I knew he'd have been able to get a ride out of town faster than we'd been able to get in four hours earlier. It was good of him to leave the jeep for me.

The end of my Saint-Lô story came several months later when I came back to Paris from up near the Rhine River. Col. Ensley M.

Llewellyan called me into his office in the *Paris Herald Tribune* building.

Llewelyan held in his hand a small box and a piece of paper.

"Well," he said lamely, "I see we have another hero with the paper." I took the box, opened it, and it was the Bronze Star, a medal that falls in rank somewhere between the Medal of Honor and the Good Conduct Medal. (I had already received the Air Medal for the five trips I'd made on bombing raids—three with the B-26s and two with the B-17s.) It's a good medal to get, though. The citation read:

TECHNICIAN FOURTH GRADE ANDREW A. ROONEY ARMY SERIAL NO. 32135400, INFANTRY, UNITED STATES ARMY FOR MERITORIOUS SERVICE IN CONNECTION WITH MILITARY OPER- ATIONS AS CORRESPONDENT FOR *THE STARS AND STRIPES,* SPE- CIAL SERVICES DIVISION, ADVANCE SECTION, COMMUNICATIONS ZONE, EUROPEAN THEATER OF OPERATIONS. TECHNICIAN FOURTH GRADE ROONEY PENETRATED TO THE HEART OF SAINT LO UNDER SMALL ARMS AND OPEN RANGE ARTILLERY FIRE AND GATHERED, WITHOUT REGARD TO HIS OWN SAFETY, FIRST HAND DESCRIPTIVE MATERIAL FOR A COMPLETE AND ACCURATE STORY. ON SEVERAL OCCASIONS HE LIVED WITH THE MOST FOR- WARD ELEMENTS OF OUR TROOPS TO GATHER THE ACTUAL FACTS FOR HASTY PRESENTATION TO KEEP UNITED STATES SOL- DIERS INFORMED. ENTERED MILITARY SERVICE FROM BUFFALO, NEW YORK.

I was simultaneously pleased and embarrassed. I knew that there were a lot of heroes in the war and knew I wasn't one of them. I was someone with a good job as a reporter who could pretty much go where he wanted to go and that included getting out of the way when the shooting got too close. I thanked Colonel Llewellyan, shook his hand as if he'd given me a diploma, and left. I wouldn't have dared mention it to anyone in the newsroom and I noticed, in subse- quent days, that Llewellyan never did either.

I don't know why the people of Saint-Lô don't hate Americans today. We destroyed their town. We didn't damage it, we annihilated

it. What buildings the infantry and artillery didn't knock down, the
Air Force, with its low-level strafing of German positions, did. It
didn't seem to embitter the citizens of Saint-Lô. Every year, on the
anniversary of their liberation, they hang banners across their main
street and make a festival of thanks to the Americans for coming to
their rescue. They don't mention that, in the process of the liberation,
we destroyed what we were liberating.

Saint-Lô was taken from the Germans forty terrible days after the
young men waded ashore on the beaches. Those were the worst forty
days. By then the Allies had suffered 40,000 casualties.

"Casualties" is an official designation that doesn't mean much
because it is too broad a word. Those included in the category are not
a group who have much in common except that they are no longer
fighting. It includes the dead, the wounded, the captured, the missing,
and the cowards who couldn't take it. I use the word "coward," but I
never heard a frontline soldier use it.

In this case, too many of that 40,000 figure were killed in action.
About 20,000 men died before the Breakthrough at Saint-Lô. Very
few were taken prisoner because the Germans had no facility for
keeping prisoners in their desperate attempt to hold their ground.

The German defeat in the town of Saint-Lô itself was a good victory for us but the Germans didn't withdraw far out of town before
regrouping. It was not unexpected, and Gen. Omar Bradley had been
planning a huge offensive operation named Cobra, which was
designed to open a gap in German lines that the Second and Third
Armored and the First Infantry Division riding half-tracks could race
through. On July 24, four U.S. divisions near Saint-Lô had been
ordered to pull back. It turned out, in documents found later, that this
was very confusing to the German high command. They couldn't figure out why we were retreating. They hoped we were quitting but
feared some trick, and of course it was a trick. Our troops had been
pulled back to allow for the saturation bombing of German troops
just a few hundred yards in front of them.

On the morning of July 25, the Allies mounted one of the greatest air raids in history. It was part of the plan to break out of the
cramped position Allied forces had occupied along the French coast
since D-Day.

I say that air raid was "*one* of the greatest" but I don't know of one that had more heavy bombers in the air dropping so many bombs on so small an area in so short a time. There were 1,021 B–17s and B–24s from the U.S. Eighth Air Force and 1,056 big RAF Lancasters, Wellingtons, and Halifaxes. They dropped 5,000 tons of explosives.

The first wave of bombers accurately dropped their loads on German positions. The general who commanded the Panzer Lehr Division described the experience:

Back and forth the bomb carpets were laid, artillery positions were wiped out, tanks overturned and buried, infantry positions flattened and all roads and tracks destroyed. By midday the entire area resembled a moon landscape, with the bomb craters touching, rim to rim. All signal communications had been cut and no command was possible. The shock effect on troops was indescribable. Several of my men went mad and rushed around in the open until they were cut down by splinters. Simultaneously with the storm from the air, innumerable guns of the American artillery poured drumfire into our field positions.

Unfortunately for U.S. forces, there was a strong wind blowing from east to west. The heavy line of smoke and dust heaved into the air by the first wave was blown in a uniformly straight line directly west. Clouds of it obscured the new positions to which American forces had withdrawn. The second wave of bombers dropped their bombs on U.S. troops, and it ended up as the highest number of casualties from friendly fire of any incident in any war. One three-star general, Leslie McNair, who had gone farther to the front than most generals to observe the effect of the bombing, was killed that day along with several hundred GIs.

And my friend and roommate at Grandcamp, Bede Irvin.

It was two days later before I learned of his death.

I had moved out of the Ninth Air Force facility at Grandcamp when I got my First Army credentials, and into the First Army press camp, but I'd left in a hurry without taking a barracks bag I had and some other belongings.

When I returned to the house at Grandcamp to pick up the things I had left there after hearing of Bede's death, all Bede's belongings in our room had been packed up and sent to the Associated Press office in London for shipment to his wife back in the States.

I glanced around the room, sat down on the edge of my bed and shook my head in disbelief. I don't know why death brings disbelief. I looked at my own possessions and recall wondering whether I'd have wanted them shipped home if I had been the casualty.

My eyes stopped at the top of the four-drawer dresser Bede and I had shared. The picture! The picture of Margie that I had put there was gone! They had shipped my wife's picture along with Bede's possessions, back to *his* wife. When she unpacked them, she was going to be confronted by a picture of a pretty stranger that Bede had never mentioned to her.

I made half a dozen frantic calls to the AP in London. The package had already been sent. Fortunately, it went by boat and had been sent, not directly to Bede's wife, but to the AP office in Rockefeller Center and I was able to get them a message. They removed Margie's picture before shipping it on.

The Army handled reporters well. The press camp had food, cots, transportation, and transmission facilities for newspeople traveling with the Army. A staff of enlisted men and three officers made life easier for newspeople although there were also two censors present to make it harder. Copy was sent via Press Wireless, a company which dealt exclusively with transmission of news stories.

While censorship was seldom onerous we all understood that pessimistic reports, reports of great losses, or negative stories about our own men were seldom passed. Actual censorship—that is, times when the censors forbade a reporter from transmitting a story he had written—were rare because reporters knew what they could and could not write. It was the case of self-imposed censorship again. Military people are convinced that they always have to be winning the war in stories sent home.

Press-camp headquarters in Normandy was the twenty-room Château d'Hamel in Vouilly, where we lived with the wonderfully friendly French family whose home it was. The Army had set up six tents, three on each side of the broad, poplar-lined lane leading to the great wooden door of the château. We used the main rooms of the house, with their great, long, walnut tables, to work and eat in. We slept in the tents. The Army supplied a few typewriters but most of us used our own. The typewriter of choice was the compact, portable, Swiss-made Hermès.

Of the twenty-five to thirty reporters there at any one time, only a couple had covered the air war from London so I made a lot of new friends. They all seemed much older than I was, but in fact most of them were only in their late twenties or early thirties. A few were in their fifties, but all of them had been excused from Army duty for one physical reason or another.

We had some great times together in large and small groups. Our common purpose bound us together and the competition to get stories that no one else had was intense but friendly. At night, eight or ten of us often sat around talking, and even though no one found the war funny there was, inevitably, a lot of laughter.

One night several correspondents started making up limericks. The name of *Collier's* correspondent Frank Gervasi came up, and Hal Boyle had the winning limerick that night. It was done as a friendly joke on Gervasi, whom Hal had been with in North Africa.

> *There once was a whore from Bengazi*
> *Who slept with a frog and a Nazi*
> *A wog and a dog*
> *And a razorback hog,*
> *But she drew the line at Gervasi*

While the reporters were civilians and nominally, at least, equal, we all knew who the important ones were. In the three press camps that were set up before we reached Paris, the first tent—the one nearest the château—was in each case occupied by the same six people. They were Ernie Pyle, Hal Boyle of the AP, Hank Gorrell of the UP, Jack Thompson of the *Chicago Tribune,* Bill Stoneman, and a photographer, Bert Brandt, of Acme Pictures.

Ernie Pyle was the den mother for the tent. Although breakfast was available at an army mess set up in the château, Ernie often made breakfast on an open fire in front of the tent, frying eggs he'd picked up in the countryside and bacon he got from the kitchen.

As a person, Ernie lived up to his reputation as a reporter. He was so normal, so decent, and so good to be around, and he knew how to do what so many of us did not. When the other correspondents rose early and headed for the action as near the fighting front as they dared go, Ernie was more casual. One day just a few weeks after the Invasion when the rest of us were giving our attention to the fighting in front of us, he went back to Omaha Beach. It was stacked with ammunition, mountains of ration boxes and crates of replacement clothing, and equipment of every kind. Ernie came upon a shoe-repair company just a few miles from where other American soldiers were dying in the hedgerows and made a wonderfully warm feature story from talking to soldiers whose contribution was putting new soles and heels on army boots. No one thought of it but Ernie.

Several weeks after I met him, I was in the same tent with Ernie, which didn't happen often. I'd come back to lie down on my cot and read and rest after a long day. Ernie was lying on his cot directly across from mine. I hadn't been reading long when the sound of a bee in flight got too annoying to ignore. I put my book down and looked for the bee. Ernie folded his book on his chest and looked.

It turned out that there was more than one bee and their nest was in the ground in the middle of the tent. We both watched the activity for a few minutes and then I got up, scuffed a pile of dirt over the hole, and went back to my cot to lie down. Ernie was lying on his left side and I was on my right side, watching the bees that came back looking for the small hole leading to their hive.

Before long there were ten or twelve bees in frantic flight over the site of their former home. Ernie and I didn't say anything but it was apparent that we were thinking the same thing. There were obviously a lot more bees trapped in the underground nest than there were hovering over it. Something about the intensity of their activity made it seem as though the bees outside were concerned, not about getting in themselves but about the safety of the ones trapped under the pile of dirt I'd heaped over the hole.

Ernie Pyle is third from the left; John MacVane, an ABC correspondent, is at the far right. The cumbersome tripod and heavy 35mm camera in the foreground make it apparent why there were not many motion pictures of real front-line action.

Finally, after perhaps two minutes, Ernie spoke.

"Aw, Andy," he said, "let 'em out."

It was Ernie's compassion for life in any form and his attention to details that seemed insignificant to the rest of us that made him the best of the war correspondents.

THE HEDGEROW WAR was over after Saint-Lô but the bulk of the German army was in front of us even though they were badly disorganized. The next major event was what military historians call the Falaise Gap. I've tried to compare what I've read in the history books to what I saw and there's no comparison. "The failure to close the Argentan-Falaise gap allowed 50,000 Germans to get away," writes one very good historian. What do you historians want, anyway? In an area thirty miles long and twenty miles wide, 30,000 Germans were killed and 92,000 were taken prisoner. A lot of them were from the elite Fifth and Seventh Panzer Divisions. Is that a big failure?

A better name than "Gap" would have been "Trap." "The Falaise Trap." I saw no gap, and when the carnage was over the better part of all forty German divisions that had been in Normandy was chopped up and sent into disorganized flight.

I guess what I saw of the Falaise Gap was a small part of it but I can't believe anything in the war, including Stalingrad, was any worse for German troops. The trap the German Seventh Army was caught in was in or near the small town of Chambois, not far from Falaise but closer to Argentan. A lot of German infantry, armor, and artillery had been hiding in the nearby woods that were called by the French "Le Forêt Gouffern."

They had emerged en masse from the forest during the night to try to escape and it was necessary for them to travel along a main road that cut through a small valley surrounded by low mountains or hills that were no more than a few hundred feet high. Unfortunately for the Germans, we had anticipated their move and hundreds of U.S. artillery pieces were in position every ten yards on the hills all around the valley. It was a shooting gallery. And if that were not bad enough for them, the P-47s were strafing them all day long. The only limitation on them was the care they had to take not to hit our troops.

U.S. gunners poured thousands of rounds of 105mm and 155mm shells into the endless lines of German vehicles whose frantic drivers were trying to get them out of the valley at the far end where the road led through a narrow pass. The history books say we allowed 50,000 Germans to escape at Falaise but no historian who saw the killing that I saw that day would repeat that phrase I've seen in print: "We let the Germans escape." It was the worst slaughter of the war, a massacre vastly more deadly for the German soldiers than D-Day was for ours.

The German soldiers in horse-drawn wagons, trucks, command cars, and a few tanks moved along the road in a straight line like clay ducks on a track in a carnival tent. As the slaughter started, big white flags started flying over their vehicles. Under ordinary circumstances the Germans would have been taken prisoner, but white flags on vehicles meant nothing at the 600 yards between them and the U.S. troops up on the lip of the saucer. The white flags only seemed to make them better targets.

Horse-drawn artillery compounded the awfulness of the day. It is easier to get used to dead men than dead or wounded and dying horses. At one point a line of hundreds of horses was strafed by P-47s and they bolted, ran, bucked. Most of them were still hitched to wagons or field-artillery pieces. The live ones, still trapped in their harnesses, dragged the dead ones and dragged their wagons and guns and dragged dead and wounded German soldiers. Some soldiers who had not been hit were crushed or trapped by the action of the crazed horses. There cannot have been many gorier days in history.

At one point as many as a dozen horses had bolted and ended up tangled together bleeding and dying in the Dive River, their blood coloring the water red. The wounded horses were unable to get themselves up the steep bank, and many were drowning in their traces. One U.S. infantryman, a humanitarian I guess you'd say, stood on the bank of the river shooting the wounded horses. I thought of Hub Zemke.

Our medics were there but overwhelmed. I tried to talk to a doctor, Maj. Clifford Vinson of Tampa, but he didn't have much time for conversation with a reporter so I watched. Vinson was working alongside a German doctor who must have been six feet five, and they were attending Americans, Germans, Poles, and French with absolutely no priorities given except in relation to how badly the man was wounded.

One German officer was lying on the ground with the lower part of his face shot away but he was alive and it was the only time Major Vinson displayed any emotion.

"He should die," he said. "I hope he dies but I'm going to try to keep him alive."

In the valley hundreds of horses had been torn open by shell fragments and another GI walked through the ruins pouring rounds of shot from his Browning automatic rifle into the bodies of those he thought might still be alive. He was careful not to hit any of the wounded German soldiers, leaving them instead, without any evil intention, to a less kind and slower death.

I never got used to seeing horses slaughtered. Wherever that happened, the civilians came out with their sharp knives an hour after the battle had passed and carved the carcasses of the horses into meat-market-sized pieces. Like most Americans, I don't think of horses in terms of chops and steaks.

The following day I went into the valley again with an inspection team from First Army headquarters and it was like walking into a slaughterhouse. Most of the wounded had been taken out by our medics but the dead remained. Burying our own dead always took precedence over burying the German dead. Our Graves Registration units were numerous and efficient although it always surprised me that young men would do so unpleasant a job.

Many of the German officers riding in the Wehrmacht equivalent of our command cars, which looked most like old Ford phaetons, had obviously been taken by surprise when they were attacked as they entered the valley because some had been killed still sitting upright, four to a vehicle.

It seemed incongruous but I had a pleasant thrill in the midst of all this. It will probably end up being the only serious brush I'll ever have with great wealth. On the ground near one of the command cars I saw a small black, grained-leather satchel. It looked like the ones doctors carried their stethoscopes in when doctors made house calls.

The bag had obviously belonged to the officer in charge of paying the German soldiers, although it's hard to imagine now what a Wehrmacht soldier could have done with German marks deep in France, surrounded by the enemy.

The leather bag was crammed full of mostly large-denomination German marks. Each bundle was three or four inches thick and tightly bound with wide, brown paper tape.

I had that greedy sensation I've had a few times in my life when I've been suddenly and unexpectedly enriched. It was like finding a $20 bill in a raincoat pocket multiplied by ten thousand. At one point I laid out some of the bundles on the backseat of my jeep and estimated that it was worth more than a million dollars.

Worth a million to whom had not immediately come to my mind, and it is frustrating to note all these years later and with all the tiny things I recall so well and clearly, that I cannot remember what I did with the only million dollars I ever held in my hand.

Most of the prisoners taken were the badly wounded but Germans in groups of a hundred or more had abandoned their vehicles and some of them had scrambled up the few dirt roads that led from the valley to surrender. Many were taken prisoner but many were not because our military police had more Germans on their hands than they could guard.

Lt. Gen. George S. Patton got everyone's attention for the first time after Falaise. He moved his Third Army into an area between the British and the Americans that Bradley wanted to leave open to eliminate any possible unfortunate contact between the two forces. Bradley ordered Patton to get out.

Anyone who knew nothing about Patton but his legend might think he stormed ashore on D-Day and drove across Europe until he'd taken Berlin. The facts of the matter were that Patton, his dog, Willie, and his small Third Army didn't get to France until after Saint-Lô had been taken. Did you know Patton brought his dog?

Patton's role in the Invasion was, nonetheless, important. He was the highly visible fake commander of a nonexistent force of forty-five armored and infantry divisions called FUSAG, First U.S. Army Group. Its only purpose was to confuse the Germans about where Allied forces were going to strike.

Eisenhower wanted the Germans to think the Allies were going to strike the Pas de Calais area, and Patton was the perfect military man to attract attention to himself and to the Army that wasn't.

FUSAG had bases, training grounds, orders of battle, communications facilities, and a specific target for its landing in France. All this information was leaked to those known German spies so that the

Germans would certainly get hold of it and be misled into thinking Patton was heading the Invasion. We were even suckered into the diversion at *The Stars and Stripes*. One headline read:

PATTON IN UK TO LEAD INVASION FORCE!

The only thing Patton's FUSAG didn't have was soldiers or weapons. The whole operation was a gigantic fake, and FUSAG was a paper tiger.

Patton's First U.S. Army Group was equal in size and military complexity to the "Twelfth British Army," which was just as fictitious. I suspect it was the product of British wit that one of the major units in that nonexistent fighting force was called the "Seventh Polish Infantry Division." There were Polish pilots flying with the RAF, but there were hardly enough Poles in Great Britain to make up an infantry division.

Patton was very good playing his part as commander in chief of his nonexistent army. While he was waiting to invade France with it, he made a speech that was typically bombastic and self-serving. It wasn't much of a speech, but it was picked up by the *New York Daily News* because its principal point of interest was the profanity in it.

Patton was reported to have cautioned his "troops" not to mention his presence. The purpose of the speech was, of course, to call attention to his presence.

"Let the first bastards to find out about us be the goddamn Germans," he was quoted as saying to his troops. "I want them to look up and howl 'It's that son of a bitch Patton again.' "

I don't know whether those lines were written by Patton himself or by someone in a propaganda unit, but they were perfect because they sounded so much like him and he was widely quoted.

Even after the Invasion, there were people who thought Patton had led the charge. The plan fooled Congress and the chairman of the House Military Affairs Committee, who you'd think would have known better. On August 1, the very first day on which Patton's Third Army was put into the line to fight, but before it had fought at all, Congressman Andrew May of Kentucky said, on the floor of the House, "I have a hunch that 'Ole Blood and Guts' is leading that steamroller offensive in Normandy and, if so, he'll win it." Lt. Gen. Courtney Hodges, who was doing the work and actually leading the offensive in Normandy, must have burned when he read Patton's press notices suggesting he was winning the war single-handed.

Many of the soldiers in Patton's army hated him and hated that nickname, "blood and guts." Their line was "Yeah, his guts and our blood."

No one I know is neutral when it comes to George S. Patton. It should be made clear right away that I met him only twice, but I followed closely what he did during the war and came away disliking him intensely. He was a loudmouthed boor who got too many American soldiers killed for the sake of enhancing his own reputation as a swashbuckling leader in the Napoleonic style.

It's my opinion that a great many Americans who idolize Patton confuse him with George C. Scott, who played the Academy Award–winning part of Patton in the movie with that title.

After I said some of these things on a CBS broadcast called "The Generals," I received one of the best—and certainly the shortest—critical letters of my career in television. Patton's daughter wrote me and her message was all in one sentence.

Dear Mr. Rooney,
    My father wouldn't have liked you, either.
                    Sincerely,
                    Mrs. James W. Totten

He not only wouldn't have liked me, he didn't like me. On one occasion when I wrote a story questioning a Third Army statement about exactly what day they had crossed the Rhine River, he wrote a sharp rebuke to *The Stars and Stripes* and addressed it not to me but to Colonel Llewellyan. People often think they can get you fired if they write an I'll-never-read-your-newspaper-again letter to your boss.

At the symposium conducted by the Naval Institute at Col. Robert McCormick's Chicago château a few years ago, an eminent historian, who had written a biography of Patton, said that the success of the campaign in Normandy owed a great deal to General Patton.

I stood up and begged to differ with him. Inasmuch as Patton's Third Army was not committed in France until August 1, seven weeks after the D-Day landings and eight days after we'd taken Saint-Lô, I thought it could hardly be true that Patton had anything whatsoever to do with victory in Normandy. I'm not sure where the boundary of Normandy and Brittany is in relation to where Patton's army was when it was committed but it's probable that the Third Army never fought in Normandy at all. If it did, it was a skirmish of one or two days because, if Patton was there, it wasn't for longer than that. His orders were to head south and east, away from the concentration of German troops facing the First Army.

There was stiff competition for headlines between correspondents for the First Army and those with the newcomer Third Army, and as a result the public got a wrong impression that Patton was winning the war because he was traveling so fast. A few irresponsible correspondents, looking for headlines, blew his progress full of hot air. Patton himself complained that he could have gone even farther if they'd given him the fuel for his tanks and trucks.

The fact is, Patton was making an end run with little opposition and the troops fighting the war needed the fuel. Everyone was fed the idea that Patton had the tanks. For most of the time, Patton had two armored divisions at the same time the vastly larger First Army had seven.

There's no question that Patton had a genius for getting his name in the papers. You wouldn't find many Americans who know that Courtney Hodges, a fine and responsible general, fought all the major battles in France and Germany with his First Army.

Without Eisenhower's backing, we'd never have made it through the war as an independent news source for the troops because Patton repeatedly tried to censor *The Stars and Stripes* and *YANK*.

"This newspaper," Ike had declared when the paper started publication, "should be the equivalent of a soldier's hometown newspaper, with no censorship of its contents other than for security, the same as for any civilian correspondent's copy in this theater."

Ike may have taken his lead from the boss, Gen. George C. Marshall. Marshall had said, "A soldier's newspaper is a symbol of the things we are fighting to preserve and spread in this threatened world. It represents the free thought and free expression of a free people."

Patton had a running feud with Bill Mauldin, *The Stars and Stripes* cartooning genius. Mauldin kept drawing blood with deft strokes of his pen. One of many Mauldin cartoons that Patton hated showed an ornately dressed general with a smorgasbord of medals on his chest, looking strikingly like Patton, standing at the rim of a picturesque valley somewhere in Germany. In Mauldin's caption, the general is speaking about the view to his aide, standing at his side. He asks:

"Is there one of these for the enlisted men, colonel?"

It was pinpricking pomposity that, being himself pompous, made Patton uneasy.

Patton demanded that if *The Stars and Stripes* didn't drop Bill Mauldin, he'd prohibit distribution of the paper in his Third Army area. His demand made the civilian newspapers and turned into a big story.

Harry Butcher, a Navy captain who was Ike's eminently sensible aide, reported that Ike called him in and said, "Get George out of this mess, Harry."

It was agreed all around that it was General Patton, not Sergeant Mauldin, who was in trouble although Mauldin was understandably uneasy about it. All of us on the paper had nightmares from time to time about ending up back in the infantry on the complaint of some chickenshit officer whom we'd displeased. (That was another irreplaceable vulgarity that was part of the language of World War II.)

Patton was in Luxembourg before he was to cross the Rhine. With Mauldin listening in on an extension in his office, Butcher telephoned Patton and told him that the best thing to do was for him to get Mauldin up there and have a talk with him.

It was not comforting to Bill when he heard Patton on the other end of the line yell, "All right. Send the little sonofabitch up here."

When Mauldin got to Patton's headquarters, he was escorted to the general's office in a grand palace in Luxembourg. Bill describes the scene as something out of a movie. As Bill came in the door of an ornately decorated, cavernous room, Patton was seated behind a huge desk at the far end and a visitor had to make the long, lonely walk to face him. It was an old belittling trick of kings.

Bill said he'd left all the clothes he usually wore in his jeep and got himself a regulation GI outfit for the appearance.

"I even took off my paratroop boots," Bill says. "Fellows in the Eighty-second Airborne gave them to me because they liked something I did about guys who wore paratroop boots who weren't paratroopers." Bill enjoyed the irony of that.

Patton lectured Mauldin on the necessity for authority in the Army and said that Bill was undermining that authority with his drawings.

Mauldin was finally dismissed by Patton but Patton was the clear loser. Bill never backed off. His cartoons continued as sharp as ever, and *The Stars and Stripes* was never barred from Third Army distribution.

One of *The Stars and Stripes'* good reporters was a man named Earl Mazo. Earl, a first lieutenant, had been the public-relations officer for the 385th Bomb Group in England when I flew on a raid with them. That trip was not so eventful as the raid on Wilhelmshaven had been. He desperately wanted to be a *Stars and Stripes* reporter and, because the policy was for all reporters to be enlisted men, he offered to resign his commission to get the job. He finally got it without giving up his commission and, after Saint-Lô, he was assigned to cover the Third Army along with Jimmy Cannon, who had been a popular New York sportswriter, and Jules Grad. They were both enlisted men but with correspondents' credentials.

When Patton discovered one day that Jimmy and Jules were eating in the officers' mess and using the officers' latrine at Third Army headquarters, he hit the roof, demanding that they never set foot in either place again.

Earl Mazo, Lt. Earl Mazo, in protest, began eating in the enlisted men's mess and used the enlisted latrine with Jimmy Cannon and Jules Grad. Inevitably Patton heard about Earl's modest little gesture of protest and threatened to have all three thrown out of his headquarters. He finally backed off when he was told that if the three were expelled they would not be replaced and there would be no Third Army coverage appearing in the only newspaper his troops could get hold of.

Following that appearance on the CBS broadcast "The Generals," I got many letters condemning me besides the one from Patton's daughter.

"His men would gladly have followed him anywhere," one man wrote.

Well, sure. A frontline soldier would follow Patton anywhere because, chances are, Patton was headed back, with Willie, for the safety of his safe command headquarters, well behind front lines. What kind of a jackass general brings a dog with him wherever he goes? Patton was not a frontline soldier—not that any general should be—but neither should he have the reputation for being one when he was not.

Meeting Patton, I was surprised how tall he was and how broad his hips were. That feature was accentuated by the flaring, cavalry-style pants he wore with leather puttees and the ivory-handled pistol in its leather holster, protruding from his right side.

"He lost fourteen jeep drivers," another man wrote me and then went on to suggest that they were all shot while taking Patton to the front. For what reason I don't know, but that's the kind of myth that grew up around this dangerous charlatan.

I have talked to John Eisenhower, the general's son, about Patton. He's soft on him because, as he says, Patton was almost an uncle to him growing up. Patton never grew up. John, a fine historian, defends Patton because he says that, if his father put trust in Patton and Patton was a bad general, that doesn't reflect well on his father's judgment.

Patton and Eisenhower were classmates and their paths had crossed frequently during their long careers in the Army. I don't think putting Patton in charge of anything was one of Ike's most distinguished moves, and I don't think Ike liked doing it. Loyalty overcame judgment.

In Sicily, a group of thirty-six Italians, some of them civilians, surrendered while Patton was there. There was some sort of confrontation during which the Italians ignored the order of an American officer and they were lined up and shot.

When Gen. Omar Bradley heard of the incident and demanded an explanation, Patton, according to historian Martin Gilbert, instructed his men responsible to "tell Bradley that the dead men were snipers or had tried to escape or something, otherwise it'll make a stink in the press and make the Italians mad."

"Anyhow," Patton added, "they're dead so nothing can be done about it." He was consistently Mr. Nice Guy.

When I said some derogatory things about General Patton's disregard for the lives of men under his command on another television broadcast, in 1992, Blair Clark, a friend of mine and former vice president of CBS News, wrote me to say that he had been the historian for Patton's Third Army.

"I know for a fact," Blair wrote, "that casualties in Patton's divisions were lower than those of Courtney Hodges' First Army."

Well, of course they were. Blair Clark's statement was true. The First, Second, Fourth, Ninth, and Twenty-ninth Divisions of the First Army suffered casualties of 200 percent. There were 18,000 men in an infantry division and before the war ended each of those divisions had more than 36,000 casualties. A large percentage of them were suffered in those first fifty days after the Invasion. How many casualties did Patton's Third suffer in the Invasion? None. They weren't there. How many Third Army men went down trying to break through German defenses at Saint-Lô? None. They hadn't been committed to battle yet. Their casualties were low because they didn't encounter the same opposition and didn't do anywhere near the fighting that the First Army did, despite Patton's attempt to grab headlines right after Falaise.

The first major contribution Patton's Third made was when it was called in during the Battle of the Bulge and, at that time, it was an important force in breaking the German counteroffensive at Bastogne. The men under Patton's command were as good as any. It was the commander who was the problem.

I have nothing but contempt for Patton.

After Falaise and Argentan there was little German resistance—reporters turned their attention to Paris 100 miles away. There was nothing tactically important about Paris and soldiers aren't much moved by psychological victories, but taking Paris back from the Germans was vastly more important than its significance as a military victory. The name Paris is magic.

ON AUGUST 22 a horde of reporters descended on the charming little Grand Veneur Hotel in the town of Rambouillet, anticipating the liberation. After Col. Monk Dixon's briefing, which alerted us to the imminent Allied move into Paris, we had all raced to that designated press headquarters. Lt. Roy Wilder, known to one and all as "Chitlin," had taken an excursion with A. J. Liebling. When they returned to the press camp and found that the rest of us had left, Roy said that Liebling broke into tears under the mistaken impression that we'd all actually gone right into Paris. His fondest wish was to see our entry into Paris.

It was an exciting time, the weather was pleasant, and we all felt good about everything until about four o'clock that afternoon when someone came back from northwest of Paris with the bad news that Tom Treanor of the *Los Angeles Times* had been killed earlier in the day. Tom was crushed to death by one of our own tanks. I never heard exactly how it happened, but a tank driver has limited vision and it was no surprise. It happened a lot.

Although it was the U.S. First Army that had reached the outskirts of Paris, reporters from Patton's Third Army, Maj. Gen. Manton Eddy's Seventh Army, and General Montgomery's British forces flooded the town. Like all beat reporters, the First Army regulars resented the influx of strangers trying to get in on our biggest story of the war and one for which we felt a proprietary interest. It was as if they were the enemy. I remember hating people like the chief INS correspondent, Pierre Huss, for no reason at all except that he was assigned to the Third Army and was intruding on First Army turf.

Some of the strangers had credentials and permission to be with the First Army for a brief period and some did not but came anyway. I was lucky to get a room that I shared with Rex Taylor, an Army public-relations lieutenant whose father, Sec Taylor, I knew as the leg-endary sports editor of the *Des Moines Register.*

A lot of the reporters had to sleep on straw spread over the floor of the hotel dining room. When a reporter who had been covering the First Army from the beaches was displaced by one of the interlopers from the Third Army, it was not a happy lobby.

It was there in the hotel dining room that evening that one of the great unchronicled skirmishes of World War II took place. Bruce Grant was fifty-five years old, six feet four inches tall, and weighed 175 pounds. That's tall and thin. He had been city editor of the *Chicago Sun Times* and looked as though he'd led an indoor life until he came to France. Ernest Hemingway was five feet ten, 185 pounds, and both fit and strong.

Bruce Grant had been unable to get a room in the hotel and he knew that Hemingway, who had arrived in Rambouillet several days ahead of our soldiers to play war with his Free French friends, had tied up ten rooms for himself. Some of the rooms were stacked with weapons and other equipment.

After being turned down on his request for a room, Grant found Hemingway in the dining room where he was holding forth as a small group of correspondents listened with respectful attention to the most famous writer among them. He had a .45-caliber pistol strapped to his side, something no sensible correspondent wore. Even though I was a sergeant in the Army, I carried correspondent's credentials and never carried a weapon. It seemed safer.

I was talking to some friends over some coffee we'd made from K rations and wasn't paying any attention until I heard some kind of a ruckus in the middle of the room. Hemingway was bellowing at Grant to "get the hell out of here."

Grant was threatened with raised fists. The correspondents watching didn't behave a lot differently from the recruits at Fort Bragg who gathered around in anticipation of my fight with Wray Funderburk.

Seconds before fists flew, Harry Harris, the popular AP photographer who wasn't more than five feet five, stepped between them. With one hand reaching up and braced against Hemingway's chest and the other on Bruce Grant's, Harry tried to shove them apart with all the might of his 145 pounds.

Hemingway turned abruptly and walked to the lace-curtained French doors at the side of the room leading to a small garden. Ernie Pyle was already lying on his bed of straw on the floor and had come to a sitting position to see what was happening. We all thought it was over when Hemingway left but ten seconds later he threw open the doors and bellowed at Grant:

"Well, are you coming out and fight?"

Bruce Grant was restrained by friends from going out to a slaughter in the garden. You should never meet one of your heroes. I had greatly admired Hemingway when I read *A Farewell to Arms* and *The Sun Also Rises* but after that night in Rambouillet I laugh whenever I think of him.

There was a rumor that night that Eisenhower was going to make what amounted to a political, rather than a military, decision about which force would go into Paris. We were very aware that the French forces with the Allies and the British both wanted to go in first for public-relations reasons, but the political implications were of no interest to me. Some of the heavy-duty reporters in Rambouillet were trying to write that story, but for me it was the kind thing they wrote back in the newsroom in London where they had access to better information than we did on the scene. Even though *The Stars and Stripes* was publishing in the good-sized city of Rennes in Brittany by now, a lot of the paper was still being put together back at *The Times* in London.

An infantry division of 18,000 men can occupy or move forward along a front about three miles wide. After Saint-Lô there were fifteen to eighteen divisions in the First Army. It wasn't constant, but the First Army was a broad force moving across France. Patton's Third Army was on our south flank. The U.S. Seventh Army wasn't committed until after Paris in early September, when it took up the front between the British and our First Army. The British could have gotten to Paris as soon as we did, and the fact that Eisenhower didn't allow that to happen was apparently a sore point with Gen. Bernard Montgomery. I mean, *everyone* wanted to take Paris back from the Germans.

Montgomery had a reputation, like Patton, for being hungry for publicity but unlike Patton, Montgomery erred on the side of being too cautious. Ike could never get him moving.

At the press camp, we were routinely briefed by Col. Monk Dixon from Twelfth Army headquarters about the progress of the war around us. Each of the correspondents made his decision about where to go looking for stories based on that information.

One of hundreds of pieces of yellowing paper I have in several boxes of notes is an official SHAEF summary for August 24, 1944. It is typical of thousands like it that were handed out to the press:

In U.S. First Army area, XIX Corps moves closer to Elbeuf and is interdicting Seine crossing sites with artillery fire. In the XV Corps area, 5th Armored Div. reaches Houdebouville. In V Corps area, French 2nd Armored gets closer to city limits of Paris against strong opposition. 102nd Cavalry Group units, screening for 4th Inf. Div., reach Seine South of Paris. Ordered by Gen. Bradley to push into Paris at once, 4th Div., less one RCT, attacks toward the city from South in conjunction with French attacks from SW. ONE RCT of 4th Div. retains mission of securing crossings of Seine South of Paris.

A soldier fighting a war knows every intimate detail of the hundred yards around him but that's about all he does know. If his friend Eddie Jacobs next to him is shot, along with three other men in his platoon who were out on reconnaissance, the frontline soldier would disagree with the briefing the reporters would get. It might explain, in optimistic detail, how well everything went as our forces moved forward more than 600 yards on a broad front with relatively few casualties the previous day.

Eddie Jacobs and the three men dying in the field do not seem like "relatively few" to that frontline soldier.

While correspondents were somewhat better informed than soldiers, those of us actually on the scene never got the big picture. To that extent, we were as ignorant of how the war was going as the GIs were. When I read the lead story describing the progress of the war in *The Stars and Stripes* each morning, I felt resentful because, while I was remote from the war the editors were reading about on their news wires, I was familiar with the details of the battle that I'd watched being fought and they knew nothing of that. Neither the communiqués from SHAEF nor the lead stories in my own paper read anything like the firefights I'd seen the day before. The dead in the road had not been run over by the tracks of the Sherman tanks in any of the communiqués.

The whole business of reporting makes me suspicious of history. It is far from an exact science and by the time the story of an event or the description of a person has been set down on paper, the truth about either is changed or distorted, even by the best reporter. It's a fact that accounts for the popularity of revisionist history. The Gospels are a good example of how difficult it is to get a story straight. No two people tell it the same way.

In 1965 two young reporters, Larry Collins and Dominique Lapierre, wrote a very readable book called *Is Paris Burning?* The title is said to be the question Hitler asked Gen. Dietrich von Choltitz, in command of German forces in Paris, when Hitler realized Paris was about to be taken from him and wanted it destroyed. This is literature with great detail—too great for my skeptical nature.

I entered Paris in the early morning of August 25 with the very first troops of Gen. Jacques Philippe Leclerc's French Second Armored Division and stayed there for the next ten days, but if I were to write a book on the recapture of Paris by French and U.S. soldiers, there is hardly a detail that would be the same as those in *Is Paris Burning?* The authors did a lot of good research but added too much to the factual material they had by writing it in the style of a novelist.

There is a whole literary genre that specializes in use of synthetic particulars in books that purport to be nonfiction. While it makes books more readable, it doesn't serve history very well. The justification for the style is to say that at least people who know nothing of the event will read a somewhat fictionalized account of it and get to know something about it. I'm irritated when I read a slick book about the war, perhaps because people I interview never give me as succinct and dramatic quotations as they gave writers like Collins, Lapierre, and Cornelius Ryan. Connie practically invented the style with his classic *The Longest Day.* Maybe it's the difference between a writer and an author. I think I fall short of being an author.

The great line I recall in a war book by an author I choose to forget because he was a friend and he's dead described Eisenhower the night before the D-Day invasion:

"That evening, Ike went alone to his tent and sat dejectedly on the edge of his bunk.

" 'No,' Ike said to himself, 'I cannot do that. I WILL not do that.' "

I think of the old radio comedian Baron Munchausen who was famous for tall tales. When his friend Charley doubted him, he'd always come up with his favorite tag line:

"Vas you dere, Cholly?"

I've read the Collins and Lapierre description of how de Gaulle arrived in the little town of Rambouillet, twenty-five miles from Paris, and took over the government residence there, the Château de Rambouillet, where, according to the authors, he spent the evening reading a leather-bound volume of Molière's *Le Bourgeois Gentil-*

homme. I, too, was in Rambouillet that night, although I wouldn't be able to say whether de Gaulle read from a leather-bound or paperback copy of Molière.

(To say I was in Rambouillet with de Gaulle reminds me of the CBS News correspondent David Schoenbrun. David was a good reporter but an incorrigible name-dropper. Harry Reasoner used to talk about the time David began a conversation with him by saying "When Eisenhower and the pope were in Rome with me . . .")

I had never been to Paris, and I was unaware that I was about to experience three of the most eventful days of an eventful life. It's better if you don't know you're going to be in on history.

The following morning, August 24, we were briefed about plans for the attack to be launched to free Paris. The city was occupied by about 11,000 German soldiers, although many of those were headquarters workers, not warriors. Gen. Jacques Philippe Leclerc was to take his French Second Armored Division, comprising a force of 16,000 men and 2,000 tanks and other vehicles, into Paris from the west and cross the Seine at Port Saint-Cloud while Maj. Gen. Raymond Barton's U.S. Fourth Infantry Division, led by the 102nd Cavalry Group, was to go in from southwest of the city.

For no real reason except that most of the correspondents chose to stay with the Fourth Division, which made it more of an American story, I decided at the last minute to go with the French. I was unaware of the choices made by any of the other correspondents.

The route to Paris wasn't a drive in the country that day. There were half a dozen German pillboxes set strategically on top of hills that dominated the road and about six tanks with their 88s looking out from behind carefully camouflaged positions. I was in my jeep well back of the leading elements when suddenly there was heavy artillery fire from the front of the procession. I left my jeep on the double and raced into the field on our right in a bent-over position. I question how many soldiers ever saved themselves from death or injury by running that way but that's the way I ran. The tanks ahead of me and behind me fanned out into the field and a few of them fired, although I don't think any of them could see what turned out to be a small, concrete-and-steel bunker from which the German shells had come.

I scrambled down a small embankment hoping to get out of the line of fire and ducked down behind the stone wall that some farmer, perhaps two centuries before, had built with the rocks he'd cleared from the field. There were scrubby shrubs growing up out of it, but it was nowhere near as tall or as substantial as the hedgerows we'd left behind a month ago. The wall was somewhat closer to where the firing came from but still seemed like the safest place to be.

It was just high enough so that by slouching down I was below any enemy gunner's line of sight, and I knelt there, gasping for air after the sprint and looking apprehensively over the top of the wall toward the enemy fire. It always seems as if they must be looking in your direction. I was aware of another figure, just one, also crouched behind the wall, about fifty feet from me. He was wearing the darker green Canadian battle jacket and an officer's cap. In my rush to get out, I'd left my helmet in the jeep.

"There's another one right over the hill," the figure down the line yelled to me. "We're going to be here a while." He meant another German gun position and, although his voice was not immediately familiar to me, as I heard what he said I realized who it was.

"Jesus," I thought to myself. "Here I am behind a stone wall with Ernest Hemingway." I would have been more impressed if it hadn't been for the fiasco in the dining room the evening before.

It was a ridiculous thought to be having in the situation but the idea of being there with Hemingway blotted out for a few minutes my thoughts about getting into Paris. I was closer to the road than he was and he gradually edged closer. When he was quite near he took some papers from his pocket and told me where the other danger points were ahead of us. It was apparent that he knew what he was talking about because he'd been out scouting with his FFI friends from his base position in Rambouillet for the better part of ten days. You could tell he was having the time of his life playing war.

No matter how well informed Hemingway was, it wasn't information that interested me much. I was going with the armored column anyway. After less than half an hour Ernest went back to a half-track he was riding in with some French soldiers and I went back to my jeep. One of the good things about jeeps then was you never had to look for the keys because they didn't have keys.

By late afternoon the French Seconde Division Blindée had reached the sharply inclined cobblestone street of Saint-Cloud, and tanks and trucks were lined up from the bridge down by the Seine all the way up the hill and back for miles out of town. I don't know how many miles of road it takes to accommodate 2,000 vehicles.

The people of Saint-Cloud were wonderfully friendly to the French soldiers of the Second Armored. They could hardly have been expected to feed a division but they kept bringing out cheese and cakes and wine. I was more in need of a bathroom than something to eat and since it seemed out of order to relieve myself in the streets of such friendly people, I mustered all my French to ask one family standing around my jeep if I could use their toilet. It was my first experience with the basic French toilet that has since amazed so many American visitors. It consisted of two stone pads for placing the feet and a hole in the ground lined with a five-inch clay pipe. It occurred to me that it probably wasn't much different than doing it in the street.

Outside, I had several boxes of the little Cracker Jack–sized K rations with me and after some fun trying to understand what the French were saying and trying to make them understand what I was saying, which wasn't much, I offered two boxes of the rations to the family whose facilities I'd used. K rations were designed to be carried by combat troops but everyone used them as a matter of convenience. There were three different kinds, breakfast, dinner, and supper K rations. The high command that worked those out must have been from the South where they had dinner at noon.

The breakfast package consisted of some compressed cereal—if you can visualize compressed corn flakes—crackerlike biscuits, an egg and meat mixture in a tiny can, a fruit bar, chewing gum, some water purification tablets, and toilet paper.

Dinner consisted of a small can of compressed meat or fish—you could call it pâté but that would be giving it too much—a packet of crackers, a chocolate bar made with a lot of flour so it wouldn't melt in the heat, an envelope of powdered coffee, sugar and four cigarettes.

The supper menu wasn't much different but I remember one can in that package I could never stomach. It was canned pork with a mixture of apple and carrot. It had more biscuits, cheese, a candy bar, lemon or grape powder, sugar, a wooden spoon, cigarettes, matches, and salt tablets. It was always a mystery to me why the French, who could make a gourmet meal out of almost nothing, loved to get one of our K rations.

In exchange for the K rations, the French family brought me half a loaf of small, crusty bread, a piece of Camembert cheese, and a bottle of unlabeled red wine. I've seldom had a better dinner. It was the first time I had ever tasted wine and I still look for an unlabeled bottle of French wine when I go into a liquor store now. There are none, of course.

As it grew dark, I made some notes on a hardcover pad I carried called Reporter's Notebook. I had dozens of them back at the press camp, and they were handy because they were eight inches long and only four inches wide so you could slip one in a back pocket. My entries that night had something less than headline-news value. I still have those notebooks and the deathless notes I made in them:

"Tanks hard on cobblestones. Cobblestones hard on tanks," I'd written

"Dogs the same in Buffalo, Dayton or St. Cloud. What dogs eat?"

"Many more women than men in French houses."

Half a dozen times in the years since that night, I've returned to France and I invariably look for places I saw in August 1944. "You can't go home again" means you can't go back to where you were during any glorious time of your life. The place is almost always gone or so changed that it's disappointingly unrecognizable. Perhaps you're memory made it into something it never was. When I'm in Paris, I cross the Seine near Saint-Cloud hoping to see some remnant of that old cobblestone street winding up through town but I don't. It's gone, replaced now by a major highway with no more history behind it than a California freeway.

The on-line commander of the French tank division was Lt. Col. Pierre de Langlade. I liked the name but never saw him and when I wrote it in a story, I didn't know whether the "de" should be capitalized or not and I didn't know whether it was part of the last name or more like a middle name that could be dropped.

Word came back from the front of the column—from de Langlade, presumably—that we were going to stay on the Saint-Cloud side of the Seine for the night and proceed into Paris in the morning. My jeep was in line, sandwiched between two Sherman tanks, and I didn't dare leave it to find a comfortable place to sleep because I knew there was a possibility the column would move. There was sporadic gunfire all through the night, and at one point I thought we were starting into Paris because there was a giant fireworks display in the direction of the bridge. We never budged, though, and I got what sleep I could in the driver's seat.

The only smart reporter that night was Don Whitehead of the Associated Press. He had the good sense to ask one of the residents if he could use their telephone. He got the number for the U.S. Embassy, called, and got a caretaker who had been there all during the German occupation. The caretaker, peering out the window overlooking the Place de la Concorde, gave Whitehead a firsthand report on what things looked like as the Germans scurried around preparing to defend the city. It never occurred to any of the rest of us that anything so normal as telephone service was available and we wouldn't have thought to call the Embassy if it had.

Just before dawn, de Langlade gave the order to move out. Tank after tank coughed to a start with a throaty rumble. My God, it was exciting.

WITHIN FIFTEEN MINUTES I could see tanks crossing the bridge in front of me as the column turned down the long, gentle curve of the road running through Saint-Cloud. As we got closer, I saw, by peering around the armored car in front of me, some kind of commotion on the bridge. From half a mile away it looked like an accident. By now I could hear the grinding sound of the tanks' treads on the open steel grillwork of the bridge's surface. Then I saw "the accident." Some accident! Two German troop-carrier trucks had tried to make a run for freedom during the night. What sounded like a small firefight hadn't been a fight at all, it had been a slaughter. German soldiers caught in Paris obviously had no information about the Second Armored's position across the river and they'd comandeered the two trucks and tried to flee. They'd been met head-on by the high-velocity 75mm gun and the machine guns of the Sherman tank sitting impatiently first in line at the western end of the bridge.

The front ends of the two Wehrmacht vehicles had been destroyed and thirty German soldiers hung in grotesque positions off the sides of the trucks or lay dead on the bridge, their blood still dripping through the grillwork into the Seine. It was not a first entry into Paris that I enjoy recalling when I visit the city now.

In view of the number of correspondents who claimed, over the years, to have been the first to return to Paris after the German occupation, I should have been more careful to note my place in the column entering the city. The reporters who came into the city with the U.S. Fourth Division, down past the Notre-Dame Cathedral, ignored the fact that those of us with Leclerc entered more than an hour earlier from another direction. When I go to Paris now, I rent a car and I always come into town the way I came that day, through Saint-Cloud. It thrills me still.

Who got to a town or across a river first was a silly game the newspeople played. I'd never realized how intense the competition was for datelines. Reporters for the Associated Press, United Press, Reuters, and the International News Service would often reach a road sign on the outskirts of town but marking its technical boundary and rush back to the press camp to write their story with that dateline.

Harry Harris, the AP photographer, and Bert Brandt of Acme always called one UP reporter, Hank Gorrell, "X-ray Eyes" because they said he had a bad habit of writing stories with datelines of towns we had not quite reached when he wrote about them. Many people back home were following the war closely, just as they might have followed a pennant race in peacetime, and with the maps newspapers ran, even small towns were news when we took them.

Most of us didn't hear about the most egregious journalistic fraud concerning our entry into Paris until we were in Paris ourselves. While most of the reporters had been drinking, talking, arguing, and watching Hemingway in the dining room in Rambouillet, we discovered that the CBS correspondent Charles Collingwood had been in his room writing a detailed account of the Allied entry into Paris—an entry that had not yet taken place. Collingwood was a bright, charming, and knowledgeable reporter who had been in Paris frequently before the war and knew the city well. It wasn't difficult for him to compose a fictitious report, complete with landmark buildings and street names. Collingwood sent his story to London and exactly what happened is not clear but Ed Murrow, the CBS bureau chief, either ignored or did not know that Collingwood had put a Hold warning on his story, meaning that it should not be released until Paris had actually been retaken.

Richard C. Hottelet, another CBS correspondent totally innocent of doing anything wrong, thought the story was legitimate and read it on the air more than twelve hours before the actual event took place. Hottelet, one of the most conscientious reporters who ever lived, takes the blame for it now but he was totally blameless. It was probably true that Collingwood put a Hold on the story but that does not seem like a mitigating factor in his decision to write it before it happened.

The story might have received less attention than it did if King George had not heard the Collingwood report in his quarters at Buckingham Palace and taken it upon himself to make a formal announcement of the liberation of Paris over the BBC and offer his congratulations to Gen. Charles de Gaulle. At the time, de Gaulle was not in Paris. He was waiting in Rambouillet with the rest of us. All very embarrassing.

Ed Murrow staunchly defended Collingwood, saying that Charles had clearly marked his story Hold for Release but that the note had been lost somewhere. Murrow more than defended Collingwood. He actually got quite worked up over it in an argument he had with Colonel Dixon, the briefing officer.

Collingwood had a great many friends. I saw a lot of him after the war and we were friends and I liked him but there was always this small memory of that event that intruded on our friendship. I knew, and he knew I knew.

After the war, Charley became the last of the big-living network correspondents in the days when expense accounts were seldom questioned. Someone did ask about two round-trip tickets from Geneva, Switzerland, to London that appeared on Collingwood's books, and he explained that an ingenious combination toilet and bidet, complete with warm-water spritzer, had been installed in his London flat and the only plumbers who knew how to repair this sophisticated bathroom appurtenance lived in Geneva and he'd had them come over to attend to a problem he was having with it.

For all of that, Collingwood was one of the all-time best television reporters. He had a way of making contact with important sources wherever he went. One of his best contacts was the seriously beautiful actress Louise Albritton, whom he married. Collingwood did the kind of original reporting that has almost disappeared from television. Like all the rest of us, he was capable of being two people.

Not long past dawn on August 25, a jeep carrying Bob Reuben of Reuters, G. K. Hodenfield of *The Stars and Stripes,* and Lee Carson of INS entered Paris. Bob always claimed he was the first correspondent to enter the city by virtue of the fact that he had been careful to be the one sitting in the front seat of the jeep.

Lee Carson, an attractive, knockabout reporter for INS, had to settle for saying she was the first *woman* reporter into Paris. All the newspeople who came in with Leclerc ignored the reporters who had entered Paris with the U.S. Fourth Division and we ignored them. Each group was totally unaware of the movements of the other and, consequently, there was always an argument about which reporter actually took Paris. It was a silly debate.

Bud Kane, another *Stars and Stripes* reporter, had entered Paris with the Fourth Division and I was as unaware of where he was as he was unaware of Hodenfield and myself.

The column of vehicles I was in came down the Avenue Clichy toward the Arc de Triomphe through a friendly gauntlet of frenzied French citizens deliriously happy to be free. It was an experience that could not be duplicated. They shouted with joy, they laughed, they hugged, they kissed, they threw flowers, they held out champagne.

Down closer to the Arc de Triomphe the celebration turned ugly and I had mixed emotions about it. Several of the buildings on Avenue Foch and other main arteries leading to the Arc were occupied by German soldiers. The Germans were led out of the buildings, by French soldiers, with their hands clasped over the soft, green wool hats they all wore. They did not look like killers—although I guess killers hardly ever do. Most of them appeared to be office workers, not

This was taken late in the day on August 25th, the day we liberated Paris. It looks orderly but I watched on several occasions when angry French citizens, often women, broke through the guard of French and American soldiers to strike, with sticks and bottles, German prisoners being marched off to a compound in the Boie de Bologne.

warriors, but that fine distinction was lost on the citizens of Paris. To them they were the detested enemy under whose jackboots they had lived a sullenly submissive life for four years.

As the German prisoners were led to trucks that were to take them to detention areas, they had to pass through a gauntlet of angry French men and women. I was revolted but fascinated as I watched one burly Frenchman grasp a wine bottle by the neck and swing it with all his might over his head to bring it crashing down on the skull of a German just in front of where his hands were clasped over the crown of his head. There was a sickening thud. Blood spurted from the German's head and down his face as he sank to the ground. With a French soldier on each arm, he was half carried to the truck and thrown up into it. He may have been a corpse by then. I'd never seen hatred so deep.

French soldiers made a halfhearted attempt to protect the Germans and get them safely to the trucks but they must have felt as I felt. If it made my stomach uneasy to see human beings treated that way my head felt that nothing too bad could happen to these people. The occupational forces were spit on, punched, and hooted at as enthusiastically as the French crowds had cheered us. There were German women in uniform, too, called by Parisians "souris grise," a term of contempt meaning "gray mice," and the German women got much the same treatment as the men got, although I didn't see any of them hit with bottles.

After the French soldiers had filled several trucks with Germans, a crowd of civilians, men and women, appeared from around the corner of a small hotel where some of the Germans had lived. The crowd was pulling and shoving three Frenchwomen. I've seen so many pictures of the act since that it no longer shocks me but I was shocked at the time to see them force the women into straight-backed chairs they had brought from the building.

It was several minutes before I understood that these were not German women but Frenchwomen who had consorted with the occupying soldiers and, in so doing, had lived better during the Occupation than the average Frenchman.

One of the men had a pair of long scissors. He forced one of the women, who was sobbing and protesting her innocence, to bow her head almost to her knees and then started chopping off huge locks of her hair. He kept at it and at it until the woman was all but hairless to the scalp. There were several small patches of blood where his scissors had cut skin along with hair. All during this rough haircut both the men and the women were jeering and taunting the three women although they never struck them.

I left when they finished with the first woman and sat the second one down in the same chair. A Frenchman who had been standing by grabbed for the scissors and insisted he be allowed to take over. I understood the anger they felt for these despicable collaborators who had traded friendship and sex with the enemy for more food and probably a better place to live. I hope they got the right women because there was no such judicial nicety as a presumption of innocence.

By late morning, I had a notebook filled with what seemed to me at the time to be great details of our entry into Paris. The trick now was to get my story back to the paper in Rennes where *The Stars and Stripes* was being printed. I envisioned it being splashed all over page one the next morning. There were not yet any communications facilities set up for transmission of stories, so I had to find a way to get mine back to the paper in Rennes about 300 miles from Paris by messenger of some kind. I dismissed the idea of trying to make the drive in time myself because I didn't want to leave the scene in Paris.

I found a French army message center that had been set up to coordinate liaison with American infantry units, and the sergeant assured me he could get my copy to the press facilities at Rambouillet.

While I was at the message center, an American pilot of a Piper Cub came in. He was ferrying important documents from frontline commanders to rear-echelon headquarters. He was flying back to Rennes within the hour, and I implored him to take a copy of my story. He promised to do what he could.

Satisfied that my report would reach the paper, I tried to make my way through the bedlam in Paris streets to the Scribe Hotel near the Place de l'Opéra. We'd been told the night before in Rambouillet that press facilities would be set up there as soon as possible and that there would be rooms for us. En route to the Scribe Hotel near l'Opéra, I met Larry Lesueur of CBS and he asked if I'd do an eyewitness radio report for them. I was elated to be able to use some of the material I had and the idea of doing a network radio broadcast seemed very big-time to me. I went to the Tuileries, somewhere near where that new modern glass addition to the Louvre is now, and spoke for three minutes about what I'd seen that morning.

If anyone asks me how long I've been with CBS, I suppose, in the spirit of the claims reporters made of when they got to Paris during the war, I could answer, "Since August 25, 1944."

It was late afternoon by the time I got to the Scribe Hotel. I didn't see anyone I knew but across the street, standing on the balcony on the third floor of the gilt-edged Grand Hotel, surveying the wild scene in the street below, was Ernie Pyle.

I had become friendly with Ernie coming through Normandy, so I made my way across the crowded street and up the stairs to his room. He was still out on the balcony with several other reporters. Ernie's language was refined compared to that of many of the correspondents, but he looked down that day, as French girls threw them-

This picture, which I took the day of the Liberation, sure illustrates Ernie Pyle's remark.

selves with wild abandon at American boys, and said, "Any GI who doesn't get laid tonight is a sissy."

In 1994 I was interviewed for an ABC News documentary on the U.S. entry into Paris. The interview lasted half an hour and I knew my part of the broadcast would be only a few minutes. I've done it myself so often to so many people—chopped a half hour they gave me into a twenty-second sound bite—that you'd think I'd have known better and stopped talking but I rattled on, caught by the sound of my own voice. I told that Ernie Pyle story, never thinking that the producer would leave it in.

They did leave it in, and when the documentary was broadcast I got more than twenty complaints about having told it. I was surprised that only two of them objected to my use of "laid." The other eighteen complained about the implication of the word "sissy."

After watching the scene from Ernie's balcony, I went back across the street to be assigned one of the rooms set aside for the press at the Scribe. It was the only time I encountered any problem being a soldier instead of a civilian reporter. Maj. Jack Redding, who later became postmaster general, refused to let me stay in the hotel with the other newspeople. It was hurtful and particularly inconvenient because in the days ahead, after Press Wireless facilities were set up there, I had to come to the Scribe to use them.

I saw Redding half a dozen times after the war at events in New York and Washington, and he always said hello to me as though I was an old wartime friend. From my point of view we were acquaintances. I reserve the word "friend" for someone I like better than I liked Redding. I don't know whether he'd forgotten what he did to me but I never forgot.

My story of the entry into Paris never got to the paper. It was the single most disappointing event in my three years as a war correspondent. I don't know what happened to the copy I gave the French but I heard two days later that the Piper Cub pilot was forced down with engine trouble shortly after he took off from an open field in the Bois de Boulogne. I met him again several weeks later. He apologized for not getting my story to Rennes and tried to make amends by telling me how much he'd liked the story, which he'd read in the field where he'd slept that night. It was small consolation. I'd spent all that time, all that effort, and devoted all those emotional hours thinking about getting into Paris for the biggest story of my life—and for nothing. I blew it. I had failed. It didn't matter that there was good reason. I hadn't paid off on the biggest story of my life.

Bud Kane, another *S&S* reporter who had come in several hours after I had with elements of the Fourth Division, got his story back to the paper, and it was Bud's report that appeared in *The Stars and Stripes* the next day. I liked Bud Kane but when I picked up the paper the next day and saw his story and not mine I felt sick. It was small consolation that Hodenfield hadn't been able to get his story out either.

My failure to get my Paris story into print was not unique. None of the six reporters who parachuted into Normandy in the early morning hours of D-Day got stories out within twenty-four hours and the day was a disaster for the twelve reporters who waded into Omaha and Utah with the infantry. Each was to have been limited to a dispatch of 125 words—hardly adequate for a story of that magnitude—and there were to be radio facilities set up for their use. The Publicity and Psychological Warfare Section of the First Army even arranged to have several crates of carrier pigeons. The idea was that reporters could write stories on pieces of paper the size of cigarette wrappers which would be put into tiny canisters and attached to the birds which, on their release, would fly back across the channel, to their coops in England.

After the pain of not getting their stories out subsided, Jack Thompson of the *Chicago Tribune* and several other D–Day correspondents laughed about the pigeons. When released, they said, they were last seen headed for Germany.

Even though I wrote hundreds of stories for the paper over three years, they were only a small part of what I saw and what I should have written. The only consolation a writer has is that whatever he or she does get out and into print is magnified ten thousand or a hundred thousand times. This thought occurs to me writing for television. A televised report is almost always shorter than the same report would be in a newspaper, but those fewer words strike a vastly larger audience. It's a bad trade you make.

IF AUGUST 25, 1944, the day of the Liberation of Paris, was the most dramatic I'd ever lived through, that record didn't last long. August 26 was more dramatic.

It was as if there had never been any Germans in the city. The people of Paris wandered the streets, still smiling and kissing everyone in sight. Charles de Gaulle, the six-foot-six-inch French leader with an ego to match his height, was determined to make certain the French people gave him credit for liberating their city, and toward this end he staged a parade from the Arc de Triomphe one mile and a quarter down the broad expanse of the Champs-Élysées to the Place de la Concorde, the great square with the obelisk for its centerpiece.

The Champs is the greatest avenue in the world for a parade, and this was the greatest parade ever staged there. Recently parades in America are most often staged by some special-interest group so all the people interested are marching and no one else gives a damn and the sides of the streets are lined with curbstones and not much else. The marchers are lucky if they get a few casual observers who happen to be in the neighborhood.

On this day, everyone in Paris watched the parade.

De Gaulle was perfect. His stature fit his imperial air and, for all his pomposity, he was a great man. When people accused Eric Sevareid of being a hypochondriac, he said, "Hypochondriacs get sick, too, you know." De Gaulle may have been egotistical and pompous, but egotists can be great, too, and he was great.

On his regal head, he wore one of those pillbox French officer's hats that emphasized his size. He marched alone at the head of the assembled troops, sharing the honor with no one although it was clear that General Leclerc was one angry Frenchman because he had not been asked to march at de Gaulle's side. I guess it was Eisenhower's decision, after conference with the British, that we'd recognize de Gaulle as the de facto French leader. The organizers of the parade, taking a chance that the Germans wouldn't counterattack during the march down the Champs-Élysées, committed the entire French Second Armored Division and some token elements of several American units to the celebratory event. It was a foolish—and French—thing to do from a military standpoint but it paid off for de Gaulle and for the French people. We all need to mark some of the events in our lives with a cake, a gold watch, or a parade, and the French needed an event to mark the Liberation of Paris. They got it with unexpected fireworks.

The day of the march, with all sorts of press credentials, I parked my jeep with my back to the Seine, looking up the rue Royale toward the Madeleine. I was sandwiched in with as many as 100 tanks of the French Second Armored Division that flanked three sides of the Place de la Concorde. The tanks were made in the United States and many of them were what we called "Honeys." They were not only small and lightly armored, their weapon was the ineffective 37mm gun. You sometimes see one, placed as a decoration, outside an armory in a small town now. The gun was about as dangerous for the enemy during the war as it is now to civilians walking past the armory. I could see the solid column of soldiers as it started its march down the Champs because, among other advantages it has for a parade, the Champs from the Arc de Triomphe is all down a slight incline so it is as though the marchers were coming toward you out of a motion-picture screen.

Charles de Gaulle in the Place de la Concorde after his triumphant march down the Champs-Élysées and shortly before gunshots coming from the top of the Hôtel Crillon sprayed the area.

This was the scene in the Place de la Concorde seconds before the gunfire which sent the panic-stricken crowd diving for cover.

It isn't simply the road in the middle that's wide. The pedestrian areas and two subsidiary roads that run parallel to the center part are wide. The whole thing is 230 feet from building to building, and this day the whole avenue was packed solid with people fifty deep on both sides. I have never seen such joy with cheering French men and women—more women than men, and more young and old than middle-aged.

As the leading elements of the parade came closer, the roar of the crowd grew and I could see, alone and in front of everyone, the imposing figure of Gen. Charles de Gaulle. He was perfect for the part. MacArthur could have done it and maybe Winston Churchill, but few men in all history could have cut the figure de Gaulle did as he strode that historic mile. He didn't walk, he strode.

It was one of the few times I had my camera with me and, while they didn't seem like significant pictures at the time, they've been good snapshots to run across in some basement box over the years.

Everyone had known in advance that the parade was dangerous. We were still at war, and the Germans had an air force and terrific firepower on the ground. It was foolish to take that many men off the front line and it was personally dangerous for de Gaulle. Paris had,

nominally at least, been cleared of Germans, but who knew how many SS snipers lurked at the windows of the buildings along the Champs-Élysées or stood in the crowd, waiting for him to approach before pulling their weapons? He was an assassination waiting to happen.

De Gaulle had just entered the outer perimeter of the square that forms the Place de la Concorde. He had waved to a million people along the way, and then what everyone feared would happen, happened. There was the staccato crackle of gunfire from the direction of the massive columns of the Hôtel Crillon or, possibly, from the roof of the U.S. Embassy next to it. Everyone dove for cover. Or at least everyone I saw did. I confess that I did not watch de Gaulle at this point. I've read that he remained erect as if facing a firing squad, but he must have had more sense than that even if it is hard to imagine this proud giant scrambling under a truck.

I grabbed my helmet from the back of the jeep and hit the ground as though I'd been shot. There were more people scrambling to get under tanks and trucks than there were tanks and trucks to get under.

After the first outburst of gunfire there was silence. I rose and moved, bent double in my life-saving crouch again, to hide behind my jeep. I was so uncertain about exactly where the gunfire had come from that I didn't know for sure which side of it to crouch behind. I sometimes felt toward my faithful old jeep the way cavalrymen must have felt toward their horses when they lay behind them on the ground for protection. I hoped it wasn't going to be hit, but better it than me.

Everyone, except de Gaulle I guess, was down on the pavement when there was a second burst of gunfire. At this point every French tank in the square, several hundred I suppose, turned their guns toward the Crillon and started blasting away at its facade.

French officers in charge quickly assembled a squad of a dozen or so soldiers to run up into the Crillon and onto the roof of the U.S. Embassy to find and kill or capture the snipers. There was a lull of perhaps ten minutes. People slowly pulled themselves out from under their cars or out from behind the French tanks.

WHEN I GO to Paris every few years now, I always rent a car, and French drivers have consistently failed to appreciate my expertise behind the wheel so I'm often the object of horn blasts, rude gestures, and what I assume to be blasphemous remarks. Inasmuch as I don't understand blasphemy in French, it rolls off my back like eau off a canard. I like taking the walk from the Arc de Triomphe down the Champs to the Place de la Concorde. Standing there in the center of the Place de la Concorde on those visits, I look across the cobblestone-paved road toward the Crillon and I can see the cement-filled pockmarks on the great stone columns. I smile. It's a smug smile. I'm smiling at the thought of all the French drivers who don't think I know Paris. I know something about their city they'll never know. I was there the day they got it back.

The *New York Herald Tribune* had published the *Paris Herald* at 21 rue de Berri before the war, and when *Stars and Stripes* executives got to Paris a few days after the Liberation they found the printing plant and editorial rooms not only usable but in first-class shape. The Germans, with no use for the facilities, had not bothered it, and on September 5, just ten days after the retaking of Paris, *The Stars and Stripes* started printing there. Although the paper was still printed in London for the Air Force personnel left there, the operation in Paris became the main source of the paper for our troops. We eventually had editions in London, Paris, Rome, Nancy, Liège, Nice, and Strasbourg. The European edition ended up in Pfungstadt, Germany.

The Stars and Stripes took over most of the rooms in the Hôtel Haussmann just a few blocks from both the Arc de Triomphe and the office at 21 rue de Berri. The fellows who edited the paper lived there, and reporters like myself could always get a room when we came to town, but we spent most of our time with the troops moving toward Germany.

Jimmy Cannon, who already had a big reputation as a New York columnist, was assigned, along with Earl Mazo and Dan Regan and Jules Grad, to cover the Third Army for *The Stars and Stripes*. Jimmy had obviously been influenced as a writer by Damon Runyon, and Jimmy's writing style must have, in turn, been the model for the popular columns written for *New York Newsday* now by Jimmy Breslin. Cannon was an experienced reporter and a colorful writer, but his quotes from soldiers often sounded more like Jimmy than like soldiers, and Bud Hutton couldn't stand his work. His reports were relentlessly well written, but there was some resentment of him by others of us on the staff who had a limited appetite for what seemed like the intrusive effect of too much good writing on reporting. You don't notice the best writing.

Jimmy spent a lot of time with the Third Army but he often came back to Paris and stayed at the Haussmann. Another resident there was a prototypical dumb blonde, a former New York showgirl named Gay Orloff. She was the kind of character Jimmy would have invented for his column if he hadn't found her.

Gay hung out in the bar off the lobby of the California Hotel a few blocks from the Haussmann and almost directly across the street from the *Paris Herald* on the rue de Berri. She always attracted a crowd. She was reputed to be the girlfriend of Mafia leader Lucky Luciano. Lucky was doing twenty-five years to life in Sing Sing for various gang-related crimes of which he'd been convicted.

Cannon was late getting to the ETO and he'd been in New York within the past few months when he first met Gay at the California bar. For fun and for conversation, Cannon started regaling her with stories about having recently visited Lucky in prison. I don't recall whether he actually had or not but he went into elaborate details, none of which were true, about what Lucky's cell looked like.

"I seen him, Gay," Jimmy said. He enjoyed talking like a character out of Runyon. "I went up the river to see him, Gay."

"Pictures," Jimmy told her. "He's got pictures of you everywhere, honey. You'd be surprised you ever had so many pictures taken—the pictures of you he's got on the wall of his cell. Everywhere. He can lie flat on his back on his bunk and look up at the ceiling at you. He's got a picture of you up there looking down at him."

Cannon told her about Lucky and his plans for their life together after he got out in twenty-five years. Gay was not the kind of girl who looked forward to the day she'd be starting her life at age sixty.

Every night Cannon would add more details to the story. It went on until the morning he read the page-one story in *The Stars and Stripes* that must have made him turn ash gray. Gov. Thomas E. Dewey of New York had pardoned Luciano, and he was going to Italy where Dewey hoped Lucky's Mafia connections could bring about the release of American prisoners being held in camps there. And first,

Lucky was being allowed to stop in Paris to see his girlfriend, Jimmy's bar companion, Gay Orloff.

The idea of running into Lucky after Gay had related his concocted stories to him didn't appeal to Jimmy, and he quickly packed up his duffel bags and got back up where the Third Army was fighting the war and where he felt a lot safer.

I came in from the field and stayed in Paris for a few days once in a while, writing some longer story from notes and soaking up a little of the atmosphere of the great city. It had it even then under difficult conditions.

None of us spoke any French worth mentioning and I'm afraid we adopted the GIs' style of shouting English louder and louder until the French understood. Joe Fleming often amused himself by approaching several Frenchmen in animated conversation on the street and saying to them, "Vous parlez bien Français." They usually looked up, surprised, and said, "Merci."

The Stars and Stripes had arranged to have meals in a small restaurant on the other side of the Champs-Élysées. It was a good meeting place for those of us in the field to talk with staff members and editors stationed in Paris.

There are people who are always broke in the Army and people who always have money. It's usually a matter of attitude toward cash. Dick Wingert, our very good cartoonist who had been with the paper since it started publishing, always had money. Ben Price, our colorful picture editor, was always broke.

At lunch one day I was in Paris, Benny came up to Dick in the dining room and asked if he could borrow a hundred francs.

"What do you need it for?" Wingert asked. Dick was careful with his money and "need" was his word.

The question struck Benny wrong and he was furious. He still had some money, so he took a hundred-franc note out of his pocket, held it up to Dick's face, and, as he tore it into confetti and let it float to the floor, said, "That's what I think of your goddamn hundred francs."

The meeting place for correspondents was the small bar downstairs in the Scribe Hotel, and even though I didn't have a room in the hotel, I went there because many of the press facilities were available only there.

I stayed in Paris for a week or ten days after our entry to savor the city and write some easy stories about what Ernie Pyle called "the greatest day of national joy I ever witnessed." I was surprised that there were restaurants serving great French food, and I had the feeling I was getting a look at the real Paris, not just a wartime Paris. I wasn't but I thought I was. Like most people my age interested in writing, I'd read all about the expatriate Americans like Gertrude Stein, Alice B. Toklas, Henry Miller, and F. Scott Fitzgerald who lived there at one time or another in the 1920s, and I walked all around the Left Bank and imagined that I knew what it had been like for them as I drank coffee at the Deux Magots.

The French genius for living was evident to me even then. There are a lot of things they don't do well but the French are experts at living and enjoying what they have. The small bakeries in the little towns we destroyed and then rolled through in Normandy were not yet functioning as they once did, and my first experience with the warm, crusty, fresh-baked bread that the French pick up twice a day was in Paris.

William Saroyan, who was already famous for having refused the Pulitzer Prize in 1939 for *The Time of Your Life,* was one of the Army's best-known sergeants, attached to a film unit. Collie Small, a *Collier's* writer, was walking into the Scribe one day with Saroyan when they passed Hemingway going out. Hemingway nodded at Small but gave no indication he knew Saroyan.

"Don't you fellows know each other?" Collie said. "Ernie Hemingway, Bill Saroyan." Hemingway gave Saroyan a perfunctory handshake and kept going.

"Hadn't you ever met?" Collie asked Saroyan.

"Yes," Saroyan said, "but it was several years ago and he had a beard then so he didn't recognize me today."

V

GERMANY, AT LAST

B Y THIS TIME the infantry and armored divisions were rolling without much opposition through the Argonne Forest and places like Verdun and Reims where, just one war ago, tens of thousands of men had died in trench warfare in World War I. We had taken Luxembourg and Belgium by the middle of September and, although we were not let in on any of the arguments, reporters realized that there was a difference of opinion at SHAEF about how to go about winning the rest of the war. The split was between those generals who thought we should push one strong force forward as far and as deep into Germany as it could get and those more conservative generals who thought we should move forward on a broad front. Patton always contended that, while he had huge losses at the beginning of an offensive, losses quickly tapered off and, he claimed, he ended up losing fewer men. There's no evidence this was true.

Our children know more about World War II than I ever knew about World War I. When I was growing up, World War I had been over for about fifteen years but it seemed like ancient history. Here I am writing about a war I watched being fought fifty years ago, and it seems like yesterday. That's partly the old-fogey syndrome but I think it's also because of the technological advances we've made in preserving evidence of our past on film and tape. It hardly seems so when you see how uninformed so many kids are in the schools of this country, but it *is* easier to know more than it used to be. The kids seem to be waiting for the day they can take knowledge intravenously.

The next press camp after the Scribe Hotel in Paris, from which I had been excluded, was in Spa, Belgium, where I was finally just one of the guys again. The First Army press group took over the Portugal Hotel and it was from this base that the thirty or so correspondents operated all the way across the Rhine and into Germany.

Charley Kiley and Carl Larsen, two of the best *Stars and Stripes* editors, had been sent to Liège, Belgium, not far from Spa, to set up an edition of the paper there. After a day at the front I often returned to Liège with my story instead of going back to the press camp and sending my copy to the United States via Press Wireless. If I did it that way, my story went from Spa to New York, from New York to London, from London to Paris, and then Paris dispatched it to the other *S&S* editions, including Liège. That was the long way around, and I preferred to send it backward to London. By way of Liège and Paris.

Back in London, each major newspaper or wire service was allotted just three minutes on the single telephone cable under the Atlantic Ocean at the time. Three minutes isn't much, and some of the reporters weren't good at reading their copy quickly, either. The *Herald Tribune* came up with the most ingenious idea for getting more copy across the ocean. They hired a former vaudeville performer whose act was fast talking. He could read something like 500 words a minute, which amounted to four times average reading speed. You couldn't understand much of what he said but in New York the *Tribune* took it in on a wire recorder and then someone played it back slowly and transcribed it.

This was the kind of real *Front Page*–style journalism that I loved being in on.

THERE HAD BEEN a gradual change in the editorial thrust of *The Stars and Stripes.* It was my first experience with what seems to be the gradual decline in quality of any enterprise any of us is ever involved in. There must be some natural law that covers it. "It isn't what it used to be" is more than a trite phrase representing reverence for the past by the people who keep saying it. Too often it's true.

The paper, which in its early years in London had been edited almost exclusively by Bob Moora and Bud Hutton, was more and more under the influence of several officers in charge who joined the staff. It wasn't a dramatic change and if there was a grand plan by the Army to use the paper as a propaganda tool I didn't know of it but the paper was different. It became easier to do feature stories than stories about the progress of the war. We took most of that from the wire services because all of them kept reporters in the kind of high-level offices from which press releases emanated. No reporter could know much about the progress of the war on a front that reached all across Holland, Belgium, Luxembourg, and France. The wire services followed the official line of what happened that day in a way no single newspaper could have, and they were competent if aseptic. Quite often the editor would give a story I'd written to the rewrite man on the desk and he'd fold my material into the lead story, using information and paragraphs from it. I never minded that although it meant I didn't get a byline and I had already acquired a warm feeling for mine. I was never told to stick to features, but if you work for a newspaper and want to get your stuff in print, you see what they're printing and you write that. It was probably true, too, that by both temperament and intellect I was better equipped to write feature stories. Hard-news accounts of the action on a broad front would have been censored, and none of our soldier-readers wanted to be constantly reminded by gruesome details of battle that they might buy it the next day. "Buy it" was a euphemism they used meaning to be killed.

In Belgium, our forces drove the Germans out of Maastricht on the border of Belgium and Holland, and I followed along after the troops looking for stories. I met a captain from Saint Louis who had been left behind in Maastricht with a unit whose job it was to help restore the local government to power in the vacuum left by the German departure. The captain said he knew of a good story but he wouldn't tell me what it was. I went with him to a place a few miles outside town. He led me to a small mountain—which had been honeycombed years before with wide paths or corridors when the Dutch mined it for a substance called marl, rich in minerals, which they used as a fertilizer. The cave was no longer a mine when I went in, it was a gigantic mushroom farm. The Dutch hauled horse manure into the corridors that crisscrossed the inside of the mountain and dumped it in ten- and twelve-foot-wide strips along the sides of the tunnels and grew mushrooms in it. I'd never seen so many mushrooms or so much horse manure. People sometimes ask me why I peel mushrooms.

My guide walked me more than a quarter mile into the mountain and we finally came up on a door constructed like the entry to a bank vault. My guide gave some kind of password and we went in. I shook hands with several American officers and some Dutch citizens who seemed to be in charge, although up to this point I didn't know what they were in charge of. Through still another door, we entered a room carved out of the mountain and there, on one side, up against the hard sides of this man-made cave, was Rembrandt's *The Night Watch.* The Dutch, putting first things first, had preserved their national treasures and prevented them from being hauled back to Berlin by their German occupiers. Until that point in my life I would not have been able to tell a Rembrandt from a Van Dyck or a Rubens from a Vermeer, but if I'm ever on a quiz show and they ask contestants to identify *The Night Watch,* I'll know it.

We reached the German border during the first week of September, and it was a strange introduction to Germany for me. In the British sector, correspondents were so worried about snipers when they entered Germany that they were given Sten guns, the small British machine pistol, with which to protect themselves from snipers and random German soldiers who had escaped being killed or captured. This made those correspondents liable to execution as spies if they'd been captured, and after a few days in Germany, during which time there was not a single incident of sniper fire from village windows, reporters turned in their guns. That's what was strange. There was no danger at all to an American in a German town once our troops had gone through it.

Within fifteen minutes of our entering a German village, people were hanging white sheets or pillowcases out their windows as a sign of surrender. They didn't want any more. There wasn't a single sniper, and within fifteen minutes German kids were out in the streets going up to the crews of the tanks, which now had their hatches open, asking for candy or gum. It was the first nice thought I'd had about anyone German in months. Although, of course, they weren't Germans, they were kids. On that first day, I was talking to an American Army doctor, Capt. Jack Blinkoff, who had studied medicine in Marburg, Germany, before the war, when an elderly German man carrying a small pig under his arm approached us. He had evidently heard the American captain speaking his language. He asked a question in German, nodding toward the pig as he spoke. I didn't understand the question or Blinkoff's answer, and I couldn't figure out what the pig had to do with it.

The German walked off and I asked what that had been all about.

"He wanted to know who he had to go to for permission to kill the pig," he said.

"What did you tell him?"

Blinkoff laughed. "I said, 'Go ahead. Kill the pig.' "

On September 12 when I headed for Aachen, the first major German city we reached, I was with a column of tanks of the Third Armored Division led by Lt. Col. William B. Lovelady. The incredible First Infantry Division was to our left, still on the line since D-Day. It was always a comfort having the Big Red One in your vicinity. You knew no one was going to get at you from that direction. It was quite possibly the single best, most experienced infantry division of any war, any time. The Big Red One was so good it was heartbreaking to see it being given the toughest assignments all the time as a reward for its excellence. It happened to all the good divisions.

This was in the area of the old Siegfried Line, and even though that kind of defensive construction had been proved ineffective when the Germans walked through France's Maginot Line four years earlier, the obstacles didn't make advancing in the opposite direction any easier. The Seigfried Line had been cleverly constructed by the Germans so that it led any attacking force into one of dozens of well-set traps. Lovelady was one of the best, but that day his task force from the Third Armored took the line of least resistance through a deep gorge dotted with thousands of six-foot-tall, triangular concrete tank obstacles. The engineers out front planted TNT at the bases of what they called dragon's teeth and tipped them out of the way to make a path for the tanks and half-tracks. It was slow going but they kept moving.

We got into the tiny town of Roetgen, three and a half miles inside the German border, before Lovelady realized he'd been mouse-trapped. German antitank and self-propelled guns opened up on Lovelady's armored vehicles. In my jeep again, it seemed as though they'd opened up on me. The German 88mm, mounted on a Tiger, could cut through the armor of a Sherman tank like a knife.

Fortunately, Lovelady had more firepower even if his guns were not, individually, the match for an 88, and the U.S. armored unit overpowered the relatively few German defenders. Most of them abandoned their vehicles and fled on foot or on bicycles or on horse-back.

We were moving along with less opposition now. There were German strong points and pockets of tanks and infantry, but the German line was no longer a solid phalanx as it had been back in Normandy. Getting through a forest area was still difficult, and every stream and river posed difficulties where bridges had been destroyed—and they'd been destroyed at almost every crossing.

The appearance of the towns and cities we went through varied depending on whether they had been wiped out by fire or high explosives. Many were no longer cities or towns but areas where they had been. Whereas towns in France had been badly damaged, many towns in Germany had been obliterated.

Cities that were hit with incendiary bombs were generally in better shape after the war passed through them than those destroyed by high-explosive bombs because the bombs destroyed the water mains, the sewer system, and the electrical conduits, which fire did not.

The engineers were great at throwing down passable pontoon bridges or repairing arch or truss bridges. Their pontoon bridges were exciting to cross because they swayed and bucked in the river's current, but they were serviceable and they got us across the water. The engineers were proud of their work and exhibited their enthusiasm for the job they did by putting up a sign in front of every bridge, proclaiming its excellence and pointing out the difficulty under which it had been erected.

The sign in front of one bridge across a small stream read, in large, hand-printed letters:

YOU ARE CROSSING THIS STREAM THROUGH THE COURTESY OF
THE 342ND ENGINEER COMPANY. IT [the bridge] WAS ERECTED
IN LESS THAN 72 HOURS UNDER HEAVY ARTILLERY FIRE AND HAS
ENABLED THE FIRST DIVISION TO MOVE DEEP INTO GERMANY.

The bridge was over a body of water only a few miles from where
British and American lines met. At a point where the stream wandered
back into British territory, British engineers took a lighthearted shot at
their American counterparts. In front of their bridge, which was comparable to the Americans', they had their own sign. It read simply:

THERE IS NOTHING REMARKABLE ABOUT THIS BRIDGE.

Aachen was the first major German city we reached, and although
it was burned out, it hadn't been so heavily bombed as the industrial
cities we came to later in the Ruhr Valley. Its buildings were charred
shells but they were largely intact. Streets looked like those false-front
Hollywood sets.

American engineers never missed an opportunity to make sure everyone crossing one
of their bridges knew who built it.

The smaller cities, Düren and Jülich, on the other hand, were industrial targets and they had received the full treatment from heavy bombers. Cities are where roads go to, and because our Army traveled mostly on roads, not across open fields, the Wehrmacht was still making last-ditch efforts to defend these hub cities. Because of this, those cities were more apt to have been bombed and shelled than burned out. I was with a military-government team when we came into Düren and they couldn't find a building standing in which to open an office—and they weren't very fussy.

I talked with a lieutenant named Ron Lightner. "These people would be smart to move somewhere else," he said. "They oughtta start over if they want a city called Düren. It would be easier to start a city on dirt than to dig out this stuff."

Essen, Wuppertal, Dortmund, and Düsseldorf were similarly destroyed. Seven and a half million German civilians were killed during the war, and most of them died during air raids. You looked at these cities and wondered how the German people who had lived in them could keep from detesting Adolf Hitler, who had brought all this down on them.

The fight to get into Aachen was rough and dirty. It lasted for more than a month until we took it on October 25, and I was driving back and forth between the front and the press hotel in Spa every day. Occasionally I'd stay up front overnight with the soldiers, either because I didn't get a story and had no reason to go back or because I couldn't get out. Sometimes, I didn't dare go back through the territory we'd so recently taken because I knew there were still patches of enemy soldiers back there.

Aachen was heavily defended and the terrain was difficult. Geography plays a decisive role in a battle. A hill, a woods, a river can make all the difference, and most terrain favors the defenders. I never realized how important topography and environment were to armies until I got to France and realized what a wide variety there was in any country. Heat, cold, rain, snow, daylight, dark are huge factors. Gen. Terry Allen's Fourth Infantry Division made a reputation for itself by attacking at night. The tactic terrorized German soldiers and Allen's men got familiar with it and were so successful that they didn't want to fight any other time of day.

Anytime there are forests to be fought through, it's tough because shells hit trees and explode, splattering slivers of metal everywhere in a random and unpredictable way. You can't hide from enemy fire if you don't know where it's coming from. Tree strikes produced an effect the equivalent of a hundred snipers shooting down from high up in the trees.

Hugh Baillie, president of the United Press, and Bert Brandt, an Acme Newspictures cameraman, were returning from Aachen to the press camp in Spa one night when they hit an axle that had been left in the road after a truck was blown up. Baillie went through the windshield and was saved because he was wearing his helmet. I had a helmet but seldom wore it because I always thought it limited my view and perception of everything around me and I felt safer with it in the back of the jeep. There were plenty of times I grabbed for it and put it on for a brief period.

David Lardner, son of the famous Ring Lardner, had just joined us at the press camp, writing for *The New Yorker* magazine. David's brother, James, had been killed fighting as a volunteer with the Lincoln Brigade in Spain a few years earlier. Several of the correspondents had known James and talked about him with David his first night at the Portugal.

David went up to Aachen where the action was the next day, October 19, along with Dick Tregaskis of INS and Russell Hill of the *Herald Tribune*. On their way back that night, their jeep hit a Teller mine that had been buried in the road by the Germans for the purpose of blowing up our tanks or trucks. Russ Hill broke his arm, Tregaskis, who had already been wounded several months before, was wounded again. David Lardner was killed.

There's no question it was a dangerous war for reporters. From the First Army press camp alone, in addition to David Lardner and Bill Stringer, William Makin of the Kemsley Newspapers had been killed before we got to Paris and Peter Lawless of the *London Telegraph* was killed near Remagen.

The thirty or so reporters and photographers tended to go to the fighting units they were comfortable with and where they had established some contacts. It was the same as we'd done covering the Eighth and Ninth Air Forces in England. We often traveled in pairs. I enjoyed the company of Bill Walton of *Time* magazine, among others, and we frequently went out together.

I thought I got to know Bill well during the war. We spent one night together well behind the front lines, sleeping on the floor of a Red Cross doughnut truck being operated by Ginny Sherwood and Tatty Spaatz. I should make it clear that they weren't on the floor with us.

Having seen Bill occasionally since the war, I realize I hardly knew him at all. During one period of both their lives, he often ended up in newspaper pictures escorting Jacqueline Kennedy Onassis to some social function. Certainly, if we had been as good friends as I thought we were, he would have introduced me to her.

The Stars and Stripes had an office in New York staffed by about five people whose function was to supply the papers in London and Paris with news-of-America stories. The reporters were chosen from among those of us in Europe who had been away for more than two years. Toward the end of November 1944, I got the good news that I was being pulled off the job at the front and sent back to New York for six weeks. It was a happy day.

Part of the pleasure was the sense of relief I felt. I hadn't sensed anything you'd call battle fatigue but there was no question that I'd been living on the edge of danger most days for six months. Ira Wolfert, a friend who worked for the North American Newspaper Alliance, had pulled out a few weeks before. When he left, he wrote, "I'm bored with the war. A person gets bored with being afraid all the time. Fear is such a simple emotion that it fills your whole mind. It gets monotonous."

The thought of getting out of the line of fire, seeing Margie, and living a civilized life for two months was enormously appealing. I'd worked hard, too, if not always well or wisely, and it was nice to have someone recognize that. Colonel Llewellyan made the decision about who got to go back to New York, and I suppose I was more aware of not having produced all I should have than he was.

I was sent back on a DC-4, the big, four-engined brother of the DC-3, which, with its limited range, stopped in Goose Bay, Labrador, Reykjavik, Iceland, and Gander, Newfoundland. In idle moments on airplane trips in later years, I've tried to name places I've been and these stops helped extend the list but did little for me at the time. Each airport had a little gift shop of some kind, and I looked for something to bring home to Margie and my parents. I've often thought, on subsequent transatlantic flights, how much more satisfactory those small places, with genuine native crafts for sale, were than the so-called duty-free shops are today in which something "duty-free" often costs more than it does on the streets of the city you're leaving.

Margie had quit her job in Albany, and Carl Larsen, who was running the New York bureau, gave her a job as a secretary. During the year she spent there, she got to know a lot of my *Stars and Stripes* friends as they came and went from the ETO. Nepotism never looked so good. We rented a small third-floor walkup on East 27th Street and after work on 42nd Street walked the fifteen blocks home, stopping on the way to shop for something for dinner. I don't recall that money was much of a consideration. We didn't have enough to eat out very often, but we had all we needed and it was a treat, after the way I'd spent the last three years, to be able to walk into a store and buy what I wanted. If good things were scarce in wartime America, it was not apparent to me. Joe Hug's delicatessen, one of the good ones in a city with hundreds, was right around the corner from the apartment, and a trip to Joe's was like Christmas every day.

In New York I was surprised to find myself vaguely unsettled about missing the action. I'd been home less than two weeks when the Germans started their last serious counterattack, on December 16, in what became known as the Battle of the Bulge.

I devoured the reports every day because I was so familiar with the terrain over which the battle was being fought and because I knew my friends at the press camp were in the thick of it. It was a miserably cold and snowy winter in Europe. The press camp in Spa was perilously close to the action, and it was a strange feeling to be warm and safe in New York.

For all the pleasures of being back in New York and away from the battle, I didn't like missing one of the big stories of the war. I'd given up my front-row seat to go back into the lobby and buy a Coke during one of the most exciting parts of the show, the Battle of the Bulge.

While I sat at a desk in *The Stars and Stripes* office across from the *Daily News* on 42nd Street, word came tapping in over the AP wire just before Christmas that the press camp and its occupants had been forced to run from their quarters in the Portugal Hotel as the Germans advanced toward it with a force of twenty-four divisions they managed to get together for one last, desperate counteroffensive in the Ardennes.

I could tell, even at a distance, that this was no skirmish to be dismissed as nothing more than the place where an American general, Anthony McAuliffe, answered "Nuts!" when asked by the Germans to surrender his encircled troops. For those under the age of fifty, "nuts" was a slang term we used in that context to mean roughly "the hell with you."

It never rang true to my ear but I never found out what McAuliffe actually did say. *The Stars and Stripes* reported that the French were puzzled about why a general would yell "*Noix!*" at the enemy.

The best assignment I got while I was home was going to Washington where I got credentials that admitted me to the White House press conference of Franklin Delano Roosevelt.

It's easy to forget that there were people who hated FDR as vehemently as others liked him. My father disliked him intensely, although I never knew why. Dad was a good guy but he enjoyed hating things and people sometimes. He wasn't the only one who didn't like Roosevelt, though. After they started making dimes with Roosevelt's picture on them, we knew a woman who threw them on the ground when she was handed one as change.

"I won't have that man's picture in my pocket," she liked to say.

At the White House I was determined to ask a question about the exchange rate between francs and dollars that was unfavorable to GIs. I didn't know what I was talking about, and fortunately I never got the opportunity to ask.

After the press conference ended, I met the president and he asked *me* two questions.

"How are things going over there?" and "Is everyone ready to come home?" Not really penetrating questions and I gave two non-answers, but I was excited about having met and shaken hands with Franklin Delano Roosevelt.

The other story I covered while I was home was the paternity suit brought against Charlie Chaplin by twenty-three-year-old Joan Berry, who charged that the fifty-nine-year-old comedian was the father of her child.

In court, her lawyer said that she was "an attractive young girl of limited intelligence" and he said Chaplin was "a runt of a Svengali with the instincts of a young bull."

The big story one day was a witness who testified that Chaplin had spent two hours in the girl's bedroom. When Chaplin's lawyer denied anything went on, her lawyer said, "What was he doing for two hours? Painting her toenails red?"

It was the kind of trial America loves, and it was fun to write, but it seemed terribly wrong to me that the guys were over there, surrounded, cold, and getting killed while Chaplin was driving them off the front page.

The story had a way stories have of getting better all the time. One day after a tough session in court, Chaplin went to his Hollywood home and found he didn't have his keys. In a rage, the comedian kicked in his plate-glass front door to get in and, in the process, slashed his leg to the bone and had to spend three days in the hospital and two weeks in a wheelchair. There were a hundred delicious elements to the tawdry story.

All my experience in journalism was writing about the war, but gradually I caught on to what *The Stars and Stripes* wanted from New York. We were providing a touch of life at home as the soldiers overseas liked to remember it. In the stories we sent, waters rose and flooded Ohio; crack trains crashed, killing nineteen, injuring thirty; the nude bodies of beautiful models were found murdered in their swank Park Avenue apartments.

I rewrote a lot of warm, fuzzy homefront stories taken off the AP, UP, INS and Reuters wires or lifted from one of several dozen local newspapers we got from around the United States. Rewrite was a new art for me to learn, although it wasn't hard work because many of the stories had a familiar ring to them:

• A twelve-year-old boy in Des Moines wrote a postcard to the king of England thanking him for how well the British were treating his older brother, who was stationed there, and the boy got an answer from the king. In newspaper stories, no twelve-year-old boy's plaintive letter to a king, a queen, or a president ever goes unanswered.

▪ Two young people went to the famous Stork Club in New York and afterward, for a lark, went to the Bronx Zoo. The socially prominent young woman waved a white handkerchief at a bear in its cage. The bear reached out with his paw, grabbed the girl, and bit off her right arm at the shoulder.

▪ The mother of an infant with a rare disease in England wrote a letter to her friend in the United States saying her infant son needed bananas, if anyone could send some.

▪ The Electrolux Corporation was given permission to start making vacuum cleaners again after a wartime prohibition.

▪ One story I liked and kept a copy of all these years was about names in the Army. In 1944 there were 72,000 Smiths, 1 percent of all the soldiers in the Army, 48,500 Johnsons, 39,000 Browns, 33,600 Millers, 31,000 Davises and Joneses, and a lot of Wilsons, Halls, Andersons, Martins, and Lewises. You couldn't beat a story like that for attracting soldier readers to *The Stars and Stripes.* Everyone with one of those names was interested, and everyone who knew anyone with one of those names was interested.

▪ Two captains and a major from Chicago were trying to keep from being shipped overseas shortly after they were married. A chaplain tried to help them by quoting the Bible to authorities.

"When a man hath taken a new wife, he shall not go out to war . . . but he shall be free at home for one year and shall cheer up his wife which he hath taken."

It didn't work.

▪ Siamese twins were born to the widowed mother of a soldier killed on a bombing raid on Germany.

▪ Otto Huttenen, an American soldier who was blinded and lost his left hand in North Africa, married a nurse at the British hospital where he was taken and brought her back to Warren, Ohio, just before all travel from the British Isles was stopped.

▪ Doctor tells Roosevelt to take it easy.

▪ Americans are asked to eat more eggs because of an egg glut. Farmers are being paid fifteen cents a dozen for eggs.

▪ The price of a stamp is raised to six cents.

- Comedian Red Skelton is drafted.
- Safecrackers get away with ration coupons for 2,000 tires, 4,500 pairs of shoes, and 100,000 gallons of gas.
- Further training of women pilots is stirring a battle here at home.
- A priest named James Gillis told the League of Catholic Women that "Hollywood weddings, Reno divorces, jitterbugging and obscene literature are driving civilization back to the jungle."
- *Random Harvest* was voted the best film of 1944. *For Whom the Bell Tolls* was second best.
- American cheese, 490,000 tons of it, is being shipped to England.
- A separate Negro draft quota is upheld by the U.S. Circuit Court. It is ruled not discriminatory.
- Coach Lou Little of Columbia says pro football is ruining the college game.
- Max Baer, Billy Conn, and Jim Braddock all want to fight Joe Louis for the heavyweight championship. (That was back in the days when everyone knew the name of the heavyweight champion.)
- The University of Arkansas basketball team beats City College of New York 39–37.
- A Utah man, seventy, is charged with kidnapping a girl, fourteen.
- A mailman in Kansas City was charged with having thrown away huge amounts of mail over a two-year period. Authorities found a garage he'd been using filled with it. In court the mailman said he only threw away second- and third-class mail.
- Three boys on a raft were saved at the last second from going over Niagara Falls.

Margie and I took the train 150 miles up the Hudson River to Albany to visit my parents and hers, and I recall feeling an emotion similar to loneliness because of all the action I was missing in Germany. I looked out the train window at the magnificent Hudson River and thought how like the Rhine it was in many ways. My mind was more on the Rhine than the Hudson. When I was fourteen or fifteen, one of the biggest events of the summer on Lake George was the boat races at Ticonderoga, twenty miles north of us on the lake. My father was away and our neighbor, Bert Robinson, had a big mahogany speedboat and he was going to the races but he had five children of his own and, with other friends, the boat was full and I wasn't invited. I wandered around most of the day with tears in my eyes. Events big and small in our lives evoke the same emotion out of proportion to their importance. The extent to which we are moved doesn't seem to be in relation to the significance of the event. I had the same empty feeling about being away from the war as I had when I missed the Ticonderoga boat races.

In Albany I met E. Howard Hunt, an author who had written several books, and, while we never knew each other well, I always cherished the meeting because it was Hunt who, as a member of President Nixon's team, led the break-in at the Watergate complex in Washington some thirty years later. He went to prison for several years and, on the occasion of his release, and because we had met during the war, I received an invitation from some of his Albany friends to attend a "coming out party." I didn't go.

Considering how clearly some things stand out in your mind in specific detail, it's surprising how frequently weeks of your life disappear into some memoryless limbo. I don't remember much more about that sojourn in New York. We ate and drank in a German café on the corner of Third Avenue and 42nd Street called Volk's, although both German and Japanese restaurants were trying to make people forget their heritage.

We often went to Costello's, a popular newspaper hangout on Third Avenue. After the war, it was at Costello's where a group of liberal writers I'd known during the war set out to try to help Henry Wallace get elected president. One of the instigators was a man named Marc Blitstein who had written a successful Broadway play called *The Cradle Will Rock*. Saul Leavitt, a very capable writer for *YANK*, was part of the group, and I didn't realize until more than a year after Wallace had been defeated that several people in the group that met in Costello's were communists. I was more amused than frightened, although several congressmen, part of the House Un-American Activities Committee, were already after anyone suspected of being a communist with as much fervor as Sen. Joseph McCarthy was ten years later.

I was interested in socialism and communism. In The Albany Academy, I had read a book about John Reed, the Harvard graduate who had gone to Moscow and become an important factor in the communist revolution there in 1919. Reed wrote the good book *Ten Days That Shook the World* and, just as I had thought I might be a conscientious objector in 1941, in 1945 I thought I might be a communist or, at least, a socialist.

Fortunately, I was never certain enough of what I believed to join an organization. I stayed clear of the crowd at Costello's while I was home and then later when I came home after the war.

On February 1 I left New York and flew back to Paris, this time by way of Reykjavik and Prestwick, Scotland.

Like Norway, Scotland is a country no one dislikes. Even during the war Prestwick had a duty-free shop that was one of the best. I bought shortcake in a plaid tin box—everything was plaid—plaid neckties, a knit tam-o'-shanter, and smoked salmon. The label on the salmon was plaid. We lost something when they started making airplanes that could make the flights from New York to London or Paris without stopping in Reykjavik, Shannon, or Prestwick.

My interest in duty-free shopping in those stopovers was a brief diversion. I was itching to get back to my war.

BY THE TIME I got back, all the speculation in the press about whether General McAuliffe had actually said "Nuts!" or something stronger had subsided and the German counterattack was a thing of the past. The press headquarters was back at the Portugal Hotel in Spa and all was right with the world. For me, it was as if the Bulge had never happened. One of my friends, Jack Frankish of United Press, was missing because he'd been killed two days before Christmas near Malmédy.

The 106th Infantry Division was all but wiped out during the Battle of the Bulge. The longer an infantryman was in the line, the better his chance of survival became because of his experience. The green 106th had come up to replace the veteran Second Infantry Division shortly before I left for home, early in December, in an area called by a name I always liked, the Schnee Eifel. I had been spending a few days with the Second Division. The replacement process took a couple of days in order to make certain that an area was never left defenseless. Elements of the 106th had come up on the Second Division's right flank.

The word for veteran GIs who'd been on the line for months was "cool." They were cool under fire. They didn't panic. They trusted the guard detachments assigned to all-night duty and slept soundly on the cold ground unless there was some action that called for them, in which case they woke up and fought.

Part of being cool in infantry warfare meant not only watching but listening. Sounds were important, and experienced old soldiers (who might have been as old as twenty-two) were familiar with every sound made at war. They could distinguish between the sounds of six different rifles and dozens of hand and machine guns. They could differentiate the sound of a General Motors truck from any German troop carrier, and the roar of a Wehrmacht Tiger sounded nothing like a U.S. Sherman to them.

Old soldiers let the mortars do a lot of work for them, too. If they heard Germans in front of them or trying to move up on them, they didn't turn and run. They called for the men just behind them with the mortars to lob some shells in the direction of the enemy. A mortar shell could be thrown as short a distance as 100 feet by increasing its trajectory to almost straight up. It then came almost straight down, too, and made an indescribably flat noise, something like slapping hard ground with a long, thin board.

On the night I spent with the Second, a reconnaissance squad from a division on its flank that had been on the line only three days came up on a small German weapons dump and picked up several dozen Schmeissers, the handy-dandy little German machine pistol that everyone loved. The Schmeisser stood out as a weapon because where the gunstock would have been on an ordinary machine gun or rifle there was nothing but an empty, long triangle framed by a half-inch steel rod bent to surround the opening and form a sort-of handle. It looked broken but it was a light, deadly efficient, fast-firing little weapon with no frills.

In the middle of the night, there was some movement in front of the 106th coming from the direction of the enemy. Several soldiers, in the line for the first time and not yet familiar with the sounds of war, reacted by firing into the night with their newly acquired Schmeissers. They might as well have been seen walking toward the Second Division in Wehrmacht uniforms. Over to their left, Second Division veterans, standing watch for the night, were not alarmed. They calmly did what they had done a hundred times before. They estimated the direction and distance of the sound of those German guns and dropped a dozen rounds of mortar fire on top of them.

Half a dozen soldiers of that green division were killed before word reached Second Division headquarters that it was firing on friends.

It was easy to make a dumb mistake during the war. Ken Koyen, another of the capable public-relations officers, represented the Fourth Armored Division, Patton's principal weapon that did an outstanding job getting through to the 101st Airborne when it was trapped near Bastogne. At about that same time, Bob Capa of *Life* magazine, the war's best-known photographer, showed up looking for help from Ken. The PRO could usually tell a reporter where to get some action without getting killed.

On this day that Capa approached Ken, he was wearing a fur coat he'd appropriated from a Wehrmacht supply dump. The effect wasn't much different from that of the Schmeissers the 106th had come upon. If there were fashions in war, that coat would have been featured in the fashion section of the Sunday paper style sections that week because every American soldier wanted one. The fur was on the inside, the skin on the outside. They were not only warm but very trendy, and Capa dug trendy.

Koyen warned Capa that the front was no place for an American to be wearing any article of German army clothing but Capa couldn't be pursuaded to take it off. Shortly after that, Capa appeared again, a little the worse for wear this time, and told Koyen he'd been fired at by American troops. He took off the coat.

Capa was Hungarian by birth and, while he was a brilliant photographer and a linguist, the joke about him among the other reporters was that he spoke seven languages—all badly. One British writer with a Hungarian background said Capa was hard to understand in Hungarian.

Capa had a good sense of humor in any language. I recall his advice to amateur photographers like myself: "If your pictures aren't any good, you weren't close enough."

On one occasion when a large number of Germans, including several generals, were surrendering wholesale, one of the high-ranking Wehrmacht officers objected to having his picture taken. He was a defeated general, and you could understand why he objected. The highest-ranking American officer got in on the argument the German was making on grounds that the Geneva convention prohibited that sort of picture taking.

Capa and the American officer talked it over and the officer finally told the general that he felt our tradition of freedom of the press took precedence over any Geneva convention position on this sort of thing.

The general, who spoke broken English, said, "I am tired all this talk freedom of press."

Capa laughed. "I'm tired taking pictures all these defeated German generals."

EVERY TIME WE thought the Germans were beaten, as we thought when the Battle of the Bulge ended, we were faced with another major obstacle. The next was the Rhine River. By the end of January, with that last-gasp German offensive out of the way, SHAEF was directing all its effort toward getting to and across the Rhine. The engineers were all geared up for throwing dozens of emergency pontoon bridges across it. No one knew for sure where we'd be able to do it but it was assumed it would be done either by Montgomery in the British sector or by our own Seventh Army.

There were engineers with every outfit who were prepared to construct pontoon bridges in a few hours, but with concentrations of German infantry and artillery dug in all up and down the east bank of the Rhine with guns pointed across the river, it seemed to those who had to do it as though it might be another bloody D-Day landing.

The German city of Cologne is on the west bank of the Rhine, our side then. It was a huge transportation center with a major bridge across the river. The Cologne cathedral sat majestically about a hundred yards from one end of the bridge. Still does. I say "still does" because amid the rubble of the bombing that all but destroyed Cologne, the cathedral was scarcely damaged. It was strikingly similar to what happened to St. Paul's Cathedral in London. It too emerged virtually unscathed after three years of bombing and German V1 and V2 pilotless buzz-bomb attacks in the area around Ludgate Circus, which was heavily damaged.

The British had contrary explanations for why St. Paul's and the Cologne cathedral were saved from destruction. They considered St. Paul's to have been impervious to German bombs for four years because of the intervening hand of God. They claimed that the Cologne cathedral went untouched because of the accuracy of RAF bombers and a civilized decision on the part of the Royal Air Force Bomber Command to spare it.

Through the last week of February and early March, I'd been traveling during the day with the Third Armored again as it fought its way toward Cologne. On March 6, I followed the tanks to a point well inside the city limits but still a distance from its center. It became apparent we weren't going in that night, and I decided to head back to Liège and spend the night there instead of at the press camp in Spa. The next day I drove back toward Cologne because its fall was imminent and taking any big city on the Rhine was a major news story. The very name had a cachet about it.

I was careful to stay well behind the lead tank in the column of tanks and I wasn't much worried. It didn't seem likely that there were any snipers left in the buildings on either side of the street. It would have been suicide for any lone gunman to shoot at a tank commander standing up to his armpits out of the top turret of his Sherman or even at a couple of unarmed newsmen. I could see the spires of the cathedral over the tanks in front of me and the pace was so slow that I drove my jeep up on the sidewalk and left it because it was less frustrating to walk. Under those circumstances, jeeps did not get stolen.

While I was traveling alone, there were other newsmen in the area, and during one of the long waits several of them who were familiar with the fame of the Hotel Excelsior's wine cellar went into the once-grand lobby and made their way down three flights of stairs to one of the best wine cellars ever assembled in Europe. It was the greatest collection of wine and booze anyone had seen since the discovery of that mother lode in the railroad tunnel outside Cherbourg. While I appreciated everyone's interest in the liquor, I didn't bother to take any because it didn't interest me.

Eventually the column resumed moving. As the lead tank reached the street in front of the cathedral, which ran parallel to the river, several blocks inland from it, there was the sickeningly unmistakable thud of a shell's impact on the lightly armored side of a Sherman tank. The surprise shot came from a Tiger sitting no more than 100 yards north of the cathedral. Who knows how long it had been sitting there near the Rhine, waiting for that first American tank to show its nose as it pulled into the intersection.

I ran for a doorway and, peering out, saw the top turret pop open. After a second, acrid black smoke started belching from it in spasmodic puffs as though some mechanical monster was trying to blow smoke rings. Two crewman pulled themselves out and fell to the street choking. A third man pulled himself up to his armpits and could get no further.

The men on the ground climbed back up to the turret and, as I ran toward the tank, lifted and dragged the third man to the ground. It was the tank commander, a major, minus his left leg. There was nothing but a ragged pant leg, wet with blood where his leg had been. There were no medics near us. One of the soldiers who had pulled the major from the tank took off his shirt, and I held the major's leg just above where his knee had been while the soldier made a tourniquet out of the sleeve. The major stared at me as though he was blind, but he was alive. Alive for the last minutes of his life. I don't think the soldier had ever applied a tourniquet before but it wouldn't have mattered. Three of us lifted the major to a protected place by a doorway and put him down. He died. I had never been present before at the moment someone died. I didn't know whether to cry or throw up.

There was frantic action in the tanks to the rear as one of the commanders organized a bazooka team to get down to the river from another direction and take out the Tiger waiting at right angles to our column. Within minutes we heard the sound of a bazooka hitting metal and a puff of dark smoke rose above the broken buildings down near the river. It was the direction from which the fire had come that had taken out our lead tank—and the major's leg and life with it.

When we reached the cathedral half an hour later, we found German demolition crews had somehow broken the bridge immediately behind it in a way that made it look as if it had been stomped on in its middle by the foot of a giant. The two ends of the bridge sloped gently down toward the water in the middle of the Rhine. It was useless for any kind of transportation, but with care soldiers could thread their way across it by using its fallen trusses as catwalks.

I had a camera with me and took pictures that still turn up every once in a while. I cannot say why I didn't carry a camera everywhere and use it. I regret it because the war was one great photo op after another. The pictures I took of the cathedral and the bridge at Cologne are not so arty as my St. Paul's Cathedral pictures but they're among the few action pictures I have. They show American soldiers scrambling down one side into the middle where the bridge rested in the water and then up the other side to the east bank of the Rhine.

WITHIN AN HOUR of that episode other correspondents had moved in on the story and also on the wine cellar in the Excelsior Hotel. It was shortly after one o'clock when I heard from a company headquarters radioman that U.S. troops were crossing the Rhine twenty miles down the river at Remagen.

The Ludendorff Bridge at Remagen had been discovered intact and crossed by elements of the Ninth Armored Division on that same day, March 7. It was the single greatest stroke of luck of the war because it saved thousands of American lives that would have been lost in any opposed crossing of that wide river.

The Ludendorff Bridge at Remagen was one of the great railroad bridges of Europe, built during World War I. German engineers had set charges designed to destroy it, but the charges were never detonated and U.S. engineers were able to deactivate the explosive bundles that had been tied to key structural places on the steelwork of the bridge. It was one of a great many good jobs done by the engineers.

It took me more than an hour to drive the twenty miles but when I got there German artillery shells were still plopping into the river all around the bridge. It was an event in progress and the Ninth Armored Division was making every effort to take full advantage of the facility by jamming across as many men and vehicles as possible. It looked like the George Washington Bridge across the Hudson at rush hour.

The public-relations officer for the Ninth Armored Division was Charles Gillett, who ended up after the war a fixture in New York City as head of its Hotels and Convention Bureau. He was a good help that day, arranging for me to actually get across the bridge. There was just one other newsman there that day, Howard Cowan of the AP. We had an exciting time together crossing the railroad bridge while German shells rained into the Rhine all around us. The German artillerymen were firing blind from behind the hills on the other side of the river, but there was always a chance they'd get lucky and we were plenty nervous running across the bridge, stepping on the wooden ties with six-inch gaps between them.

Finding a bridge that was intact across the Rhine was better luck than the most optimistic SHAEF commanders had expected. It enabled them to push thousands of U.S. soldiers across the river in a few hours and, as soon as that happened, and as soon as the Germans knew it had happened, German lines all up and down the river were threatened with being attacked from their flanks or even from behind. There was nothing for them to do but retreat and try to regroup further back.

I was excited about the story I had. The crossing of the Rhine was one of the most important events of the war and Howard Cowan and I had it exclusively. I wrote my story and looked for a courier going in the direction of Paris who'd take it back to the paper for me and had better luck than I'd had on the entry into Paris.

At the west end of the bridge, I interviewed a lieutenant in the engineers named Marcus Hoffman who was working to make the railroad bridge better for wheeled vehicles. In the course of the interview, he brought out a camera and said he'd taken what he hoped were some good action pictures of the very first men to cross.

I implored him to give me the roll so I could get it back to Paris and have our lab develop his pictures so we could get it into the paper the following day. I knew if they were any good at all the editors would use them with my story. He was reluctant to turn the roll over to me but I finally convinced him I was trustworthy and that I would get his pictures back to him.

I was able to get my story to Paris and it ran the following day, along with Marcus Hoffman's pictures. Now the bad news that I write reluctantly: I never got the pictures back to Marcus Hoffman.

It has been a lifelong source of embarrassment for me, and I've made several attempts to find him but cannot. Marcus Hoffman, where are you?

Because it was obviously of prime importance to Hitler, the Luftwaffe kept diving in at the bridge in an attempt to take it down. The engineers, anticipating the eventual success of the German artillery and air force, threw up a long pontoon bridge 200 yards upstream from it that ran from shore to shore, pushed by the flow of the river into a long, graceful loop. I recall crossing it twice, both times with Gordon Gaskill, who was writing for a magazine called the *American*. Gordon was tall and rangy with long legs, and by the time we reached the opposite end he was twenty yards ahead of me and gasping as shells continued to drop into the Rhine around us. They fell like huge raindrops into still water, exploding, for reasons I don't understand, as they struck the water.

The second day I wrote a story about the great parade of infantry, tanks, and armor crossing the Ludendorff Bridge. It was exciting to be in on so dramatic an event. The bridge eventually did collapse, but the fact that men were still crossing the Rhine at Remagen on the pontoon bridge the engineers had built apparently caused some confusion. A good reporter named Marshall Yarrow reported that the Ludendorff Bridge had been rebuilt. He was not there.

Well, I was standing within a hundred yards of the bridge when I read his story, and I was angry and a little worried that my editors would think I didn't know what I was talking about. I found Charley Gillett and asked him to please find a way to send a highest-priority message over military lines to the paper. My message was necessarily brief but to the point, and it got through. *The Stars and Stripes* ran it along with a dramatic photo of the bridge, and an excerpt from Yarrow's dispatch. By the evening of March 7, 100 Americans, including Howard Cowan and me, had crossed the bridge under heavy fire from German artillery, which still had an observation point on a promontory further down the river. I heard from a major who was a history buff that no invader had crossed the Rhine since

She's Up:

PARIS, March 19.—A magnificent job by First Army engineers has already restored the Ludendorff Bridge, leading into the Remagen bridgehead, after its collapse. It was announced here today that traffic is expected to be resumed "very soon."—*Marshal Yarrow, Reuter special correspondent.*

She's Down:

AT SITE OF FALLEN LUDENDORFF BRIDGE, March 19.—If the Ludendorff Bridge is "already restored" and ready for use, I'll swim the Rhine with the Reuter special correspondent who wrote the story, on my back.—*Andy Rooney, Stars and Stripes Staff Writer.*

This is how the Ludendorff Bridge at Remagen, Germany, looked when an Army Signal Corps photographer reached the site shortly after the bridge collapsed last Saturday. The span was weakened by constant shelling and heavy traffic.—*(Other Pictures on Page 3.)*

Napoleon in 1805, and I also remember editing that information out of the story I wrote before I sent it because I didn't think it was anything GIs reading my story would know or care about.

Our crossing the Rhine at Remagen shook the German high command and Hitler fired von Rundstedt because of it. Von Rundstedt was one of the best German generals and he had nothing to do with the failure to take down the Ludendorff Bridge before we crossed it but logic was not a Hitler strong point.

There's a small mountain above the Ludendorff Bridge, looking across the Rhine, west toward Remagen. I remember it well because when the first company across the bridge tried to get to the top of the hill to secure that important gun location, the men found almost no opposition from the top. Suddenly they were taking fire from behind and to the right, down the Rhine, from where they were climbing. It was a strange kind of action but they couldn't stop, turn back, and go down the mountain so they kept going up until they were out of range.

I never saw it in 1945 but when I returned many years later I climbed the promontory again and discovered a brass plaque in a small park up there. It was riveted to a boulder and was put there to honor Count Ferdinand von Zeppelin. It had been from that position that he had launched the first lighter-than-air airship. There was no plaque for the American who led his men up the hill.

Howard was another wartime friend with whom I reunited many years later under markedly different circumstances.

We hadn't seen each other in more than thirty years but I'd heard he'd moved from Tulsa, Oklahoma, where he worked in the publications division of an oil company, to Boothbay Harbor, Maine, where he was running the local paper, the *Boothbay Register.* In 1988, we were sailing down the Maine coast with Walter and Betsy Cronkite on their comfortable, forty-eight-foot sailboat, *Wyntje,* when a storm loomed and we pulled into Boothbay Harbor.

We wanted to get a car and look around but there was no rental agency so, recalling that Howard lived there, we phoned and said we'd like to see him. We also said we'd like to borrow a car. Old AP reporters are not famous for being wealthy and we had no idea what Howard's situation was but within minutes he showed up driving a

Mercedes and leading a man in his employ who was driving another. Howard insisted we come to their house and have dinner.

We took the borrowed car, put on clean clothes but still sailing clothes, and headed for the Cowans' house, following directions Howard had given us. We arrived at what turned out to be one of the grand homes in all of Maine, situated on a promontory over the Atlantic, and were greeted by Howard and his charming and mildly daffy wife, Marylouise.

We were ushered into the house and walked down a long hallway whose walls were hung with paintings. We were slow to recognize that the paintings, all originals, were done by three generations of Wyeths. The hall was a museum in itself and we knew then that Howard was not living on an AP pension. He had left the AP and worked in public relations for an oil company in Tulsa, and after his wife died he had married Marylouise, the widow of the founder of the Radio Shack chain of electronic stores.

On March 28, 1945, I made the long drive from Bad Wildungen up to where the Third Armored Division was approaching Paderborn. The name Paderborn had a special mystique about it because it's where Werner von Braun and his team of scientists and engineers had made the V1 and V2 self-propelled bombs that hit London. I was familiar with the Third Armored Division because of my experience with them at Cologne and I decided to go up there alone. It was good to have another reporter along sometimes, but there were journalistic advantages to being alone. If I felt like stopping and staring, I could stop and stare. I found out where Third Armored was and caught up with them on their move north, near the Netherlands. It was a long drive under difficult conditions. The roads were an obstacle course with the walls of stone homes falling into the streets of the small towns where they'd been hit by shells, overturned trucks, burned-out tanks, and the dead bodies of men and animals everywhere.

By the time I had a story, it was late afternoon. The tank columns had moved so fast through the countryside and gone through so many tiny villages that they couldn't afford to leave behind detachments in all of them to secure the areas. I started back for the press camp and I knew it was going to be a rough, lonesome ride. I was careening along a narrow, paved road vaguely nervous about the lowering sky and concerned about whether I was going to make it back before dark. I knew there had to be small groups of German soldiers still roaming the countryside.

Suddenly I saw a uniformed figure a few hundred yards ahead of me running across the field toward the road. He had both hands over his head as he ran but he clutched a rifle in one of them. It was apparent that he was going to intercept me on the road but there was nothing for me to do but keep going. There was no place to turn, and by this time I was so close that my back would have been an easy target for him if I'd tried to head in the other direction.

With my heart in my throat, I screeched to a stop in a cloud of dirt that covered the road. It was instantly apparent to me that he didn't want to kill me. He was as scared as I was and only wanted to surrender. I don't know why he hadn't dropped his rifle. With no German at all at my command, I indicated, in as stern and authoritative way as I could with nothing but gestures, that he should drop his rifle in the ditch. He did. I told him to climb into the jeep next to me. He did.

As I shifted into low, I looked over at him and noticed he still had a pistol strapped to his side. This was going to be the final test of whether he wanted peace or war with me. Again, with all the authority I could fake, I indicated that he should hand me the pistol.

All he had to do to have a jeep of his own and an American uniform to wear—with a bullet hole in it—would have been to shoot me. My mother told me never to pick up hitchhikers.

He didn't shoot me. Without a pause he reached down, took the gun out of its holster, and handed it to me muzzle first. It was obvious he'd never had much training on how to handle a gun safely. He could have hurt me. It was the first time I'd felt any sympathy for a German soldier. I thought of how many like him had been shot and left to turn green in the ditch. He seemed like a decent man and I knew that, while he might escape with his life now, he faced some unpleasant times ahead as a prisoner.

I took him to the nearest prison compound more than ten miles from where I picked him up. He put his hands up and clasped them behind his head and then turned to me. He took one hand down, reached across the jeep, and extended it for a handshake. It seems unkind now that I didn't shake it.

The pistol, a handsome Walthour, had—still has, if you want honesty here—a beautiful, nut-brown walnut handle. My son Brian and I took it up in the woods behind the house years ago. We each fired it once. The German soldier I "captured" may never have fired it, so that gun hasn't had an active life. I know I ought to throw it out or turn it in before someone gets hurt with it, but how many pistols do you have that were handed over in person by a German soldier surrendering to you?

Maj. Gen. Maurice Rose, who had been with the Second Armored at Saint-Lô, was now the commander of the Third Armored and he may have been the best tank commander of the war. He was a leader down where they fight.

Not all great generals were recognized. Maurice Rose was a great one and had a good reputation among the people who knew what was going on, but his name was not in the headlines as Patton's so often was. Rose led from the front of his armored division.

I was still alone when I joined Rose's Third Armored near Paderborn on March 29. My intention was to stay with the division until I had a story and then decide whether to go back or stay overnight. In view of the harrowing experience I'd had the day before, I was inclined to stay, so I brought along a bedroll.

There were tanks in front of me and tanks behind me as we traveled at ten to fifteen miles an hour along a two-lane road through a heavily wooded area. In daylight it didn't seem dangerous. Occasionally the column would stop and I'd hear gunfire from up front, but it was never long before we started to move again. Nowhere along the route of the war from the beaches to Berlin did German soldiers who had been overrun hide and continue firing on stragglers in the rear elements of our divisions. I never understood why. Once German soldiers were overrun, it was as if they considered that we had won and the game was over. They put down their guns, lifted their hands over their heads, and looked for someone they could surrender to. Snipers were rare so I felt relatively safe in the tank column during the day as we went through the narrow streets of small villages. I hadn't considered the night.

It got dark early in Germany in the last days of March, and in the afternoon that day it became apparent to me that, with tanks occupying one lane of the two-lane road and supply trucks occupying the other, there was no way I was going to be able to return to the press camp against an outgoing tide. Toward evening the tank column stopped and we got the order that we were not going any farther. When you're with the Army, no one you're in touch with ever knows why you're moving or why you're stopping.

The most felicitous event of the Third Armored's advance that day was the two hours we stopped near the battered brick factory that had been the major producer of blowtorches in Germany. There were still thousands of torches in storage areas near the recently vacated production line, and every tank crew helped itself to several. For the rest of the war, they hopped out of their tanks every time there was a stop of more than ten minutes and made coffee or heated food from their rations in their mess kits. Some crews even used them inside on the steel floors of their tanks. I laugh now when I think of air bags in relation to the danger those crews exposed themselves to.

To the crew, a tank was like a small apartment. They stuffed personal items in every empty corner of it. The interior of each tank reflected the personality of its crew. The housekeeping in some was better than in others. For me, being in one was more claustrophobic than being fifty fathoms deep in a submarine.

The tank crews felt sorry for the infantry and the infantry felt sorry for the tankers. Inside the tank, the crew was immune to small-arms fire. Their worst enemy was the modified 88mm rifle mounted on the German Tiger tank. The Tiger was a lumbering giant, well built, heavily armored, and armed with the great 88mm gun, but for all its virtues it often lost the tank-to-tank battles with the Shermans. The gun protruding from its turret had to be hand-cranked, on well-made gears, into position to fire, so aiming at anything took a minute. That was almost a minute longer than it took the U.S. gunner to aim with the 75mm gun with its push-button controls. The Sherman was quick on its feet. The difference was the difference between a car with automatic steering, hydraulic shift, and push-button window control on one hand and a car with none of the modern conveniences on the other. The one thing the Tiger had was that high-velocity, armor-piercing gun. When a Tiger and a Sherman came on each other unexpectedly, the U.S. tank could often zero in on the Tiger with its electronic controls and fire off five shots before the manually operated

Tiger could bring its gun into position to aim and shoot. In those encounters, the Sherman won. If shots were exchanged at the same time, the German gun could do more damage.

In the evening of the second day I was hanging around with a tank crew along the side of the road near Paderborn when a major came up in a jeep and said General Rose would like to see me in his headquarters, a German house he'd taken over for the night.

The general had a fine taste for command posts. He always chose a comfortable castle or mansion, and somewhere in it there was a good-sized room he used as his office. He put his desk in the center of the room, always facing the door, and laid out his maps on another desk. His situation map was mounted on the wall opposite his desk so all he had to do to review his situation was look up. It all looked that way the night I talked to him.

Here I was a sergeant reporting for the Army newspaper and this tall, handsome, forty-five-year-old general was inviting me into his command post for an interview.

"When do you hope to reach your objective?" I asked General Rose, a little stiffly. We didn't talk about specific objectives because of censorship and I wouldn't have been allowed to name them in my story anyway.

"Tomorrow," he said.

"Wow," I said. "You think you'll be there tomorrow?"

"You said 'hope,' " he said. I was amused by this play on words by the general. When a general is even a little funny it's an event.

"I sent Yeomans a message today," he said, referring to another general, a friend of his. "I sent it in the clear so the Germans must have picked it up. I told him I'd give him a case of Scotch if he captured von Rundstedt, Kesselring, or Guderian and one bottle of Scotch for Hitler, dead or alive. The message got garbled and someone put Goering in for Guderian. Now I suppose if he brings Goering in here I'll have to give him a case of Scotch." We both laughed.

"I take orders from the corps commander," he told me. "He just tells me where he wants the Third Armored to go. He doesn't tell me how to get there."

Maurice Rose was killed by machine-gun fire the next day and I felt as if I'd lost a friend. He wasn't a friend but he'd made me feel that way in our conversation. Niceness is not an attribute they instill in generals at West Point, but he and Leon W. Johnson, the Ploesti leader, were very nice generals.

The U.S. Third Armored Division, without General Rose now, and the 104th Infantry Division went into Cologne with the British on our left flank. At some point the British crossed a bridge over the Rhine and, having heard that the Third Armored had already crossed at Cologne, fell into the Patton public-relations trap and named it "The George S. Patton Memorial Bridge." They made the mistake of thinking the Third Armored Division, which belonged to the First Army, was Patton's Third Army. He was more than a hundred miles to the south.

AFTER WE HAD crossed the Rhine, it seemed as if everything from then on would be an easy, downhill trip to the end of the war. There was no longer doubt who was going to win. There had been doubt only six months earlier when we were trying to break out from the beach area at Saint-Lô.

We were already running over the stalags in which American Army and Air Force men had been held prisoner. One of my friends, who had been held prisoner for several years after being shot down while flying as a waist gunner on his seventeenth mission, was a talented artist, Don Bevan. Don had worked for the *New York Daily News* before the war and I made arrangements for him to do some combat sketches for *The Stars and Stripes.* He did some very good work for the paper and one of the reasons I liked to go to the 306th Bomb Group at Thurleigh after a raid was to pick up the sketches he had drawn. That ended when his B-17 was shot down.

I don't recall the date, but one day shortly after he'd been liberated from his POW camp I ran into Don. He was with a friend, another POW named Ed Trzynski, and they seemed to have forgotten the horrors of their imprisonment in view of their enthusiasm for a play they'd written while they were captives.

They had cast the play in a prison camp, Stalag 17, and it had been done for several different audiences of American prisoners. I was more sympathetic than encouraging about their optimism for the play as a commercial venture back home, and I tried to tell them as nicely as I could that they should be prepared to be disappointed. As far as I knew, they had no qualifications for writing a play and I thought their enthusiasm was based, in large part, on their state of euphoria over being finally free again.

It seemed to me to be wildly improbable that they'd done anything that could be produced as a movie or a play back home. Bud Hutton and I had already had our book, *Air Gunner,* published by Farrar and Rinehart, so we'd made some contacts in New York and been represented by one of the most reputable literary agents of the time, Harold Ober. He had rowed for Harvard. That's the kind of agent Harold was.

I gave them Harold's name and address and forgot about the incident in the light of what was going to happen in the next few days. You can imagine my amazement when, shortly after the war, Don Bevan and Ed Trzynski's *Stalag 17* was made into a wonderfully successful and Academy Award–winning movie.

Several years later someone at CBS apparently ripped off their idea and made a television series called *Hogan's Heroes* of it. The television program had too many similarities in character and plot to be coincidental, and when Don and Ed sued the network they won a huge award.

ONCE MORE, WE were all optimistic about the end of the war, which seemed so close now. I never dreamed, as we rejoiced in the great crossing of the Rhine at Remagen, that in some respects the worst was yet to come. And soon.

On the evening of April 11, I was sitting in the big dining room of a bombed-out hotel that we were using as a makeshift press camp in Weimar, about fifty miles from Leipzig, idly typing out some notes I'd scribbled over the past few weeks. It was after nine and I was the only person there when Jack Thompson of the *Chicago Tribune* and Hal Boyle of the Associated Press burst in. Here were two hardened newsmen who had seen everything in a lifetime of reporting and they were in an uncharacteristic state of high excitement.

They had just come from a place called Buchenwald. The name was new to me.

It would have been normal for them to sit down at their typewriters and put down their stories without saying a word but on this occasion they couldn't keep themselves from telling me what they had seen. They had driven south of the First Army lines to where the Third Army's Sixth Armored Division passed through the Seventy-sixth Infantry Division and had overrun the Buchenwald concentration camp near Weimar.

Hal and Jack talked to me for fifteen minutes. It was as if they had to get it out, talking as much to themselves as to me. It was, perhaps, the story of the war, and they offered it to me. Eventually they sat down and wrote, and as the pages came off their typewriters they handed them to me.

It seems, in retrospect, a strange time for me to have become philosophical about journalism but I remember knowing that minute that I couldn't write so important a story without seeing Buchenwald myself. They described the bodies, piled like cordwood, in open graves. They told me of having seen the house in which Ilsa Koch, the camp commander and so-called Bitch of Buchenwald, lived. They described the lampshades there that they had been told were made of human skin.

I made the difficult decision not to rewrite the information they gave me as a story for *The Stars and Stripes* the next day. I liked to get stories in the paper and Boyle and Thompson had impeccable journalistic credentials but the story was so big that I didn't feel it was right to appropriate it, even with their permission. *The Stars and Stripes* ran Hal Boyle's Associated Press story the next morning, and that's the way it should have been. Hal was one of the best.

I grew up a skeptic and, while the trait has been an asset to me as a reporter, there have been times when it skewed my vision of events. In high school I read of German atrocities in World War I and decided many of those reports had been propaganda. I felt there were very likely as many atrocities committed on our side as on theirs. In college, during those sessions with Professor Boulding, I was similarly suspicious of the concentration-camp stories about which there was minimal detail and no substantiation. One of the incredible things about Hitler's Germany was how little real information about it got out. It wouldn't seem possible to bottle up a whole country and 50 million people so tightly.

Embarrassed as I am by the fact, I have to say that I was initially suspicious of all the reports of Nazi concentration camps even as we moved across France. A lot of Americans were. It seemed likely that they had been exaggerated as a way of bringing our patriotic blood to a boil.

On this occasion, rejecting what I couldn't verify personally may have been one of my best moments. I already knew enough journalistic sleight of hand to write the story convincingly without actually saying I was there but I have been pleased with myself over the years for not doing it. I was somehow vaguely aware that no one should ever be able to cast doubt on the whole hard-to-believe story of what happened at Buchenwald by being able to disprove one insignificant element of it. I've thought of it ten thousand times since on the occasions when I've become infuriated with people denying that the murder camps existed. I don't think, however, that any denial will ever be taken seriously by historians of the future because there is simply too much hard evidence. They might be able to cast doubt on the number of millions who were killed but that millions were killed they can hardly deny.

I don't think the people who have escalated the number of Jews who died in concentration camps have served their memory well. Soon after the war, the figures 2 and 3 million were used. I've read estimates as high as 8 million. I don't use the figure 8 million for the same reason I didn't use the term "the Bitch of Buchenwald." It sounds tailored for tabloid headlines.

If it can be proved, as it might be possible to do, that it was 3 million Jews who were killed, or 4 million, it would lend credibility to the doubters. If it was 4 million, can someone say "only"?

I don't use the word "Holocaust" because it sounds like a word conceived by a public-relations agency. We have a strong word for what it was. The word is genocide: "The systematic, planned annihilation of a racial, political, or cultural group." I concede that "Holocaust" has taken hold and may, in the end, be the word most used. I don't have any strong feelings about it, I just don't use it.

All this came to me again in a theater in 1994, watching the motion picture *Schindler's List,* sitting next to a pretty young girl who periodically plunged her hand into a huge box of popcorn. How strange, I thought, that we could be sitting side by side, strangers, she with her thoughts, me with mine, so close and yet so distant.

The brilliant director, Steven Spielberg, felt compelled to make too many concessions to entertainment. There were dramatized parts of the film that could lead anyone to conclude that they were over-stated. If they were overstated, might it not also be true that other parts of the story of the Nazi attempt to exterminate the Jews were exaggerated? That should never be allowed to happen.

When Hal and Jack had finished their stories that night in Weimar, they left for their tent and I sat there alone again. All I knew was that I had to get to Buchenwald myself the next day.

I did get to Buchenwald the next day, and I stared. I stared in embarrassed silence, thinking about the doubts I'd had in college and even more recently. Buchenwald represented the worst of everything in all the Nazi extermination camps. The dead and dying were still everywhere. The camp was unchanged, still the way it had been for all those terrible months except that there were cameramen there now, documenting the horror of it for all time. It was worth leaving things as they had been for a few days for that purpose.

I was ashamed of myself for ever having considered refusing to serve in the Army. If my conscience objected, it hadn't paid much attention to my brain. I'd like to have taken Ken Boulding by the hand and shown him around Buchenwald. I was angry that I'd been fooled. For the first time, I knew for certain that any peace is not bet-ter than any war.

For all the impact Buchenwald had on all of us who saw it in that first week, it was a much smaller camp I saw several days later, on April 20, that is more vivid in my mind. It was called simply Thekla for the name of the town in what became East Germany. I've been in contact with several organizations who continue to gather material about the concentration camps and almost no one ever mentions

Thekla. I think it's because it was not a death factory in the sense that Buchenwald and Auschwitz were. The prisoners at Thekla were kept alive for the work they did.

I was with Fred Graham of the *New York Times* when we came into Thekla. I was always pleased to be with Fred Graham because he was such good, easy company and he always gave me the feeling he knew what he was doing. It made me feel I did. The Fifth Armored Division had blown through Thekla the day before we arrived. It was a typical German small town with well-kept, solid-looking stone houses. Almost everyone seemed to have a little garden, and I recall noting that flowers were growing during a war.

At one edge of the town, there was a small factory that had been making wings for Luftwaffe fighter planes. Immediately adjacent to the factory was a cluster of barracks that looked like a thousand others we had seen. The difference was the vicious, thick rolls of barbed wire around them.

We found an English-speaking Pole who had somehow survived, and he went inside the compound with us. He was the only tour guide I've ever heard who was worth listening to.

The compound had housed several thousand slave laborers who worked in the adjacent aircraft factory and about 1,200 Jews, but we were never sure, from what our guide said, how the Jewish prisoners worked in relation to the other prisoners.

The burned and blackened bodies of about sixty men were hanging in contorted positions from the needle-point barbs of the wire. When one part of the body burns, the skin and muscles contract and the body, in death, lies warped like a board left out on wet ground in the sun. A few—the lucky few—had bullet holes through them.

Our Polish guide said that because of the importance of the aircraft-parts factory, there had been a small contingent of SS troops stationed in Thekla. There's no good translation for "SS," but it has a meaning I think everyone understands. It is hard to conceive of human beings doing what they did to other human beings. They were born-again Nazis who carried out Hitler's wishes and commands with religious zeal.

When these SS troops realized U.S. soldiers were going to arrive in Thekla within hours, they herded 300 prisoners into one of the barracks. I don't know where the other prisoners were. They threw pails of gasoline over the barracks and onto some of the prisoners and then tossed incendiary grenades into the building. It surely was one of the pinnacles in the annals of man's inhumanity to man.

Many of the prisoners clawed their way out of the burning barracks and ran, in flames, to the barbed-wire fence before they burned to death or were machine-gunned by the SS troopers standing around the perimeter of the compound.

We talked to a few of the citizens who spoke a little English and it was my first exposure to what we began to hear so frequently: "We didn't know."

The people of Thekla said that to us endlessly. "We didn't know." They said it until we felt like kicking them down the street and into the compound themselves. If they didn't know, which seemed impossible, they should have known.

One of the three barracks was still standing, unburned, and Fred and I went in. The wooden bunks were three high. There was one aisle down the middle of the barracks and four bunks from the aisle in to the wall. Anyone with a bunk on the third tier up against the wall had to climb up to the third level and then across three other bunks to his own.

The most gut-wrenching details were the vestiges of human effort to make some life for themselves under these conditions. These men who were about to die played chess. In half a dozen places on the bare wooden walls next to the tier of bunks up against it, the prisoners had scratched out the squares for chessboards. Pinned to the squares were crude paper cutouts of chessmen. There was no good reason to feel any worse about the death of a man with a brain active enough to want to play chess under those circumstances but, nonetheless, I could not resist thinking that it *was* worse.

It was this scene I saw on that one day at Thekla that made me so resentful of President Ronald Reagan's visit, in 1985, to the cemetery for German soldiers at Bitburg where SS men were buried. In their case, I am not willing to let bygones be bygones.

One of the devilish aspects of this crusade against the Jews was the necessity the Germans felt for making the extermination of Jews legal. I don't think Americans know about it. Whatever the Nazis

This was the scene when Fred Graham and I arrived at the small prison labor camp at Thekla. The barracks in the background was similar to one that had been doused with gasoline and set on fire with its Jewish occupants inside. Some of them ran, in flames, to the barbed wire encircling the camp and died there.

wanted to do, they first arranged to have a law passed that made the action legal. They did not, as it might seem, simply haul Jews off the streets and out of their homes without being able to justify it in their own minds and according to laws that had been enacted, and there were laws that covered every act.

In 1946 I returned to Germany for a magazine and attended part of the Nuremberg trials. Someone had a small volume produced by the Reichstag in 1935, some of which I copied.

It was called, just coincidentally, *The Nuremberg Laws on Race and Citizenship, 1935.*

There's a chapter called "Law for the Protection of German Blood and Honor."

A citizen of the Reich may be only that subject who is of German or kindred blood, and who through his behavior shows that he is both desirous and personally fit to serve loyally the Reich and the German people.

Only citizens of the Reich . . . can exercise the right of voting in political matters and have the right to hold political office.

A Jew cannot be a citizen of the Reich. He cannot exercise the right to vote. He cannot hold public office. Jewish officials will be retired as of December 31, 1935.

A Jew is an individual who is descended from three grandparents who were full Jews. . . .

A Jew is also an individual who is descended from two full-Jewish grandparents if:

He was a member of the Jewish religious community.

He is married to a Jew.

He is the issue from a marriage with a Jew.

He is the issue of an extramarital relationship with a Jew and will have been born out of wedlock after July 31, 1936.

Another section of the law starts this way:

Imbued with the knowledge that the purity of German blood is the necessary prerequisite for the existence of the German nation . . . the Reichstag has unanimously adopted the following law:

Any marriages between Jews and citizens of German blood are herewith forbidden. Marriages entered into despite this law are invalid, even if they are arranged abroad in order to circumvent this law.

Extramarital relations between Jews and citizens of German or kindred race are herewith forbidden.

Jews are forbidden to employ as servants in their households female subjects of German blood who are under 45 years of age. [The implication here is, I guess, that a German woman servant over forty-five who had an affair with the boss wouldn't have a baby.]

Jews are prohibited from displaying the Reich and national flag and from showing the national colors.

However, they may show the Jewish colors. The exercise of this right is under State protection.

These laws shall go into effect January 1, 1936.

Even doctors working in the extermination camps had the law on their side and it must have made the work easier for a doctor who did not take genocide lightly. The Reichstag bothered to pass laws providing for the "humane" deaths of anyone whose physical condition left that person with no practical hope of living.

A doctor could, legally, prescribe death by gas, and sleep at night serene in his knowledge that he had acted according to law. The fiendish quality of this aspect of genocide seems important to know because it is, in part anyway, an answer to the mystery "How could they have done it?"

FROM A MILITARY standpoint, there was one last, great event. That was the meeting of the Allied forces with those from Russia. (It was easier when we referred to it as just plain "Russia.") Both armies were driving relentlessly forward to close the narrowing gap of German territory between us. The only desire the remaining German soldiers had was to be captured by the Americans and not by the Russians, so whatever resistance the Germans offered was concentrated toward the east. The Germans had taken thousands of Eastern Europeans prisoner and had used them as slave labor in factories and fields. Many of them were Russian. Their German captors had long since lost the ability to control this labor force, and thousands of them were tagging along behind U.S. Army forces, waiting for the day we'd meet the Russians coming from the other direction. Sensing the drama of it, reporters were there too, following the Sixty-ninth Infantry Division. The name of a division is its number. It has almost no meaning to anyone but members of it, but to them it is important and I mention it here because I hope at least a few of them who were there with the Sixty-ninth will read this.

The Sixty-ninth reached the Elbe River at the small town of Torgau in the middle of the day on April 26, at the same time the Russians reached the bank of the river on the other side. It was a wild day. Russian soldiers are a little crazy and, watching them for the first time, I understood why German civilians didn't want to be overrun by them.

In Torgau I met a lieutenant named Robertson who was trying to make sure the soldiers he saw across the river were friendly Russians.

He wanted an American flag, but flags are more readily evident in peacetime parades than they are at war and he couldn't find anyone in the division who had one.

There was a drugstore in Torgau that was closed, of course, but Robertson and a few of his men broke through the front door. Inside they found jars of dye on the shelves and searched until they found a good red and a good blue. It wasn't clear what a German druggist used dye for. Robertson took a bedsheet the same way he got the colored dye and daubed crude stripes on the sheet until he had a rough approximation of an American flag.

As I recall, the red stripes were better than the stars, but it's unlikely that the Russians viewing it from across the Elbe cared.

Within hours hundreds of Russian soldiers had found boats in which they crossed the river. The town of Torgau was more attractive to them than anything on their side of the Elbe because the biggest industry in town was the factory that made Hohner harmonicas and accordions. It seemed as though every Russian soldier knew how to play and by a great stroke of luck one of the women the Germans had forced to work for them was a former star of the Moscow opera. With hundreds of Russian soldiers forming the chorus and with this woman singing the solo parts over a loudspeaker set up in the town square, it must have been one of the great musical concerts in the history of the world.

My friends Gordon Frazier and George Hicks of NBC radio always traveled with a bulky wire recorder in the back of their jeep. That was the earliest version of the tape recorder, and they were able to record part of this magnificent event for broadcast. I'd like to know what happened to that wire recording. I'm not sure the wire was replaceable or interchangeable as tape is and it seems likely that, in the last few weeks of the war, they had to erase the impromptu concert by recording over it. The technological revolution in our ability to save sounds and pictures is going to fill the world's basement and attic with an overflow of accurate records of how we lived in the twentieth century and I'm not sure who's going to be in charge of throwing some of it out, but that recording should never have been lost to posterity.

The next day I got in my jeep and drove back to Paris with a feeling the war was over.

VI

GOING HOME

A LL ANYONE CARED about now was getting home. The war was won and the only fear that lurked in anyone's head was the Pacific. They wouldn't send us there for an invasion of Japan, would they? It didn't seem like our war over there.

The formal surrender by the German high command was scheduled to take place May 8, in Reims. The single most unfortunate thing about Reims as a choice was that its name is almost impossible for any non-French-speaking person to pronounce and was also easily confused with Rennes. It didn't help that it was alternately spelled "Rheims" and "Reims."

I've returned to Reims several times since the war and was surprised to find what I had not known then: it is in the center of champagne country. In 1945 I'd never tasted champagne. Reims is the only place in the world where gas stations have racks of champagne for sale where the Coke machines stand on Route 66. I've sipped champagne on several hundred festive occasions now and still fail to find any relationship to celebration in its bubbles.

Bob Moora, the managing editor in Paris, had assigned me the job of covering the surrender for *The Stars and Stripes*. I was one of eight correspondents whose reports on the momentous event were to be pooled and used by anyone who wanted them. There was to be no exclusivity.

A few days before the signing, Maj. Fred Eldridge called me into his office. Eldridge was a personable, gung-ho officer with a flair for theatrics who had been recently transferred from command of the *China-Burma-India Roundup,* the equivalent of *The Stars and Stripes* in the CBI theater of operations, to officer in charge of the Paris operation of *The Stars and Stripes.*

He asked if I would like to go to the CBI and report back from there to *The Stars and Stripes* about what the soldiers in Europe could expect to find when they were sent there. It was assumed, at that point, two months before the atomic bomb was dropped on Hiroshima, that more than 2 million U.S. soldiers in Europe would be shipped and flown to India and China to continue the war there. There was still a possibility, as far as any of us knew, of an invasion of Japan.

It was a tough decision for me because covering the surrender was a once-in-a-lifetime assignment. I was still not really aware—or maybe knowledgeable would be a better word—of what I was involved with in relation to the broad outlines of history, but I recognized that the surrender was a major occasion.

On the other hand, I liked the idea of seeing India and China. It turned out (as it so often does when it seems as though you've been offered a choice) that Eldridge wasn't so much asking me if I wanted to go as he was telling me I was going. That made the choice easier for me. My friend Charley Kiley got the job in Reims, and he was better equipped for it than I would have been anyway.

A sergeant by the name of Fred Friendly, with whom Eldridge had worked in India, was being sent to Paris. We were to change places. It was a dramatic way of meeting Fred Friendly, a man who, many years later, was to have a major influence on my life as a friend and boss.

Over the years I've had so many bosses that I've become something of an expert on them. I know so much more about being bossed than the average boss knows about bossing that I have them at a great disadvantage. Fred was an exception. For one thing, he was smarter than anyone else at *CBS News* and that's a quality I admire in a boss. It isn't always the case.

Fred flew from India on a DC-4 carrying a major general in the Quartermaster Corps who had been deposed and was being sent home for some form of what would have been called "white-collar" crime in civilian life. What he did, I believe, was steal.

I was to go to New Delhi on the return flight of the same plane. By this time in my Army career, I'd accumulated a lot of possessions—good stuff. I had thousands of pages of notes I wanted to keep in several dozen spiral-bound notepads that opened from the top. I had pieces of clothing I didn't want to leave behind. The sheepskin bomber jacket I'd worn on that first flight into Germany was a treasure. I couldn't dream of selling, trading, or giving away the .45-caliber pistol I'd taken from the German officer who surrendered to me. There was no such thing as checking through a metal detector before you boarded an airplane, and I had a right to have a gun anyway.

My dependable jeep was my close friend. I'd driven it 20,000 miles since shortly after D-Day over every conceivable kind of terrain. I'd been pulled out of a ditch in it by an M-1 tank. I'd cowered in it that night I was stuck in the armored column near Paderborn, and I'd spent hours in it with good friends.

Joel Sayre, who had written a movie called *Rackety Rax* that we all saw three times when I was in school, drove with me in that jeep from Frankfurt to Leipzig, a distance of several hundred miles. Joel had been a crime reporter for the *Herald Tribune* in the "Legs" Diamond days and was writing for *The New Yorker*. I'm afraid I was impressed to the point of being starstruck, but it was a great trip. Joel was somewhat older than Joe Leibling but with comparable literary talent. He was less intense and more fun to be with than Joe. For part of the ride on the autobahn, during which we passed through forests on long concrete corridors, Joel jovially propounded a theory he had of the German people. He said that, while the image the world had of them was of a nation of realistic and logical humans, a great many Germans were actually possessed by trolls, fairies, and other otherworldly beings that lived in their woods. My jeep was oblivious to notions of this kind.

The thought of abandoning my four-wheeled companion was almost too sad to consider after all we'd been through together. I've always had a tendency to be sentimental about inanimate objects, and to this day I dislike turning over a car that's given me good service to a dealer who's going to sell it to a junkyard for scrap. It seems like taking a faithful old pet to the dog pound.

My friend Bill Walton of *Time* was in Paris when I returned and during a dinner one night I asked if he wanted my jeep. It was not my jeep to give away, of course. It was the property of the U.S. government, but I gave it to Bill anyway. Ownership was often vague during the war. Its serial number was on an Army list of vehicles somewhere with my name after it but it hadn't been accounted for in ten months and I couldn't imagine the Army coming to look for one vehicle in the sea of U.S. vehicles that had flooded France and Germany. For all the Army knew, the jeep might have been shot out from under me.

I gave the jeep to Bill because I wanted it to have a loving owner and Bill was a kind person. It would be comforting to me to know where it was. It was more than a year after I was discharged before I got a query from the Army about the whereabouts of my jeep, and while it would have been easy to concoct a plausible excuse for its disappearance, I ignored the query and it went away. I never heard another word.

I have subsequently asked Bill whatever in the world he did with it and he's been evasive. Either he doesn't want to tell me or he's forgotten, and I think he's forgotten.

The plane I was to fly to New Delhi in was at an airport near Nice. I flew there from Paris in a DC-3 with bucket seats. "Bucket seats" meant that each side of the aircraft was lined with a plastic bench with form-fitting indentations for passengers. I don't recall that there were seat belts. The wide center of the plane, between the two rows of seats, was often used for cargo. When there were no passengers, the seats themselves folded flat against the sides of the fuselage, opening up the whole inside body of the aircraft for cargo.

As you pass over the low mountains behind Marseilles and Nice along the Mediterranean, the wind sweeps off the warm waters of the sea and up the mountain slopes. There are strong updrafts that make flying bumpy and landing perilous.

I was seated next to an American nurse who was being assigned to an Army hospital in the area. She seemed remote and distracted and, when we finally talked, she told me that her twin brother had been missing since December and she couldn't get any satisfaction from the Army about where he was or what had happened to him.

He'd obviously been lost during the Battle of the Bulge and it was hard for me to respond in any optimistic way. It seemed certain he had been killed or he would have surfaced by then. A lot of bodies were never found or were impossible to identify when the dog tags were missing or damaged.

As those of us on the flight to Nice turned to catch a view of the Mediterranean as it came in sight, we were caught by a strong downdraft. The aircraft dropped, and all our stomachs with it, in a free fall for perhaps 100 feet. As we dropped, we and the bucket seats were suspended off the floor of the plane.

When we hit solid air again, we leveled off as abruptly as if we had hit the ground. The flap that acted as the front support of the bucket seats had folded under us while we were doubly airborne, and when we came down the seat buckled under our weight and we all hit the floor in a variety of states of akimbo. My companion broke her right arm and that ended my awkward attempt to comment in an optimistic way about her missing twin brother. Is there any wild, one-in-a-million chance that she will read this and recognize herself in my story? I suppose she'd be in her early seventies.

I was still waiting in Nice for them to service the big DC-4 that was to take me to New Delhi when the surrender was signed on May 8. *The Stars and Stripes* had an edition being printed in Nice and one of my good mementos is of a copy of that day's *Stars and Stripes* for sale at the stand in the Negresco Hotel lobby carrying a story I wrote under the four-word headline

IT'S OVER
OVER HERE!

Two days later I had word that the DC-4 was ready and we were going to take off at 6 A.M. I had two heavy barracks bags with all my worldly treasures in them. I remember thinking it would be a good idea to tie them together and sling the connecting rope over my shoulder so that, with one bag hanging in back and the other in front, I'd be balanced. That turned out not to be true. What happened was, one bumped me from the back as I put forward one foot and the other bumped me from the front as I extended the other. I untied

EXTRA

NICE-MARSEILLE EDITION

THE STARS AND STRIPES EXTRA

Daily Newspaper of U.S. Armed Forces — in the European Theater of Operations

Vol. 1—No. 56

Tuesday, May 8, 1945

ONE FRANC

IT'S OVER OVER HERE

Surrender Completed At Rheims

By CHARLES KILEY
Stars and Stripes Staff Writer

RHEIMS, May 8—The Third Reich surrendered unconditionally to the Allies here at Gen. Dwight D. Eisenhower's forward headquarters at 2:41 AM Monday.

The surrender terms, calling for cessation of hostilities on all fronts at one minute past midnight (Double British Summer Time) Wednesday, May 9, were signed on behalf of the German government by Col. Gen. Gustaf Jodl, Wehrmacht chief and Chief of Staff to Fuehrer Karl Doenitz.

Under Jodl's signature were those of Lt. Gen. Walter Bedell Smith, Chief of Staff to the Supreme Allied Commander; Gen. Ivan Susloparoff, head of the Russian mission to France who was authorized by Moscow to sign on behalf of Soviet forces, and Gen. Suvez of France.

The surrender as signed in five minutes in the SHAEF war room here, 35 miles east of Compiegne forest where Germany surrendered in the last war on Nov. 11, 1918, and the scene of the capitulation of France to the Third Reich in this war June 21, 1940.

Flew from Germany

The terms were signed in less than ten hours after the arrival of Jodl by plane from Germany, and 14 hours after final negotiations first begun with the arrival Saturday of Gen. Adm. Hans Georg von Friedeburg, commander in chief of German navy, who on Thursday headed the Nazi delegation which surrendered German forces in Denmark, Holland and Northwestern Germany to the 21st Army Gp.

Gen. Eisenhower did not take part in the actual surrender. He remained in his office with his deputy, Air Chief Marshal Sir Arthur Tedder, during the ceremonies.

Flanking Jodl at the surrender table were Friedeburg, and Maj. G. S. Wilhelm Oxenius, aide to Gen. Jodl.

Correspondents, cameramen and photographers were in the war room when three Russian officers, Gens.

GENERAL OF THE ARMY DWIGHT D. EISENHOWER

From D-Day to V-Day

'Good! When Do We Leave This Hole and Go Home?'

By ANDY ROONEY
Stars and Stripes Staff Writer

When American soldiers on furlough along the French Riviera, one of the world's most expensive and exclusive vacation spots, heard last night that the war in Europe was over, they had one reaction:

"Good! When do we get out of this hole and go home?"

In Nice, the Red Cross club posted a large red-lettered sign over its situation map which read simply:

"The war in Europe is over."

Soldiers who read it, who heard the announcement over the BBC or who got the news second-hand from a usually reliable friend, were happy but generally undemonstrative. There was very little dancing or hugging by frontline soldiers in the area. They quietly talked over what it meant among themselves.

At MP headquarters the sergeant on the desk, Julius Lavrentier, of Perth Amboy, N. J., said, "We're going to lock this place up tonight and let 'em tear the town down. That's what we'd like to do anyway."

Capt. William Vezzell, of New York, the MP detachment com-

(Continued on Page 4)

The Allies today proclaimed to the world that the war against Germany is over.

At one minute past 11 o'clock tonight (Central European time) the cease fire order will sound throughout Europe and the unconditional surrender of all German air, land and sea forces, signed yesterday at Rheims, will become effective.

President Truman and Prime Minister Churchill, in simultaneous announcements to their nations, officially proclaimed the end of hostilities.

At the same time, Supreme Headquarters issued the text of the Act of Surrender, signed yesterday at 0241 (CET) in Gen. Eisenhower's forward CP by Lt. Gen. Walter Bedell Smith for the supreme commander, Maj. Gen. Ivan Susloparoff for the Soviet high command, Gen. Suvez for France and Col. Gen. Gustaf Jodl, German Army troop chief of staff for the defeated Reich.

A Navy communique said that all German warships have been ordered to proceed to the nearest Allied port and disarm. All vessels now in port have been ordered to remain until further orders and personnel have been told to remain on board.

"This is a solemn and glorious hour," President Truman told the nation in his V-E Day proclamation.

Reminding the U.S. that the war has brought "sorrow and hardship" to thousands of homes, the President set aside next Sunday—Mothers Day—as a day of prayer.

(Continued on Page 4)

Act of Military Surrender

1.—We, the undersigned, acting by authority of the German high command, hereby surrender unconditionally to the supreme commander, Allied Expeditionary Force, and simultaneously to the Soviet high command all forces on land, sea, and in the air who are at this date under German control.

2.—The German high command will at once issue orders to all German military, naval and air authorities and to all forces under German control to cease active operations at 2301 hours, (Central European time) on May 8 and to remain in the positions occupied at that time. No ship, vessel or aircraft is to be scuttled or any damage done to their hulls, machinery or equipment.

3.—The German high command will at once issue to the appropriate commanders, and insure the carrying out of any further orders issued by the supreme commander, Allied Expeditionary Force, and by the Soviet high command.

4.—This act of military surrender is without prejudice to, and will be superseded by, any general instrument of surrender imposed by, or on behalf of, the United Nations and applicable to Germany and to the German armed forces as a whole.

5.—In the event of the German high command or any of the forces under their control failing to act in accordance with this act of surrender, the supreme commander, Allied Expeditionary Force, and the Soviet high command will take such punitive or other action as they deem appropriate.

This was my last story written for the paper in Europe. The following day I left for India.

them and lugged them, one in my left hand and the other in my right. They were all I could lift. Later I lost one treasure-filled bag somewhere between China and home.

Fortunately the plane was empty except for the pilot, copilot, and two enlisted crew members. It was the most elaborately appointed aircraft I'd ever seen. It had been done to the specifications of the quartermaster general for his use in the CBI before he was caught stealing. When I see pictures of the President waving from the top of the platform as he boards Air Force One, I always think of my own luxury trip.

I was relaxed and exultant as we took off. I had survived the war and, at that moment, realized it for the first time. There was no war to be fought in the CBI. I was vaguely uneasy about the possibility that a trip to India and China would delay my return home, but it was a chance I decided to take. No one really knew what was going to happen to anyone. It didn't seem as though there was any danger of death in the CBI comparable to what I'd experienced for ten months in France and Germany, and the prospects of the trip were exciting. I looked forward to writing from there.

If I ever knew, I've forgotten what course we took from Paris to our first stop in Cairo. I think we made a fuel stop in Rome but then I don't know whether we stayed out over the Mediterranean and headed east or crossed it and headed toward Egypt over North Africa. My memory of the trip kicks back in as we started the glide path into the Cairo airport.

The plan was for us to spend not more than an hour at the airport while the DC-4 was serviced and refueled. That plan changed abruptly when the pilot misjudged our distance from a steel light pole as he taxied toward the passenger terminal and clipped eighteen inches off the end of our right wing.

The airport accident was lucky for me as a reporter and tourist. I spent nine days and nights in the palatial Shepheard's Hotel. For me, being in Cairo was a chapter out of *Arabian Nights*. I drank a Pimm's cup feeling like Lawrence of Arabia whiling away the hours watching the other guests from a rocking chair on the spacious porch of one of the best-known hotels of the world.

Shepheard's reeked of the kind of British colonialism I'd read about but never seen. The war did not seem to have diminished it. It was a long way from where I'd been with the First Army in Germany as recently as two weeks before.

When the DC-4 had been repaired, we left Cairo and headed for New Delhi with a pit stop in Abadan, near Kuwait, at the head of the Persian Gulf. Much of the Middle East's oil production flows through Abadan into the holds of waiting tankers, and the U.S. Army had several hundred soldiers stationed there as guards.

The pilot was familiar with Abadan and took no chances with light poles at the barren little airport, laid out in the sand eight or ten miles from the gulf. I got off the DC-4 while it was being refueled and walked to a low, barracks-style building where several GIs were sitting on benches out front watching planes land. The heat was overwhelming. At Lake George, as a boy, I used to think it was hot when it hit 85 and cicadas sang in the weeds by the side of the road as we walked to the Big Dock to get the mail, but I'd never felt anything like this.

I talked to the dispirited soldiers for a while about the heat and whether they ever got used to it. They said they did not but they seemed listless and resigned to their fate of being stationed in one of the godforsaken places in the world.

"What do you guys do on your day off?" I asked one of them, trying to stir up a conversation.

He looked at me with obvious disinterest.

"This *is* our day off," he said.

The following day we landed at the airport in New Delhi.

Delhi—they called it just "Delhi," as in delicatessen—was Abadan all over. What served as a terminal at the airport was a small, attractive building with a dome over its tiny waiting room and tile mosaics on the floor, walls, and ceiling. All mosaics look to me like the interior walls of a cave with artwork to be understood only by historians.

I said good-bye and thank you to the crew and lugged my khaki duffel bags—I still had two—into the waiting room, where I sat dejectedly on one of the wooden church benches and gazed at the strange surroundings. If breathing had demanded a decision from me to do it, I wouldn't have. The heat took over. I couldn't move.

After perhaps half an hour, I realized I couldn't decide to die there and I went out front where there were taxis and said "Cecil Hotel" to a driver. I wasn't sure whether I needed a foreign language and was relieved when the driver replied in that attractive, clipped English that identifies English-speaking Indians. They all sound like Peter Ustinov doing a parody of them.

The Cecil Hotel was several miles from the airport. I had made arrangements in Paris to stay in a room there being rented by *Life* photographer Eliot Elisofon, who was on assignment in China for a month. The room was on the second floor, and sitting cross-legged on the floor of the balcony outside the room was an Indian untouchable who was Elisofon's *dobi wallah*. A *dobi wallah* was a personal servant, housekeeper, errand runner, and laundryman. I had been advised to give him a dollar every week.

To this day the idea of having my own *dobi wallah* is an appealing thought, but there are unfortunate implications of slavery that go with the job. It surely must have been a British institution from the days when Britannia ruled not only the waves but all of India.

In New Delhi I went to the offices of the *Roundup* from which my stories were to be dispatched to *The Stars and Stripes* in Paris. Colonel Eldridge had provided me with eighteen neatly typed letters of introduction to such people as Gen. Joseph Stilwell, Gen. Claire Chennault, and the Maharajah of Cooch Behar.

I didn't feel up to using my introductions to Stilwell, Chennault, or the Maharajah, but the letter to a colonel who was the adjutant in New Delhi proved to be helpful. The U.S. headquarters building in New Delhi was a one-story white stucco building with latticework openings at regular intervals that were covered with a mossy vine of some kind. There was usually a warm wind blowing. All day long four Indian men circled the building carrying what appeared to be whole pigs on their backs. What appeared to be a pig was a pigskin filled with water. Each man grasped the neck to keep the water in and then with a twist of his body, released his grasp on the neck and sent a spray of water up over the moss clinging to the lattices. They walked along the side of the building until the bladders were empty and then went to refill them and returned to continue spraying.

This was a remarkably effective air-conditioning system. The water on the moss evaporated as the wind blew through it and reduced the temperature inside by as much as fifteen degrees.

I was lost in New Delhi. It was too hot to look out the window of my hotel room, let alone go out and do any work. On the second or third day there, I was looking through the pages of the *Roundup* and saw a reference to some American soldiers who had gone to Srinagar for R&R (rest and rehabilitation).

It sounded like something I could write as a story—WHERE TO GO ON VACATION WHEN YOU COME TO THE CBI! I booked a flight on an Air Force DC-3 that was headed there with supplies for a small U.S. unit stationed nearby.

My memory of Srinagar, now part of Pakistan, is that it looked much like Venice. It may influence your opinion of my comparison to know that I have never been to Venice. I once got a postcard from the great television performer Garry Moore saying that he had been surprised that morning at breakfast to look out from his hotel balcony to see a speedboat full of nuns going by. I formed my vision of Venice from that postcard.

Srinagar is a small city of about 250,000 people—or was, anyway. I suppose it could be 2,500,000 now. What would have been paved streets in any normal city were waterways there. Everyone traveled around either by bicycle on the paths beside the canals or by boat. It was one of the dream geographic locations in the whole world. I don't know why there isn't more talk of it as a destination for tourists.

Kashmir, the Vale of Kashmir, is a valley about twenty-five miles long and not so wide that is ringed with magnificent, snowcapped mountains. The waterways in Srinagar are fed by the melting snow that produces a thousand streams that run down into the town. Its main arteries are all water, and many of the fifty-foot-long houseboats can be rented for days or weeks by anyone wanting to spend time there.

A friend named John Derr who worked for the *Roundup* and later had a role in running the Masters Golf Tournament in Augusta, Georgia, had given me the name of a houseboat he'd stayed on. When I found it, it was already occupied by two RAF pilots and an American sergeant from Pittsburgh whom the RAF men had taken in. They took me in and I spent an unusual four days in their company.

The owner of the boat spoke in that same Ustinov accent that made them all sound as if they'd learned the English language at Oxford or Cambridge. The owner was captain, cook, bellboy, and hotel maid—and good at all of them, although generally speaking I didn't find the Indian food as good in India as it had been off Shaftesbury Avenue in London.

The three people onboard had arranged a horse ride up into the mountains the following day. I protested that I didn't know how to ride a horse—had, indeed, never been on a horse—and thought I might hold them back. They insisted I go and I went.

I got myself up on what seemed to me to be a big, strong horse. He was somewhat broader than the average horse I'd seen people riding all my life, but he seemed gentle and would have been obedient if I'd known how to order him to do something. Fortunately, all I wanted him to do was follow the horse ahead of him and he did that dutifully.

The temperature was a pleasant 70 degrees in Srinagar, and in anticipation of its getting cooler in the mountains I'd brought my tank jacket, one of the most coveted pieces of clothing issued during World War II. The outside was a hard-finish gabardine cotton, and it was lined with high-grade olive-drab GI blanket wool. I'd tied the arms of the jacket around my waist and the rest of it dropped over the horse's flank.

It soon became apparent that I wasn't going to need it and had made a mistake bringing it. Within five or six hundred yards, the path turned from dirt to snow. The sides of the stream were lined with crusty snow, the running water cutting underneath it. We had to be careful to stay well in from the undercut snow crust because it probably would have crumbled and dumped us into the stream. And although we expected it should have been getting colder as we ran into increasing depths of snow, it didn't. It got warmer. I ended up not wearing my tank jacket and also taking off the light shirt and the T-shirt I wore under it.

For almost seven hours we made our way up and then down that mountain path in a strong sun with my legs across the back of my broad-beamed bay horse. We got back to the houseboat shortly before dark. I got into bed without eating and stayed in bed for the next two days. My shoulders and back were sunburned lipstick red, and I was so crotch-bound and saddle-sore that I could barely walk. It was as miserable as I've ever been in my life.

I wrote several stories from Srinagar and then flew to Karachi, where I spent three days looking for Americans and found none. By this time it was apparent to me that I was pushing a good thing too far and I returned to the Cecil Hotel in Delhi.

At the airport, I took a ride to the hotel across town in a cart pulled by what was known as a tonga pony. The word "tonga" is not in my dictionary, but that is what they were called. I remember noting that most of the tonga ponies standing in the heat waiting for a customer to climb into the two-wheeled rattan cart they drew were light-colored. It dawned on me the second day that all the darker horses must have long ago died of the heat because their dark coats absorbed more of the sun's rays. Darwin would have been proud of me.

It's a common thing for us all to feel sorrier for animals than for people, and I recall feeling worse about those horses in that intense heat than I felt for their drivers, who were enduring the same condition, or, for that matter, myself. It would not be good luck to be born a tonga pony in India.

After another week in New Delhi I flew to Calcutta. There was a sizable U.S. force there and you can't ignore a name with all the dramatic implications Calcutta has.

There may be worse cities, but Calcutta is the worst city I have ever been in. It seemed impossible that I'd ever be hotter than I was in Abadan or New Delhi. Calcutta was as hot and worse because it was dirty and the dirt stuck to your damp skin. You hardly dared eat, and it was difficult to get a drink of anything you felt safe gulping down. The natives had a good answer, as natives always do. Men with carts heaped high with coconuts stood on every corner holding long, razor-sharp machetes. When someone indicated they wished to buy a coconut, the vendor picked one off his cart, raised the blade over his head, and, with a quick motion, whacked off a small portion of the top. The purchaser gave him his money and walked off drinking the untouched-by-human-hands liquid inside, confident that it, at least, was not contaminated by man.

If I wrote a memorable story in Calcutta, I forget it—nor do I recall that I was uneasy about what they were thinking about my work, or the lack of it, back at the office of *The Stars and Stripes* in Paris. I was hardly firable at that distance.

Back in New Delhi, the clean room at the Cecil Hotel seemed almost luxurious after Calcutta, but I stayed only a few more days before heading for China by way of Chabua, Burma.

Chabua is near the border between India and Burma, and most of the troops stationed in Chabua were engineers working on the famous Burma Road through the Himalayas east into China. They were building it or fixing it. We were losing so many aircraft carrying supplies into China from the India side that the road was a military necessity if we were to make any moves toward Japan.

When I got to Chabua, the monsoon season had just ended. They had something like 100 inches of rain in two weeks. Everything was sodden but the rains were over and the engineers, anticipating being able to get back to the job within a week or ten days, were working on their equipment. Advance crews made their way back up into the mountains over the part of the road already completed to locate the huge Caterpillar tractors they'd left up there, covered with tarpaulins, when the rains came.

The Cats were nowhere to be found, and one of the war's major mysteries was what happened to them. I was in on a high-level meeting of officers and there were wild, improbable guesses made as to what had happened to the equipment. They were obviously very valuable, but who could have stolen seventy-five mammoth tractors and earthmovers out of one of the world's most inaccessible areas and got them far enough away to sell them without being found out?

The answer came three days later. I was allowed to go up the crude road with a team of engineers in a huge vehicle with wheels ten feet tall that trundled along and over anything in its path. For all I know, the balloon tires might have supported it in water. For several hours the great diesel engines churned the wheels through the mud and over fallen branches and rock slides.

Every mile or so the colonel in charge, a college professor in real life, would climb down off our wheeled platform and read the meters on his metal detectors. We'd about given up on his theory when he let out a yell when the arrows on his meters hit the far right side of the dial and quivered there. He'd found the heavy-duty machinery. In the days that followed, they located, by prodding with long metal poles, the Caterpillar tractors and the earthmoving machines. They'd gone straight down—sunk into the quagmire the ground had been turned into by 100 inches of rain in two weeks.

Although they were located, they were never recovered. The job of getting them out was more than the engineers could handle, and there was no guarantee they'd ever run again if they were extracted.

If there are any land-based treasure hunters looking for work, I know where they can find a lot of very wet and muddy earthmoving equipment. It did make the first story I'd found of any consequence since I'd arrived in the China-Burma-India Theater.

After three days in Chabua, I climbed aboard a C-46 for a flight over the Himalayas—known simply as "The Hump." I sat almost alone in a bucket seat on the airplane, with supplies of all kinds crowding in around me. It was known to be a dangerous flight and I wasn't made any easier by the graffiti someone had crayoned on the inside sheath of the plane right behind my seat:

THIS IS A THING YOU DONT SEE OFTEN
TWO ENGINES MOUNTED ON A COFFIN.

CHINA WAS A happier experience for me than India had been even though I had the second great disaster of my reporting career while I was there. Paris was the first.

There were only a handful of American reporters in China, and they were in either Chungking or Kunming covering the legends of Joe Stilwell and Claire Chennault. Their legends were about all that was left by the time I got there because "Vinegar Joe" Stilwell had been sent home and the Flying Tiger general, Claire Chennault, was no longer making news. Chennault was a retired U.S. Air Corps (so-called before 1941) fighter pilot whom Chiang Kaishek hired to assemble an air force for him. His small group of Chinese and American mercenaries, whose pilots were originally paid a $750 bonus for shooting down a Jap plane—we did not call them "Japanese"—had been incorporated into the Fourteenth Air Force by then. Our planes were largely inactive because we were no longer doing much fighting of the Japanese in Burma. Chennault was fighting his own war to become the replacement for Stilwell, whom he detested. Everyone in the CBI was waiting to see whether several million American soldiers from Europe would be dumped in their theater, in anticipation of an invasion of Japan. It slowly became apparent to everyone in China at the time that any such invasion, if it took place at all, would not come from the Chinese mainland nor would we fight a ground war with the Japanese troops in China alongside U.S.-trained Chinese divisions.

I knew little about the history of the war there and couldn't have told you the difference between Chiang Kaishek and Sun Yatsen. Neither was I much interested in the angry argument about Chiang Kaishek. I did know his wife went to Wellesley.

My work for the paper consisted mostly of feature pieces about American soldiers stationed in that part of the world and what it was like for them to be there. I had my handwritten introduction to Chennault and to Stilwell's replacement, Gen. Dan Sultan, and to Col. Frank Merrill, the leader of "Merrill's Marauders," who had become American folk heroes for their hit-and-run tactics in Burma. I never considered using the letters because I felt they were Major Eldridge's way of letting me know how important he'd been in the CBI. He knew and I knew that I'd never present them. In many cases I think I'd have gotten a blank stare from the person I presented a letter to. "Major Eldridge?"

One man I was interested in meeting was General Chennault's public-relations officer. He was Tom R. Hutton, Bud's father, who worked with Chennault's top aide, Joseph Alsop. Alsop, a Harvard graduate, had been a well-known columnist in Washington before the war and was important in setting Chennault's agenda. Tom and his son, Bud, had not spoken in years and after getting to know his father a little, I understood why. They were very much alike—by which I mean impossible. After getting to know Tom, I decided they were both right not speaking to each other.

Chennault's Flying Tigers had a glorious reputation with their P-39s in combat with the Japanese during the early years of the war and, after watching Tom Hutton at work for a few days in Chungking before I went to Kunming, I could see that no good deed by any of the Flying Tigers ever went unnoted in the press releases. He was good, and he certainly had a lot to do with the Flying Tigers' widespread and well-deserved reputation.

Wherever I went during the war, I met new newspaper friends. There was something about newspapermen and the few newspaper-women I met that appealed to me. Their curious interest in the world seemed the same as mine, and even before we were friends, we had some common ground. They all wanted to know.

The last newspaper friend I made during the war was an AP reporter named Clyde Farnsworth. I still get a start when I see the name, his son's, as a byline in *The New York Times*. I called the son once years ago but didn't get much reaction when I told him his father had been a friend of mine in Kunming. I have a feeling Clyde left his wife—perhaps with son, Clyde—but he wasn't my father or my husband and I found him good company and helpfully knowl-edgeable about living in Kunming where I'd gone.

The U.S. Army had posted signs on restaurants that met their san-itary standards and there weren't many of them. The rest of us relied more on Clyde's judgment than on that of the Army health police, and we'd often congregate in some hole-in-the-wall that he'd dis-covered had good food. His judgment on good food was better than the Army's.

Clyde always laid out his rules for the proprietor of a restaurant and the proprietor was anxious to have our business and our dollars no matter what trouble he had to go to to get them.

Clyde's first rule was that everything that came to the table had to be bubbling. His second rule was that, along with our food, we had to have one of those gigantic china bowls brought in filled, or nearly filled, with water that was still boiling. It took three waiters to handle. The bowl was placed on a short, thick board. One waiter lifted from each end of the board and the third, with cloth wrapped over his hands, steadied the load so the boiling water didn't slop out over everyone.

As soon as it was on the table, Clyde had everyone dump all the utensils and small plates into the water. None of us ever got what was known to GIs then, even in China, as "Delhi-belly." Under Clyde's gastronomic direction we ate well and stayed well.

Chinese food was a new experience for me. It's hard to remember but I don't think I'd ever been to a Chinese restaurant. I don't recall that there was one in Albany when I was growing up there. My father had made three business trips to Japan when I was a young boy, and he'd taken us to the only Japanese restaurant in New York, Daruma on West 55th Street, but I don't recall ever going to a Chinese restaurant before the war.

On one occasion in Kunming, four of us went into a small restaurant that Clyde knew and seated ourselves at a small table by a window overlooking an interior courtyard. I ordered chicken because I was already familiar with what the word looked like in Chinese and I could point to it. We were talking and idly staring out into the cobblestone courtyard after ordering our dinner when the chef came out his kitchen door and grabbed a leg of one of eight or ten chickens pecking around the yard. He swung the bird around over his head and brought it down so that its head landed on a stump of wood simultaneously with the sharp edge of the heavy cleaver in his other hand. The head fell to the ground and the stump glistened with the dark red evidence that it had been used that way hundreds of times before.

When I was a child, my mother had frequently accused me of "running around like a chicken with its head cut off" and, while it was certainly descriptive, I had never known, until that moment, that a chicken with its head cut off does actually run around for as long as thirty seconds before its body recognizes its head is missing.

I have never been much inclined to buy anything called "fresh chicken" since that day. I've always felt I know fresh chicken like few people who order fresh chicken. I'll just have chicken, thank you.

It wouldn't take much eating in China to make any sensitive person a vegetarian. I include myself among the sensitive ones. Small farmers routinely come to market with small, flatbed carts pulled by donkeys. Tied to the bed of the cart is a pig and sitting on the pig is the farmer.

There were caged dogs near some of the bigger restaurants. A patron could select the dog he thought he might like to have for dinner. I've heard people say that this custom no longer exists in China, but I always wonder if the people who think not got up to Kunming.

One of the most unpleasant sights in my memory is of the round table with a hole in its center about four inches in circumference. The table is hinged on one side so that it can be opened and closed. A young monkey is put in the middle and the table is closed around its neck so that the hole in the table forms a collar for the monkey's neck. His head protrudes above the table. I don't know whether you're ready for this, but the monkey's head is cracked open, boiling water is poured over it, and the brains are eaten with chopsticks. That practice, too, has very likely ended by now, but I've been challenged about it in the past and I can assure you it existed in 1945.

Years ago I told my children some of the things I'd seen involving cruelty to animals in China. One incident involved a man beating a horse that simply could not go on.

"What did you do?" Ellen asked.

I felt bad, but I had to say I did nothing. What *do* you do? You do nothing. You feel terrible about it but you do nothing. There is no way one person is going to change the ways of a whole culture by crying "Stop"—and in a language they don't understand.

If you got thinking much about all the cruelty in the world, to both people and animals, there wouldn't be time or inclination to think of anything else.

DRESSING WAS EASY in the Army. There weren't many sartorial decisions to make. All I had to do was dig down into those two barracks bags I'd carried with me everywhere. I had four sets of underwear, three light khaki shirts, one wool shirt, socks, the shoes on my feet, my dress jacket with the correspondent's patch on the shoulder, my Eisenhower jacket, and a highly prized leather bomber jacket with the 306th Bomb Group insignia on it. I have no memory of what I did about laundry while I was in the Army. I think probably every unit had a laundry facility, and it's strange I don't remember something so basic.

The Eisenhower jacket, so called because it was the style worn by him, was the fashion smash of the war. I believe they were originally Canadian battle jackets but when Ike started wearing one they took on his name. Everyone wanted an Eisenhower jacket even though they were only a rumor in China. Clyde Farnsworth, for all his sophisticated worldliness, desperately wanted one.

If I have extra money, I don't buy clothes, I spend it on tools, camera equipment, radios, or electronic gadgets. If something comes out that's substantially smaller or more sophisticated than the previous model, I buy it. Clyde owned a magnificent pair of Carl Zeiss binoculars that I coveted. They were the best I had ever looked through, and he kept them in their own, specially made, beautifully burnished, chestnut-brown saddle-leather case lined with green felt. We talked about a swap one night at dinner, and afterward Clyde tried on my Eisenhower jacket. We were not really the same size or shape, but my jacket seemed to fit him and we agreed to the exchange. I always thought I got the best of the bargain and I hope Clyde took as much pleasure from the jacket as I did from the binoculars. For thirty-five years they were one of my most highly prized possessions. I liked the memories they evoked, I liked their optical excellence, and I liked what they looked like in and out of their leather case. Over the years, I suppose I watched a hundred New York Giants football games with them. I took them in my suitcase wherever I traveled and whenever I was reporting on anything. If they'd been a camera and I'd recorded what I saw through those lenses, I'd have a photo archive unmatched short of the Library of Congress.

The binoculars were stolen from my car in 1987. I have a Walthour pistol I'll trade with anyone who has them.

Another reporter with whom I became friends in Kunming was Lester Walker, who was writing articles for *Harper's*. He had what he thought was a great story and he shared it with me and invited me to go along on the expedition it involved. The Air Force was losing too many planes in flights over the Hump and many of the survivors of the actual crashes that took place at high altitudes were dying of exposure in the Himalayas before anyone could reach them. Someone had the bright idea of using helicopters for rescue work in the foothills of the mountains.

I've crossed the United States four times in helicopters, twice each way. The last trip, with a cameraman and two experienced pilots, was made in a state-of-the-art, two-engined Sikorsky. It was the best, safest helicopter there is. Let me assure you the state of the helicopter art, even the best there is, to this day is primitive. They can do some remarkable things but helicopters are an invention waiting to be completed. The big Sikorsky, for instance, had that small propeller mounted on the tail that twirled parallel to the body of the aircraft. Its only purpose was to keep the helicopter itself from twisting in circles from the thrust of its main rotor blades. This small mechanical necessity alone leaves helicopters in the class of Mickey Mouse inventions.

The helicopters they planned to use in the foothills of the Himalayas were forty years before those giant choppers and not far removed from the early days of the whirlybirds' invention when they were called autogiros. The Army wasn't finished with bright ideas when it conceived the helicopter rescue plan. They had more than fifty magnificent, 2,000-pound Missouri mules shipped to China for the purpose of towing the partially assembled helicopters up the first stages of the mountain slopes to a base that had been laid out for that purpose. The mules were part donkey and part Clydesdale, and every one would be fit to appear in a beer commercial.

I jumped at the chance to go along even though it seemed to me that my story in *The Stars and Stripes* might make Lester's story less attractive to *Harper's* editors. He didn't think so. I guess he was confident that my story wouldn't hurt his, which was not exactly a vote of confidence in my reporting skill.

We spent five days on the road with the mules, sleeping in tents we pitched alongside the path we were following. Keep in mind I was experienced at this sort of thing because of the time I had spent on a horse in Kashmir. Fortunately, in this procession, we were riding in a General Motors truck.

The day following our arrival at the base, the mechanics went to work assembling and test-running the helicopter engines. It was all hard work because we were at 6,000 feet and we all noticed we were short of breath if we exerted ourselves for any reason. The crash sites were almost always in the mountains 6,000 to 8,000 feet above the base.

Finally, everything was ready. Lester and I stood by for the payoff. During the three days it took them to completely assemble the helicopters, we suppressed the idea of actually hoping for the crash of a C-46 somewhere high in the downside of the mountains, but we waited, expectantly, for anything that would make for a dramatic rescue. None came. On the fourth day, the pilots climbed in the helicopters, revved the engines, and the big, ungainly birds lifted a few feet off the runway and dropped back to the hardstand with a bump.

They lifted off again. In a matter of ten minutes, by persistent goad-
ing, the pilots were able to get the whirlybirds to a height of perhaps
200 feet.

We were puzzled when the pilots of the three helicopters put
them down, cut their engines, and walked to the Nissen hut used as
the base office.

"You know," one of them said to the colonel in charge of the
operation, "there's something we haven't considered. This aircraft has
a maximum altitude of about seven thousand feet. We're at about that
right here. We have all we can do to get them off the ground. We're
never going to get up into the mountains."

End of story. And to make it clear how inexperienced I was as a
reporter, I never wrote the story of the failure which in many ways
could have been as interesting, and a lot funnier, than that of an actual
rescue.

Lester and I went back down the mountain, found Clyde, and had
a good dinner at a place he picked where he knew the water would
be boiling when they brought it in. At least someone in Kunming
knew what he was doing.

There was very little to write about. I went out to an American
unit that was trying to train Chinese soldiers and was immediately
impressed with what an impossible job it was. The Chinese divisions
were still run like some feudal lord's private army. They were a band
of brigands and had to be because there was no food-supply system.
For the most part, they lived off the countryside they occupied, taking from farmers and the people of the small villages in the area.
Many of the soldiers the Americans were trying to train had their
own coolies who did their laundry for them. American soldiers in
semipermanent bases often paid for the same service. A small group of
GIs would get together and pay a Chinese working man $5 a month
to do laundry for all of them and press their uniforms.

I was surprised to find so much English in Chinese newspapers.
Even in relatively remote Kunming there was a cosmopolitan society,
and you would often see strikingly beautiful women who were the
offspring of White Russian, Dutch, or Scandinavian fathers and Chinese mothers. Advertising signs in front of small businesses were often
in English, or close to English. A popular brand of cigarettes was

called Chenmen, and billboards proudly proclaimed, in broken Madison Avenue English:

CHENMEN CIGARETTES; SMOKE ONE AND YOU'LL
NEVER SMOKE ANOTHER!

I wrote one story with several examples. A sign over a tailor shop read:

RESPECTABLE LADIES HAVING FITS UPSTAIRS.

A sign noting the office of a dentist said:

FALSE TEETH. LATEST METHODISTS EMPLOYED.

One legitimate news story I got involved an American private named John Breman from West Hartford, Connecticut. He and Pvt. James Cooper of Norwood, Ohio, apparently got drunk one day and decided to ride one of the tame water buffalo used to till the fields. An elderly Chinese woman, the owner of the beast, chased after the soldiers. Breman fell from the buffalo, and in the melee the woman was severely hurt and died shortly thereafter. Breman's defense was that the woman was hurt when he fell off the animal and landed on her. Witnesses said he dismounted and beat the woman for harassing him. The two privates were condemned, by an American military tribunal, to be executed.

Breman wrote to his aunt, who got his letter to U.S. Sen. Brien McMahon. That was as far as I got with the story because I left China before the case was resolved.

My assignment, to tell soldiers from the ETO what it would be like when they arrived in China, no longer made sense. In the fury over the atomic bombs we dropped on Hiroshima and Nagasaki in August, historians have tended to minimize the force with which we were already hitting Tokyo and other places in Japan. In May and June alone in 1945, bombers based on Pacific islands and fighter planes from aircraft carriers were dropping huge bomb tonnages on Japan. If anyone thinks Nagasaki and Hiroshima were our only targets, they should be reminded that our B-29s bombed thirty-nine Japanese cities in the spring of 1945.

The American soldiers left in China were puzzled because they seemed to have been left without a war to fight or any purpose in being so far from home. They'd read that Eisenhower was welcomed back in Washington as a conquering hero, and they'd heard that forty-two of the sixty-eight infantry divisions in Europe were being sent home. The suggestion was that the war was over. They wondered if they'd been forgotten and they were intensely unhappy. I wrote it but that made only one story for me.

THE ARMY DISCHARGE schedule was drawn from an elaborate point system, and although the system broke down after the first few months, initially those overseas with 100 or more "points" were assured of a quick release. Points were accumulated by number of months served, number of months overseas, and number of days in a combat zone.

On all counts I had good numbers, and my Air Medal and Bronze Star helped because bonus points were given for any medal a soldier had been awarded. It turned out to be the best thing about getting one for most soldiers who had not been previously impressed by the Army's effort to improve their morale by pinning medals to their chests.

I was still in Kunming in the early days of July 1945 when I got what I wanted most, a notice that I had enough points to be discharged and that I was to return to the United States for that purpose.

The only negative aspect to the discharge process was that I was briefly thrown back into the Army I detested and from which I had all but escaped during almost three years with *The Stars and Stripes*. Although I was a staff sergeant, I had been as free as if I were a civilian reporter. The correspondent's patch which had been so much help to me among soldiers in the field didn't have much standing in the long lines at the mass processing centers that were set up to handle the men returning. It was an abrupt reminder that I was still an enlisted man in the Army. I'd almost forgotten.

My route home from Kunming was from Chungking to Cairo to Oran, Algeria, to Santa Maria in the Azores, and then to Idlewild Airport in New York. For what reason I don't know, but they operated DC-4s carrying troops home like a ferry service between Oran and Santa Maria and then another group of DC-4s shuttled between the Azores and New York. None flew directly to the United States. When the plane carrying soldiers from Oran to the Azores landed in Santa Maria, it was refueled but it didn't continue on. It was turned around and sent back to Oran. The soldiers who had been on it waited for the next shuttle plane to come back to the Azores. Inevitably there was always a wait of twenty-four hours and sometimes as long as seventy-two hours.

When the DC-4 stopped at Santa Maria, 900 miles off the coast of Portugal, I thought it would be interesting to see what the islands looked like but the occasion to see any of them never came up. The air base where we landed was run by a small cadre of Regular Army soldiers who seemed to have only one purpose in mind: to take away from every soldier who went through there the $238 he had in his pocket as discharge pay. The operators of the gambling casinos in Las Vegas and Atlantic City would have admired their thoroughness. The shuttle system with the transfer of passengers and two-day holdover seemed designed to facilitate the fleecing of the returning soldiers, and I wouldn't be surprised if some of the permanent personnel on Santa Maria made hundreds of thousands of dollars during a six-month assignment there.

The permanent cadre on the island had put up dozens of long, narrow dice tables, each covered with a GI blanket. Overhead, hanging from cables they'd attached to poles that had been planted in the ground, were garlands of unshaded lightbulbs that lit the playing field beneath. We were all encouraged to step up and double our take-home pay. I was one of the few men who came through Santa Maria without losing his nest egg of $238 and it was neither luck nor skill. While I'd learned poker at the knee of Wray Funderburk in the boiler room of the barracks at Fort Bragg, I'd never mastered the dice game so I didn't play. I wasn't so much afraid of losing as I was hesitant to reveal my ignorance of so all-American a game. In the Army, real men played craps.

Back in the States, we were taken by bus from the New York airport to Fort Dix, New Jersey, and it was frustrating to be, for a short distance, so close to Margie in New York without being able to stop the bus, get off, and go to her. I was still dragging along one khaki barracks bag containing such treasures as letters from home, notebooks with scribbled material for stories I'd written, the binoculars, several fancy gold-embroidered women's handbags that I'd bought in India, and a few trinkets I had picked up from street merchants in Kunming or Chungking. Somewhere between Chungking and New York, one of the bags went astray and I lost half of all the things I'd accumulated during the war. I knew they were important, priceless, and irreplaceable, but I've never been able to remember everything that was in the lost bag.

Idlewild became Kennedy in the 1960s. It was fortuitous that they originally gave the airport so neutral a name as Idlewild until someone came along who was worth naming it after. There may have been some objection to naming it Kennedy, but there was no outcry from any organized group of supporters for the name Idlewild. It was a long ride home, but at least I did get to fly instead of being sent the long way around by ship. Hutton, who took his contribution to the war effort more seriously than others of us on the paper, was shipped home on a small freighter named the *Louisa M. Alcott*. In the mind of this journalist-warrior, the author of *Little Women* was not a fitting name for a ship bearing him, and Bud never forgave the Army for this ignominious end to his distinguished Army career. We kidded him about it because, while we took him seriously as a newspaperman, we took his war record less seriously than he took it. We may have been unfair but we judged his by the same standards we judged our own and not many of us in the privileged position of reporters took our war records seriously no matter what fringe dangers we'd been exposed to. Bud was already at war with the New York office because, along with Walter Cronkite and several other reporters, he had jumped into Holland with the 101st Airborne Division. The *Stars and Stripes* editors in New York got a wire-service report about him before he could get his own story out, and they wrote that he had gone from a burning glider. His complaint was that people would infer from the story that he was *forced* to jump because the glider was burning when, in fact, he had planned to jump all along. This was the kind of fine line Bud always drew.

I arrived back in the United States on August 2 and spent four miserable days at Fort Dix, New Jersey, filling out papers before being discharged and joining Margie in New York. The war seemed so close to being over that we all felt the Army should simply forget the paperwork, close up shop, and let us go home.

Margie had found an inexpensive cube of a room in the Henry Hudson Hotel on West 57th Street, more than twenty blocks from where she was working for *The Stars and Stripes* across town on 42nd Street. The war ended in a climactic fireworks of events during my first week home: on the day I was set free, the B-29 named *Enola Gay* dropped the atomic bomb on Hiroshima, killing 75,000 residents; Russia, which had been reluctant to get involved until then, declared war on Japan on August 8; we dropped another bomb on Nagasaki August 9; and, in the face of imminent annihilation, the Japanese surrendered on August 14.

The Japanese didn't sign their surrender until September 2, two weeks after I was discharged, but we were still in New York on VJ Day, staying at the Roosevelt Hotel for $4 a night. I'm amused to note that a room in the Roosevelt in 1995, now one of the more moderately priced hotels, goes for $119.

A monster demonstration, planned and unplanned, was predicted for Times Square that night, and Margie decided not to risk the crush of the crowd to see it. It seemed like a once-in-a-lifetime event and I couldn't resist walking the three blocks alone to be in on the party. When I see that classic picture of the sailor kissing the young woman he has bent backward in his arms as if they were ballet dancers, it reminds me of everything I saw that night. The atmosphere was somehow different than it had been on August 25 in Paris almost a year before. There was unrestrained joy—jubilation—in Times Square that all America felt that night, but the reaction of the people of Paris to their liberation had a depth and a poignancy to it that Americans who had never been subjected to a foreign conqueror could not possibly have felt.

The annual New Year's Eve happening in Times Square is a pale copy of that grand, if somewhat frightening evening. It was frightening because I kept thinking of Bethnal Green and the possibility of being crushed to death. In this case, I think the crowd was so tightly packed that no one *could* have fallen down and been trampled because there was no space to fall in.

We had stayed in New York because Bud and I had written a second book together called *The Story of The Stars and Stripes* and were appearing on radio shows with popular entertainers like Mary Margaret McBride to plug our new book. Mary Margaret McBride was the Larry King of her time, without suspenders.

We had worked separately on our parts of the first book, *Air Gunner,* when we were in London before the Invasion, and then we rewrote it together, although I wouldn't claim that my editorial judgment of what should stay in, come out, or be changed had the same weight as Bud's did. Before I left for India, we had written the book about the Army newspaper and had sent it off to the publisher, Farrar and Rinehart. We had laid out the sections and agreed on which one of us would write which sections, but again there was no question of my status as junior member of the writing team. While *Air Gunner* had been a legitimate report about some of the characters who fought the air war, this second book was a hastily assembled series of vignettes about the newspapermen who worked on the paper. In later years it was not a book I pushed on our kids to read with any pride, but Rinehart published it and an agent named Steve Schlessinger, with whom Bud had dealt before the war, told us he could take it to Hollywood and sell it to MGM.

Steve had made a lot of money merchandising a popular comic strip named *Red Ryder.* The artist, Fred Harmon, had been trapped in a contract with Steve that had him working in a grubby little office in the back of Steve's suite of offices on Park Avenue for a salary somewhere under $100 a week. Steve, meanwhile, had sold the rights to the name "Red Ryder" to the Daisy Air Rifle Company, and he'd sold the motion-picture rights to Republic Pictures.

Republic was in the process of making twenty-six B movies out of the strip, using Fred's characters and some of his story lines. In London I had known the good-but-difficult *New York Times* military reporter Drew Middleton, and I recall his having told me, when he first heard of my connection with Steve, that "you'll probably end up working in a garret for fifty dollars a week."

Drew was prescient.

Fred Harmon's situation of indentured servitude should have alerted us to the danger of signing on with Steve but it did not. Steve was a charming rogue and very bright, so we signed and Steve took all of us to Los Angeles on the Super Chief to sell the book to MGM. Bud had recently married a sweet but somewhat naive Red Cross girl named Isabel whom he'd met in London. With Steve, there were five of us traveling in first-class accommodations. It was my last great train ride. The New York Central had even arranged such details as stopping along the way to pick up local delicacies. We stopped in southern Colorado, I think, for ripe melons.

We had private rooms on the train, and it was the kind of luxury accommodation everyone old enough to remember yearns for now when they travel in the cramped conditions of modern flight. Bud's new wife had a bit of bad luck the first night out. She tired early and decided to go to bed shortly after we'd all had dinner in the dining car and before the train had passed Utica. Too bad, Isabel.

Shortly after Isabel retired, Bud sat down next to an attractive young woman traveling alone and feigned reading the paper for a while. Shortly after turning a few pages, he struck up a conversation with her. We left them an hour later at about eleven o'clock playing gin rummy. Apparently rummy grew to romance, because by the second night Bud was not retiring to the stateroom where Isabel was sleeping at all, although he assured her in the morning that he had stayed up all night working. We were pleased there was no bed check.

By the end of the train trip Bud's brief fourth marriage was on the rocks and we were left with Isabel, a distraught friend of ours now, who had been looking forward to introducing her new husband to her family in California.

On the morning of our arrival in Los Angeles, the lead items of the two most prominent show-business gossip columnists, Hedda Hopper and Louella Parsons, announced that "Those two sergeant authors, Bud Hutton and Andy Rooney, arrived in tinseltown today to begin work on their fabulous new production of the motion picture *THE STORY OF THE STARS AND STRIPES!*"

Hutton and I were astounded that we were well known enough to rate any mention at all, let alone the lead item in both columns. It was

several months later, during an argument with Steve over money, that
he let us know how much it had cost him to place those paragraphs
with Hedda and Louella.

We were introduced all around at MGM, given two good offices
in what was known as the "writers' building," and left alone to come
up with a screenplay. We had no idea what a screenplay was or how
to write one but we pored over scripts in the library and got the idea
of how one was set up on a page. The first thing you had to learn
about screenwriting was, you used only half the page to write on and
left the other half free for camera and stage directions, which you
entered in capital letters. We both pecked away, dividing up the pages

*An agent in Hollywood bought a small degree of celebrity for Bud Hutton and me
by paying for photographs and inserting items about us in gossip columns. This was
one of the photos designed to make us look like authors.*

in a manner that we judged, from the samples we'd seen, to be in the style of a screenplay.

We soon learned that they had professional people who turned the awkward work of amateurs into shooting scripts that were broken down into scenes for the director. We were relieved the day we learned we were not expected to know how to do that.

I ate regularly at the writers' table in the cafeteria and became friends with Lester Cole and Robert Nathan. Nathan was a novelist with a good reputation who was trying to make a screenplay of Galsworthy's *Forsyte Saga*. In school I had never been able to finish *reading* the *Forsyte Saga,* and making a screenplay of it seemed comparable to making a stage play of Conrad's *Heart of Darkness*.

Dalton Trumbo, who had written *The Postman Always Rings Twice,* was there occasionally.

Audrey Totter, a budding young star, often sat at our table, and I was smitten by her beauty and intellect although I'm willing to concede the former may have fogged my view of the latter. Lester Cole seemed worldly-wise, and when he asked me to come to a big fund-raising event for the Barsovie Hospital in Spain, I accepted. Dorothy Parker and Quentin Reynolds spoke that night, and when the master of ceremonies asked for a show of hands of those willing to contribute, the people around us at the table dutifully put theirs up. There was nothing for me to do but raise mine, and before we left that evening I wrote a check for $25 to "The Barsovie Hospital Committee." It was not until several years later, during the witch-hunt for communists initiated by Wisconsin senator Joe McCarthy, that I learned the fund-raising event was for the Communist Party and not for the hospital. One of the principal defendants in the trial of the "Hollywood Ten" in the 1950s was my friend Lester Cole, and Lester went to prison for refusing to divulge the names of other Communist Party members. I was pleased that my name was not one he had to refuse to divulge. Lester had never even suggested to me that I might be interested in joining.

Somewhere on an FBI list in a storage cabinet in Washington my name must be written down as a possible communist but I never heard anything more about it. In the 1960s I wrote the FBI and asked, under provisions of the Freedom of Information Act, that I be sent

any information about me that they had in their files. I got back a letter saying that, while my name was indeed in their files, it was in relation to someone else and it would not be proper for them to release
it in that context. I was curious but foiled by the bureaucracy.

Housing was short because there hadn't been any building during
the war, and Margie and I were unable to find a place to live in Bev-
erly Hills or Hollywood. We finally located a cottage that was for rent
in the Malibu Beach colony and lived there in number 55, next door
to the producer B. P. Schulberg. It was November now and cold along
the beach in a house with no central heating, but it was pleasant. Bud
rented number 99, just up the beach from us, and he bought an eight-
cylinder, baby-blue Packard convertible. I often left our Chrysler with
Margie and went to work with Bud in his Packard.

The actor Robert Walker was scheduled to appear in our movie
about *The Stars and Stripes* and it was to be filmed in London where
MGM had accumulated a fortune from box-office receipts that British
wartime restrictions, still in effect, prohibited them from bringing back
to the United States. MGM had planned to use that money to pay for
the production of our film and get their money out when they sent
the finished movie back to theaters in the United States.

The movie was never made, and the project fell apart for two reasons: Robert Walker died and the British announced a new policy
that prohibited any foreign company from removing property representing major property holdings from the United Kingdom. This
effectively foiled MGM's plan for extracting their money, and the
project was canceled. The idea of a motion picture or a television
series based on the Army newspaper in World War II is still a good
one, and I'm surprised no one has ever undertaken it.

Bud and I had been in Hollywood for eight or nine months of our
one-year contract when it became clear that there wasn't anything
more for us to do. Steve Schlessinger had taken half of the original
$55,000 MGM paid us, and he was taking half of our salaries of
$1,500 each. Still, as recently discharged sergeants, we felt rich.

Joe McCarthy—the other Joe McCarthy, our friend who had been
the overall editor of *YANK* magazine during the war—and Arthur
Gordon, the Air Force major with Eighth Air Force public relations
who had helped us with contacts for the *Air Gunner* book, had taken

over as editors of Hearst's *Cosmopolitan* magazine. One was called managing editor, the other executive editor. They offered us $10,000 to return to Europe and write a series of ten articles for the magazine describing what America had bought for all the lives that had been lost there and all the money that had been spent.

Somehow the brief time we spent in Hollywood so soon after my experience in China attaches itself in my mind to the war itself. It was an epilogue. More than my discharge, those months in California were the real end of the long, terrible, and fascinating episode in my life. Sitting in the living room of our house on Malibu, gazing idly at the sunset and at the seals frolicking on the beach in the foreground, I knew I'd come to the end of my war.

INDEX

Page numbers in *italics* refer to photographs.

ML

Thunderous Barrage of Bomb
Notches Coastal Belt in France

By Andy Rooney
Stars and Stripes Staff Writer

A FORTRESS BASE, Apr. 20—"The pre-invasion shuttle," the air crews were calling it this evening as they came back from giving the Nazis' West Wall its worst pounding of the war.

Fortresses and Liberators poured back and forth across the English Channel in a steady stream this afternoon, and there wasn't a moment almost up to dark that found the skies above the Channel free from the roar of the shuttling bombers or their escorts.

From the Fortress piloted by 1/Lt. Carl N. Grending, of San Leandro, Cal., I watched the group commanded by Col. George L. Robinson, of Los Angeles, join the mass of heavy bombers, mediums, P38 and P51 fighter-bombers and U.S. escorts

Calais and Dunkirk, American bombs formed a precise pattern on the already crater-pocked fields and woods of France. Almost continuously bombs were hurtling down even as the smoke climbed up from earlier hits.

Not all the bombs hit the target; ours fell in a field next to it, but other squadrons were on it.

There was some flak, but it wasn't up to Nazi standard, and their fighters were conspicuously absent, at least in our area.

While the bombers came and went, swarms of P51s, 38s and 47s were searching, mostly without luck, for German fighters. One unit of yellow-nosed Thunderbolts criss-crossed the coastal area as long as their fuel held out

---

1 D.
THE STARS AND
Daily Newspa
Forces
New York, N.Y.—London, Eng
Vol. 4 No. 145

---

men Never
lk This Way
the Movies

By Andrew A. Rooney
Stars and Stripes Staff Writer

A U.S. FIGHTER STATION, England, July 13—1/Lt. Ralph A. Johnson, of Pikeville, Ky., was shot at and hit by a German fighter in a USAAF fighter sweep over France last month. He got his P47 back but over the field he found that he could only get one wheel down, and he couldn't get that one back up. A crash landing with one wheel up and one down is suicide.

Col. Hubert Zemke, group commander from Mazuma, Mont., had landed, but when he saw Johnson's trouble he took off again "to get a better look at what was wrong."

Zemke drew up next to Johnson and the following conversation was jotted down in the radio control room.

Zemke—Have you tried to shake it down?

Johnson—Yes.

Z—Get way up and try again. If you can't shake it down you'll have to be careful. Go over to the lake and ahead. Put your landing gear in the down position, do a bank on the wing and snap it over to the me get a little ahead.

J—OK.

Z—That hasn't done it. Do som violent weaving back and forth.

J—Sir, my landing gear handle is stuck.

Z—Is it stuck down?

J—Yes, sir.

Z—Let's go upstairs, follow me. (pause)

(Continued on page 4)

Ninth's Fighters Will
'Infantry Invaders' A
Quesada Reveals Unit's
Job Will Be Support
Of Ground Troops

By Andy Rooney
Stars and Stripes Staff Writer

Ninth Fighter Command will be "the Infantry's air force," Brig. Gen. Elwood R. Quesada, 39-year-old Ninth Fighter chief, said yesterday when he ap that his command would spearhead of U.S. group make the first invasion Army will have air officers assigned to command can most effective ground troops.

Equipped in large numbers three most successful types of U.S. planes, P38s, P47s and P51s, the force is prepared to give support the ground forces in the actual invas and to move into captured airfields enemy territory soon after.

Squadrons of ground and flying personnel living in tents in England are prepared to move, at a few hours' notice, with their mobile headquarters, munications and emergency airfield equipment, into captured air bases soon after airborne units have secured the airfields.

All three types of fighters are equipped to give dive-bombing support to the offensive troops as well as providing defensive cover from Luftwaffe fighters and fighter-bombers. The P38s and P51s

---

GI Enjoyed Pa

By Andy Rooney
Stars and Stripes Staff Writer

PARIS, May 21—Between white sheets in a hotel in Nice a Joe fell asleep and dreamed:

He was assigned to a division made up of the best from the 1st, 2nd, 3rd, 4th, 9th, 82nd Airborne and a few more crack divisions. They just took the old timers. Terry Allen was division commander.

The infantry division was reinforced with tank battalions selected from 2nd, 3rd and 4th Armored Divisions, had new tanks with three feet of a all around and a quick traversing, velocity 105mm. gun.

Every man in the division kept and was given a German Luger Schmeisser machine pistol in a Each man also got a pair of Zeiss lens binoculars and a Lei

Plenty of Jeeps For Al

One of the best things about was that there was a jeep for men and the jeeps were armed twin Spandau machine-guns the tails of captured Ju88s.

The division artillery with German 88s, which a had been careful to see Department had not to modified," and with our and 240s. Each platoon by a battery of 4.2mm. and, of course, had observation planes, The division fough the men were